ABOUT THE AUTHOR

Tom Miller is a senior analyst at Gavekal Research, a global economic research service, and managing editor of *China Economic Quarterly*, published by its sister service Gavekal Dragonomics. Tom was educated at the University of Oxford and the School of Oriental and African Studies (SOAS) in London, and spent two years studying Mandarin in Beijing. A former journalist, he has reported from a dozen countries in Asia. His first book, *China's Urban Billion: The Story Behind the Biggest Migration in Human History* (Zed, 2012), was translated into Chinese. After fourteen years living in China, Tom now divides his time between England and Asia.

CHINA'S ASIAN DREAM

EMPIRE BUILDING ALONG THE NEW SILK ROAD

TOM MILLER

ZED

Zed Books

LONDON

China's Asian Dream: Empire Building Along the New Silk Road
was first published in 2017 by Zed Books Ltd, The Foundry,
17 Oval Way, London SE11 5RR, UK.

www.zedbooks.net

Typeset in Haarlemmer by seagulls.net
Index by John Barker
Cover design by Clare Turner
Cover photo © Martin Roemers/Panos Pictures

A catalogue record for this book is available from the British Library.

ISBN 978-1-78360-924-6 hb
ISBN 978-1-78360-923-9 pb
ISBN 978-1-78360-925-3 pdf
ISBN 978-1-78360-926-0 epub
ISBN 978-1-78360-927-7 mobi

MIX
Paper from
responsible sources
FSC® C020471

For Flora, Harry and Penny

CONTENTS

ACKNOWLEDGEMENTS

This book is the fruit of two years spent wandering around China's border regions and often far-flung parts of Asia. It could not have been written without the support of my colleagues at Gavekal Research in Hong Kong and Gavekal Dragonomics in Beijing. Special thanks go to Arthur Kroeber, who encouraged me to disappear from the office, and to Louis Gave, for not minding. Many thanks as well to Simon Pritchard, Tom Holland, Udith Sikand, Chris Rickleton, David Eimer, Paul Mooney and David Brown, who read through earlier articles and draft chapters of the book, pointing out errors and making helpful suggestions.

I was helped in my research and on my travels by numerous people. In Beijing: Ignacio Asenjo, Andrew Batson, Chen Long, Ernan Cui, Simon Denyer, Matt Ferchen, Thomas Gatley, Philippa Jones, David Kelly, Calum MacLeod, Pratik Mathur, Alanis Qin, Felix Roberts, David Sedney, Ruslan Suleimenov, Dina Turarova, Rosealea Yao, Wang Jisi, Joerg Wuttke and Zha Daojiong. In Hong Kong: Gavin Bowring. In Kunming: Lu Guangsheng. In Astana and Almaty: Nurbala Amiebayera, Aidar Azerbayev, Amer Durrani, Steven Freeman, John Gray, Janet Heckman, Ann Herrigan, Nargis Kassenova, Joanna Lillis, Yelena Sadovskaya, Leilya Shamell, Brian Shelbourne and Dena Sholk. In Bishkek and Osh: Bakyt Duashov, Sultan Khalilov, Uluk Kydyrbaev, Roman Mogilevskii, Nazira Raymond, Talant Sultanov and Deirdre Tynan. In Yangon and Mandalay: Jan Ano, Roman Caillaud, Nickey Diamond,

Stuart Deed, Josh Gordon, Judy Ko, Thura Ko, Aung Naing Oo, Tao Ye, Khin Tun and Wong Yit Fan. In Phnom Penh: Daniel de Carteret, Julian Rake, Sok Siphana and David Van Vichet. In Ho Chi Minh City and Hanoi: Mike Ives, Nguyen Thanh Tuan, Nguyen The Phuong, Nguyen Trung Truc, Tuong Lai and Truong-Minh Vu. In Singapore: Kanti Bajpai, Selina Ho, Huang Jing, Tomoo Kikuchi, C Raja Mohan, Alex Neill and Ian Storey. In Colombo: Krishantha Coorey, Karu Jayasuriya, Ravi Karunanayake, Vidya Nathaniel, Paikiasothy Saravanamuttu and Eran Wickramaratne. In Delhi: Rahul Bedi, Brahma Chellaney, Gurcharan Das and Rahul Jacob. In Washington DC: Michael Austin, Peter Foster, Bonnie Glaser, Michael Green, Murray Hiebert, Yukon Huang, Christopher Johnson, Scott Kennedy, Ashkok Mirpuri, Vikram Nehru, Douglas Paal and Sun Yun. In London: Agatha Kratz, Sam Leith and Rafaello Pantucci. And in Oxford: Rosemary Foot, Ewan Smith and Jonathan Ward. My apologies to anyone I have forgotten.

Finally, my love and thanks go to my family—Flora, Harry and Penny—for being there when I come home. This book is dedicated to them.

Oxford, July 2016

ABBREVIATIONS

ADB	Asian Development Bank
ADIZ	Air Defence Identification Zone
AIIB	Asian Infrastructure Investment Bank
APEC	Asia-Pacific Economic Cooperation
ASEAN	Association of Southeast Asian Nations
ASEAN Plus One	Association of Southeast Asian Nations and China
BCIM	Bangladesh-China-India-Myanmar Economic Corridor
"Belt"	Silk Road Economic Belt
BRICS	Brazil, Russia, India, China and South Africa
CAREC	Central Asia Regional Economic Cooperation
CCP	Chinese Communist Party
CDB	China Development Bank
CNOOC	China National Offshore Oil Corporation
CNPC	China National Petroleum Corporation
CNRP	Cambodia National Rescue Party
CPV	Communist Party of Vietnam
CRG	China Railway Group
CSIS	Center for Strategic and International Studies
CSTO	Common Security Treaty Organization
EEU	Eurasian Economic Union
EEZ	exclusive economic zone
EU	European Union
ETIM	East Turkestan Islamic Movement

Exim Bank	Export-Import Bank of China
FDI	foreign direct investment
GDP	gross domestic product
GMS	Greater Mekong Subregion Programme
Guangxi	Guangxi Zhuang Autonomous Region
IBRD	International Bank for Reconstruction and Development
IMF	International Monetary Fund
IS	Islamic State
KIA	Kachin Independence Army
LTTE	Liberation Tigers of Tamil Eelam
MDB	multilateral development bank
NATO	North Atlantic Treaty Organization
NDB	New Development Bank
NDRC	National Development and Reform Commission
NLD	National League for Democracy
OECD	Organisation for Economic Co-operation and Development
ONGC	Oil and Natural Gas Corporation
PLA	People's Liberation Army
PRC	People's Republic of China
PSA	Port of Singapore Authority
"Road"	21st Century Maritime Silk Road
SCO	Shanghai Cooperation Organization
SARS	Severe Acute Respiratory Syndrome
SEZ	special economic zone
TPP	Trans-Pacific Partnership
UN	United Nations
UNCLOS	United Nations Convention on the Law of the Sea
US	United States
Xinjiang	Xinjiang Uyghur Autonomous Region
WTO	World Trade Organization

INTRODUCTION

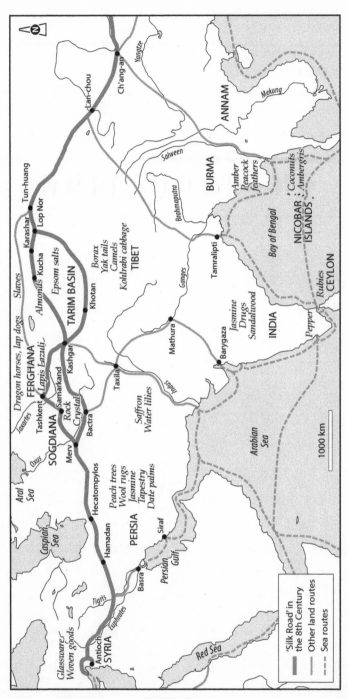

Old Silk Road

Let us begin with a thought experiment.[1]

It is 2050. Europe, once the wealthiest and most advanced civilization on Earth, is showing signs of decrepitude. Millions of tourists flock to museums in Paris and Rome, but the modern world is passing it by. Its technology is outdated, easily surpassed by innovations from China. The European Union's once mighty economy is sinking, its inhabitants addicted to social media and state handouts. Islamist rebels establish a vicious caliphate in London, which the authorities struggle to put down. Twenty million people lose their lives in the ensuing carnage.

Fast-forward a hundred years. Europe is in tatters, burnt to the ground after nearly two decades of war and occupation by the United States, its former ally. Another 20 million Europeans lie dead. China, which put an end to the war by firing nuclear missiles at the US, reigns supreme. Europe is now but a minor player in a global order led by Asia-Pacific nations, with its effective capital in Beijing. Europe's new government vows to rebuild the smouldering continent as a communitarian utopia, yet the global superpower—China—is hostile. The People's European Union hunkers down, shutting its doors to the world...

This dystopian future sounds like a horror film, but it gives us an approximation of what happened to China between the start of the First Opium War in 1839 and the Chinese Communist Party's (CCP) consolidation of power in the 1950s. China's fall from grace was every bit as unexpected and bewildering.

In 1800, China regarded itself as blessed by heaven, the world's greatest power and its leading civilization—much as the great European nations regarded themselves in 1900. In classical Chinese cosmology, China sat at the centre of the world: its very name, *zhongguo*, literally means "middle country". Poetically known as "the Celestial Empire", China filled the central sphere of three concentric circles. The second circle contained colonies and tributary states, such as Japan, Korea and Vietnam, all part of the Chinese Confucian world. The benighted third circle was reserved for foreign peoples—"barbarians" in some translations—unenlightened by Chinese civilization.[2]

China's power reached its peak in the decades before 1800. The Qing Dynasty had crushed smaller nations to the north and west, incorporating them into a much enlarged empire. This included Tibet, Mongolia and a sizeable chunk of central Asia, which it renamed Xinjiang (literally "new frontier"). It had regulated relations with the Russian Empire, the kingdoms of Southeast Asia, and the Himalayan kingdom of Nepal. Bordering states, from Burma to Korea, recognized China's pre-eminence, paying ritual tribute at the Qing court. This was not simply about kowtowing to the great emperor in Beijing: the relationship provided mutual benefits, notably in trade.

The Chinese state, still intact 2,000 years after it had first been unified, had no rival. With a population of 328 million, the Qing Empire was more populous than the British Empire, the Indian Maratha Empire, the French Republic, the Russian Empire, and the Ottoman Empire *put together*.[3] Its economy dwarfed all others, as it had done for two millennia, accounting for well over a quarter of world output.[4] It was ten times larger than the Japanese economy and substantially mightier than the combined economies of Europe—faraway places to which China sold silk, porcelain and tea, but in which it otherwise had little interest. China was indisputably the leading power in Asia, holding sway over a vast area of land and sea, and dominating the cultural order. It was a civilization on a scale the world had never seen.

Yet within the space of a few decades, China's seemingly unassailable position unravelled in a series of catastrophic events. It began in 1839, when British gunboats exacted revenge for the destruction of 20,000 chests of Indian opium in Canton port, after the Daoguang Emperor attempted to abolish the pernicious trade. The British East India Company turned its gunboats on Canton, exacting a decisive victory. In 1842, under the Treaty of Nanking, Britain forced the Qing government to pay vast compensation costs and demanded the opening of five new treaty ports, in which its citizens would enjoy freedom from the emperor's legal jurisdiction. As a bonus, Britain would also take Hong Kong Island.

In the mid-1850s, Britain and other Western powers demanded that China open further to foreign commerce, freeing the opium trade and abolishing import tariffs. When the Xianfeng Emperor reneged on a new agreement, British and French troops sailed north to the port of Tianjin. After initially being rebuffed, they destroyed the Chinese imperial forces and marched on Beijing. With the emperor fleeing the capital, the troops looted and burned to the ground his most prized possession—the exquisite Garden of Perfect Brightness, known in English as the Old Summer Palace. In the following days, the Western powers forced China to open Tianjin as a treaty port, cede Hong Kong's Kowloon area to Britain, legalize the opium trade, and pay reparations to Britain and France. For good measure, Russia pocketed 1 million square km of territory in the ancestral homeland of the Qing rulers.

The timing of the Second Opium War could not have been worse for the imperial court, which was simultaneously fighting the biggest domestic uprising in its history. While foreign troops stormed the imperial palace in the north, the rebel Taiping Heavenly Army marched through the south. Ordinary Han Chinese flocked to the cause—led by Hong Xiuquan, a religious maniac who proclaimed himself the younger brother of Jesus Christ—rightly believing the Qing government to be corrupt and ineffective. In 1853, the Taiping Army captured the eastern city of Nanjing, which was declared the Heavenly Capital of the Heavenly Kingdom of Peace. The rebels occupied large swathes of China, establishing a brutal, theocratic rule. By the time Nanjing was finally overthrown by Qing forces in 1864, more than 20 million people lay dead, ranking the Taiping Rebellion as the bloodiest civil war in history.

The Opium Wars and the Taiping onslaught demon-strated, beyond doubt, the diminished power of the imperial court. That fragility laid the way for the darkest chapter in modern Chinese history, which opened in 1895 with defeat in the Sino-Japanese War. China had regarded Japan, a former tributary state, as a little brother within the wider Confucian world. In 1911, the Qing Dynasty collapsed and the country sank into a morass of warlordism. The nationalist govern-ment of the 1920s briefly reunified the country but quickly got bogged down in a civil war with the Chinese Communist Party. In 1931 Japan invaded China's frigid northeast, setting up a puppet state. Total war broke out in 1937, as the Imperial Japanese Army rampaged across China, slaughtering up to 300,000 people in Nanjing alone during six weeks of bloody carnage. Approximately 20 million Chinese lost their lives in what China calls the Anti-Japanese War, fully one-quarter of World War II's total casualties. Chinese estimates put the figure closer to 35 million.[5]

When the Communists secured victory over Chiang Kai-shek's Nationalist Party in 1949, setting up the People's Republic of China (PRC), they took over an impoverished and depleted country: China was battered and broken. After a century of slaughter and destruction, they set out to rebuild. They took a slogan first used by Chinese intellectuals in 1915 and have popularized it ever since: "never forget national humiliation" (*wuwang guochi*).[6] Recalling the untold abuses and indignities heaped on China and its people, this visceral four-character phrase is taught in schools to this day. China must never forget, because it can never be humiliated again.

China must never forget, because the pain of humiliation must spur national revival.

The goal of national rejuvenation has been invoked by every modern Chinese leader since Sun Yat-sen, the father of the Chinese republic. The national anthem of the PRC is quite explicit:

> Arise, ye who refuse to be slaves;
> With our very flesh and blood
> Let us build our new Great Wall!
> The peoples of China are in the most critical time;
> Everybody must roar his defiance.
> Arise! Arise! Arise![7]

The point is that China must rise *again*. Its leaders talk of *fuxing*, "rejuvenation" or "revival"—to restore what has been lost. China was once the greatest civilization, the greatest state, in the world. It must be so again.

Without China's "century of national humiliation" in mind, it is impossible to understand the resonance of President Xi Jinping's "Chinese Dream".[8] Like all modern Chinese leaders before him, Xi has promised to realize "the great rejuvenation of the Chinese nation". But under his leadership, the pursuit of the "Chinese Dream" has become a guiding philosophy. It is in the first place a domestic vision—China cannot be great, after all, if it is not strong at home—but it is also intimately bound up with China's place in the world. After years of preparing the ground, China is determined to take its place as a modern world power.

This is frightening for China's neighbours, because the "Chinese Dream" is closely linked with military might.[9] "To realize the great rejuvenation of the Chinese nation," Xi declared soon after becoming Communist Party chief, "we must preserve the bond between a rich country and a strong military, and strive to build a consolidated national defence."[10] The quest for "wealth and power" (*fuqiang*) has been a common refrain among political leaders and intellectuals since the 19th century. It is shorthand for "enrich the state and strengthen its military power", a phrase that dates back more than 2,000 years to the Warring States period, which laid the way to the unified Chinese empire. In today's terms, economic development is needed to create a wealthy state that will enable the Chinese people and their ancient civilization to prosper. A powerful economy will pay for the strong military required for self-defence, so that China will never be invaded and occupied.

Military strength is also required to give legitimacy to the Communist Party as China's defender-in-chief. Party propaganda systematically picks at the historical wound of national humiliation with the aim of consolidating national identity around its own role in building a "rich country and strong army". The message that the Party seeks to project is that only *it* can lead China back to greatness. That was the logic behind the vast military parade held in Beijing in September 2015, ostensibly to commemorate the 70th anniversary of victory over Japan. The marching phalanxes of soldiers and rumbling lines of tanks—beamed on television screens around the world—were really a sign of insecurity: truly confident nations do not have to show off their military might. Yet China's leadership needed to project an image of strength, both to bolster its rule at home and to scare potential enemies abroad, especially the US and Japan.[11]

The pursuit of national glory, fuelled by this deep well of insecurity, is pushing China towards a more muscular foreign policy. Thirty years ago, the CCP could still appeal to Communist ideology to shore up its authority as the ruling party. By contrast, the nationalist logic of the "Chinese Dream" requires China to project power overseas. The victory parade was lapped up by a patriotic nation, even as it sent shivers around Asia. "The lack of confidence in internal affairs means you have to appear very assertive abroad to unite the country around nationalism—but I cannot say that openly," says one of China's leading thinkers on international relations.[12]

This marks a fundamental shift in China's foreign policy. Deng Xiaoping, China's paramount leader from 1978 to 1992, advised that China should lie low in foreign affairs and concentrate on getting its own house in order. President Xi has abandoned that humble approach. The signs were there even before he officially took power when, during a trip to Washington as vice president, he called for a "new model of great power relations".[13] Soon after succeeding Hu Jintao, Xi declared that China would play a "proactive" role in Asia. This innocuous-sounding phrase was actually a signal that Deng's dictum had been abandoned. Since then, China has prioritized "neighbourhood diplomacy" and begun to formulate concrete policies to translate its economic heft into regional leadership.[14]

Gradually—and somewhat erratically—China's geo-political muscle is growing to match its economic might. China, according to the eminent political scientist David Shambaugh, has long been a "lonely power", lacking close friends and possessing no allies.[15] Following Deng's advice, Beijing has kept its nose out of other countries' affairs, pursuing a foreign policy guided by the principle of non-intervention and non-alignment. Yet President Xi's "proactive" foreign policy requires China to work closely with other countries. Beijing is not seeking to build a formal alliance structure, but Xi Jinping has declared his intention to "make more friends" and forge a "community of shared destiny" in Asia.[16] The goal is to create a web of informal alliances lubricated by Chinese cash. As its neighbours become ever more economically dependent on it, China believes its geopolitical leverage will strengthen.

President Xi's mission is to return China to what he regards as its natural, rightful and historical position as the greatest power in Asia. That does not mean that China has to replace the US as the world's only superpower, but it does mean that Asia has to predominate in its own backyard. After a "century of humiliation", only this "Asian Dream" can bring back the nation's dignity and self-respect.[17] For China, it is a glorious vision—and one that has enormous implications for the future of Asia.

亚洲梦[18]

How will China's "proactive" foreign policy work? In the first place, it requires oiling the wheels of trade and investment. China's rise in Asia is founded on a simple fact: its vast economy, measuring US$10.9 trillion in 2015, is larger than the other economies of East and Southeast Asia combined.[19]

This mighty engine has driven regional development for at least a quarter of a century. China is the largest trading partner of most countries in Asia, including almost all of those in its immediate vicinity. This gives it enormous economic leverage.

China's next goal is to boost regional investment, which it does not yet dominate. In Southeast Asia, for example, both the EU and Japan contribute more. This is a failing that the "Belt and Road Initiative", also known as "One Belt, One Road" or the "New Silk Road", is designed to rectify. The initiative describes two hugely ambitious projects to improve connectivity in Asia and beyond. On land, the "Silk Road Economic Belt" envisages new transport infrastructure and the construction of industrial corridors stretching across Central Asia to the Middle East and Europe. On water, the "21st Century Maritime Silk Road" will encourage investment in new ports and trade routes through the South China Sea and the Indian Ocean. This will be backed by financial brawn: China's two policy banks—China Development Bank and the Export–Import Bank of China—already lend more in Asia than the World Bank and Asian Development Bank combined. By financing roads, railways, ports and power lines in underdeveloped parts of Asia, the Belt and Road Initiative aims to draw China's neighbours ever tighter into Beijing's economic embrace.

The initiative is Xi Jinping's signature policy, designed to secure his legacy. Beijing is supporting it with new financial institutions, notably the Asian Infrastructure Investment Bank and the Silk Road Fund. This does not mean that China is rejecting the global architecture, as some have suggested.[20] But it does mean that it wants to supplement and reshape it. It will use multilateral organizations such as the AIIB, the Shanghai Cooperation Organization and ASEAN Plus One, in which the US plays little or no role, to push its own regional agenda. The reality is that China is already challenging the post-World War II order established in Asia under the watchful eye of Washington. (See Chapter 1.)

China's infrastructure diplomacy aims to improve connectivity with neighbouring countries. On the border with Kazakhstan, the small town of Khorgos in Xinjiang is being transformed into a distribution hub for Central Asia, with new rail and road links from the regional capital of Urumqi to Almaty, Kazakhstan's biggest city, and on to Iran. Train links to Europe run via Kazakhstan from cities across China. To the south, vast new markets are designed to re-establish Kashgar—one of the busiest bazaars on the old Silk Road—as a regional gateway. Chinese firms have built roads to neighbouring Kyrgyzstan and Tajikistan, and there are plans to lay railway lines through the Karakoram and Pamir mountain ranges to Pakistan, Uzbekistan and beyond. Trade flows and economic activity have yet to match the building frenzy, but no one can doubt the intent.

Central Asian countries welcome investment that improves transport links and helps unlock their vast mineral wealth, especially if it decreases dependence on their traditional patron: Russia. China has replaced it as the leading economic presence in Central Asia over the past decade, even if Russia maintains deeper political and cultural roots. Vladimir Putin, who like Xi Jinping wants to re-establish his country's historical sphere of influence, is busily pushing an alternative economic vision founded on a customs union of ex-Soviet states. China and Russia claim to be strategic partners; but as China's leverage in Central Asia grows, there is potential for the traditional rivalry between the two countries to re-ignite. (See Chapter 2.)

In the Mekong economies of mainland Southeast Asia, China's biggest rival is Japan, which has long financed and built infrastructure across the region. These days the most ambitious projects are Chinese: they include a completed US$4 billion highway running 1,800 km from the city of Kunming in Yunnan province to Bangkok, and a proposed 3,900 km railway line from Kunming to Singapore, stretching down through Laos, Thailand and Malaysia. Doubts remain about the viability of the railway, but transport connections between Yunnan and Laos are already convenient enough for that country to be overrun by Chinese investors. Cambodia, meanwhile, is so dependent on Beijing's cash that it has been accused of acting as a Chinese stooge. Both countries are at risk of becoming appendages of their giant neighbour. (See Chapter 3.)

Back in 2010, the same could be said of Myanmar. After cultivating ties with the ruling military junta for more than two decades, Beijing saw Southeast Asia's most reclusive state as a bridge to the Indian Ocean—"China's California"—offering the valuable potential for direct access to a western seaboard.[21] China has built twin oil and gas pipelines from the Bay of Bengal to its border town of Ruili, which is also a planned staging post along a proposed highway through Myanmar from Kunming to Kolkata, on India's eastern coast. But China's position has deteriorated significantly since Myanmar's democratic transition led to a rapprochement with the West. Political liberalization has given ordinary people a voice to protest against China's presence, forcing the government to postpone a giant dam and railway line. It will be fascinating to see how Aung San Suu Kyi's government approaches the all-important China question. (See Chapter 4.)

Populist blowback will remain a hazard for Chinese firms operating abroad, especially in fragile states run by authoritarian regimes, where changing governments can see dramatic shifts in the prevailing political winds. After Myanmar, the best example is Sri Lanka. China lent extravagant funds to this strategically placed island, until its corrupt former president was ousted in 2015. The new government promised to review a number of dubious Chinese projects, vowing to renegotiate interest rates on loans that really served as backhanders to government cronies. But Sri Lanka is so reliant on Chinese funding that it will struggle to extricate itself from China's economic grasp.

Across the Indian Ocean, China is using economic resources to secure strategic ends. Its engineering firms have built ports in Myanmar, Sri Lanka and Pakistan that could provide vital support to Chinese warships and submarines. It has promised US$46 billion to finance an "economic corridor" through Pakistan, linking the port of Gwadar on the Arabian Sea to the deserts of northwest China. And it will soon open its first overseas military base in Djibouti, in the Horn of Africa, where it plans to install several thousand troops. Indian military analysts argue that China is deliberately threading a "string of pearls" through the Indian Ocean—though some of these fears are overdone. (See Chapter 5.)

China's presence in the Indian Ocean raises concerns in India about how rapidly its economic power is translating into military might. China's leaders are adamant that it is, and never has been, an expansionary power. This is a highly selective reading of history: imperial China grew out of the Chinese state's expansion beyond the Han heartland along the Yellow River. Moreover, since its founding in 1949, the PRC has occupied Tibet and colonized Xinjiang. But it is true that China has generally stuck to its borders since then, albeit with minor incursions into Vietnam and Indian-held territory.

The big caveat is China's recent behaviour in the East and South China Seas, where its outrageous claim to vast areas of territory far beyond its land borders is greeted with anger and fear, especially in Japan, Vietnam and the Philippines. China has negated its long-term efforts to build a positive image in Southeast Asia, proving the hollowness of its much-touted "win–win" diplomacy. Its reclamation efforts in the South China Sea, which go far beyond those of other claimants, show it is now confident enough to flex its muscles over its borders. China's determination to build a strong military capacity is militarizing the region, dragging the US into the fray. War remains unlikely, but China's behaviour is reinforcing age-old resentments, even pushing Vietnam into the arms of the US. (See Chapter 6.)

亚洲梦

China's unbending assertion of its territorial claims is about two things: self-protection and national glory. The ability to defend itself and shape its own destiny is at the heart of the "Chinese Dream". Love him or loathe him, Xi Jinping is determined that China will no longer be a country that can be pushed around. He has set a target date of 2049—the centenary of the founding of the PRC—for realizing the dream of national rejuvenation. By mid-century, Xi says China must be "wealthy and strong", both at home and abroad.[22] And as a great power, it must be an active participant in global affairs, helping to make the international rules.

Beijing claims to have no imperial ambitions. "China will never inflict its past suffering on any other nation," Xi declared at 2015's victory parade in Beijing. "The Chinese people are resolved to pursue friendly relations with all other countries."[23] Yet the "Chinese Dream" is, in its way, a dream of buiding an Asian empire. I do not mean that China has ambitions to conquer foreign lands. Beyond the turbulent waters of the South China Sea, there is little evidence of military intent for territorial expansion. I mean that the dream of national rejuvenation requires China to recover what has been lost, which means restoring its historical status as Asia's dominant power. China's new "empire" will be an informal and largely economic one, posited on cash and held together by hard infrastructure.

Re-establishing a Sino-centric order is a dream shared by many Chinese nationalists. In his book *The China Dream*, Liu Mingfu, a retired People's Liberation Army colonel, describes with nationalistic fervour how the traditional tribute system worked:

In East Asia's tribute system, China was the superior state, and many of its neighbouring states were vassal states, and they maintained a relationship of tribute and rewards. This was a special regional system through which they maintained friendly relations and provided mutual aid. The appeal and influence of ancient China's political, economic and cultural advantages were such that smaller neighbouring states naturally fell into orbit around China.[24]

Historians in those former vassal states point out that the Chinese Empire was not as benign as maintained by Liu, and by other advocates of Chinese neo-imperialism. But this rose-tinted view of China's imperial past informs the government's "win–win" diplomacy today. In essence, the goal of China's economic diplomacy is to create a modern tribute system, with all roads literally leading to Beijing.

How worried should China's neighbours be? The challenge for countries on China's periphery is how to extract as much economic benefit from China, in terms of trade and investment, without losing political and economic sovereignty. This is a precarious balancing act. All states in the region are putting in place hedging strategies to ensure they do not become Chinese vassals. Myanmar and Vietnam, for example, have moved closer to the US in recent years. Moreover, all benefit from an international system that protects sovereignty and enshrines the sanctity of borders. Nevertheless, the weakest countries on China's periphery will struggle to remain truly independent.

China's economic diplomacy is most effective in small countries, where its leverage is greater. Those underdeveloped and often fragile states are the focus of this book. Developed economies, by contrast, have less to fear: Japan and South Korea are powerful countries in their own right. Far from needing the Chinese to build and finance infrastructure, they are competitors in the game of infrastructure diplomacy. The fact that both countries are firm members of the US alliance system shows just how weak China's position truly is: while Beijing wines and dines tin-pot dictators, Washington sits at the apex of the most powerful tributary system ever devised.

China is big and it is scary, especially for its neighbours, but the continued presence of the US is the single biggest reason why it will struggle to assert itself as a regional hegemon. Beijing denies it is pursuing hegemony, which it regards as a colonialist enterprise pursued only by devilish foreigners. But one does not have to be an arch-realist to understand why China should aspire to predominate in its own region, just as the US sought in the 19th century to predominate in the western hemisphere.[25] China's problem is that, for all its talk of building a "community of common destiny" (*mingyun gong-tongti*), it will struggle to convince its partners that abandoning the US-led order for a Chinese one is a good deal. So long as its economic juggernaut rolls on—and that is no longer as certain as it once seemed—China's regional importance will deepen. But Xi Jinping's vision of an Asian empire is probably a dream too far.

CHAPTER 1

"ONE BELT, ONE ROAD"

FINANCING THE NEW SILK ROAD

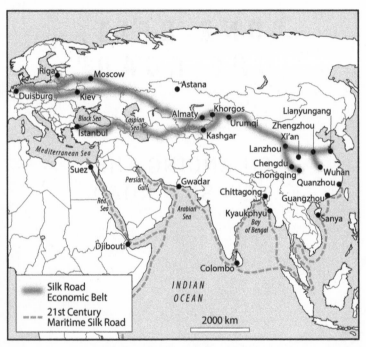

New Silk Road ("Belt and Road")

In November 2014, Beijing's habitually smoggy skies turned a brilliant shade of blue. The clean air was engineered to coincide with the first full meeting of the Asia-Pacific Economic Cooperation (APEC) forum in China since 2001. With twenty top leaders flying into the capital, including US president Barack Obama and Japanese prime minister Shinzo Abe, the government was determined to show it at its best. Factories were shuttered; shops, schools and businesses closed; cars ordered off the roads; and residents advised to leave town. Farmers were told not to fire up their traditional stove-heated beds—or risk arrest.[1] Once the dignitaries flew out and the steel mills reopened, the sky returned to its familiar grey. Cynical Beijingers coined an expression to describe the fleeting phenomenon: "APEC blue" refers to anything too good to be true.

The APEC meeting in 2014 was the most important international event in Beijing since the 2008 Olympics, and the first big meeting of foreign leaders chaired by President Xi Jinping. If the Beijing Olympics was China's opportunity to show the world that it had arrived as a modern global power, the APEC forum was President Xi's chance to show that China was finally going to start acting like one. He did not disappoint, easily

projecting the air of an international statesman and negoti-
ating confidently with President Obama. Most significantly,
he used the forum to intimate grander geostrategic ambitions
for China, announcing plans to ramp up overseas investment
to US$1.25 trillion over the coming decade. Placing China at
the heart of Asian diplomacy, he proposed new initiatives that
dovetailed with the signature foreign policy of his administration: building a New Silk Road.

Founded in 1989, APEC is supposed to champion trade
and regional economic integration, but often comes across as
little more than a talking-shop. President Xi attempted to inject
much-needed vitality into the forum by floating the ambitious
idea of a Free Trade Area for Asia-Pacific—essentially a more
inclusive version of the Trans-Pacific Partnership (TPP) sponsored by the United States, of which China is conspicuously
not a member. He also persuaded his counterparts to approve
a new "APEC Connectivity Blueprint 2015–2025" involving
the construction of new roads, railways and shipping lanes
across Asia and the Pacific Rim. Xi presented these ideas as
part of a grandiose vision for the future. "The development
prospect of our region hinges on the decisions and actions we
take today," he told 1,500 businesspeople attending the forum.
"We are duty-bound to create and fulfil an Asia-Pacific dream
for our people."[2]

No Chinese leader before Xi has had the gumption to talk
of an "Asia-Pacific dream" under implicit Chinese leadership.
China has traditionally been a passive player in the world of
high diplomacy, preferring to hide behind a mantra of "non-
interference" in other countries' affairs rather than to shape

global events. But under Xi, China is preparing to play a much more active role over its borders, and is ready to underpin its diplomacy with huge economic largesse. Just two weeks before the APEC meeting, Beijing hosted a launch ceremony for the Asian Infrastructure Investment Bank (AIIB), at which 21 countries agreed to become founder members of the first Chinese-sponsored multilateral development lender. And at the APEC meeting itself, President Xi announced the establishment of a US$40 billion Silk Road Fund specifically to finance projects along the New Silk Road.

The founding of the AIIB and the Silk Road Fund are evidence of China's deepening strategic ambitions in Asia. This first became apparent in 2013, when the new foreign minister Wang Yi announced that the focus of foreign policy would shift to China's backyard. Among its neighbours, China would seek to build a "community of shared destiny"—a vision that not only encompasses greater economic integration backed by huge spending on infrastructure, but also mutual defence of national interests.[3] China's aim is to use economic incentives to build closer relationships with its neighbours, drawing them ever tighter into its embrace. In return for delivering roads and power lines, it expects its partners to respect its "core interests", including its territorial claims in the South China Sea. This is what Beijing means by "win–win" diplomacy.

The shift to a more assertive foreign policy marks a fundamental break with the past. Since "Reform and Opening" began in 1978, Chinese foreign policy has been underpinned by the "Deng Xiaoping theory", which holds that diplomacy must serve the greater goal of domestic development. In essence, this boils down to supporting China's export growth model by attracting foreign investment and promoting a stable external trading environment. Deng laid down his famous dictum in the early 1990s, when he urged China's leaders to "observe calmly; secure our position; cope with affairs calmly; hide our capacities and bide our time; be good at maintaining a low profile; and never claim leadership".[4] This strategy is abbreviated in Chinese to *taoguang yanghui*, which is usually translated as "hide our strength and bide our time", but literally means "hide light, nurture obscurity".

Before Xi rebooted its foreign policy, China was generally happy to stand on the international sidelines. Its leaders demanded shows of international respect and were quick to accuse countries of "hurting the feelings of the Chinese people" when they felt it was not forthcoming; but they rarely sought to lead.[5] Instead they concentrated on economic diplomacy, pressing for trade agreements and supporting the overseas efforts of state-owned engineering and resource enterprises. They worked most actively with the Association of Southeast Asian Nations (ASEAN), hoping to allay fears that China was a competitive threat to its neighbours. They tried hard to present China as a responsible economic power: the decision not to devalue the renminbi during the Asian financial crisis in 1997 helped stabilize the region, and China provided billions of dollars of credit to Southeast Asian nations in the wake of the global financial meltdown in 2008.

With economic power, however, comes geopolitical clout. China's foreign policy strategists have long debated how a strengthening China should assert itself on the global stage.[6]

In 2004, China's leaders briefly began to talk about a "peaceful rise", seeking to encapsulate the reality of China's resurgence while reassuring the world that it remained a benign power. When this was deemed too provocative for foreign ears, they adopted the more innocuous-sounding term "peaceful development". Calls for a more assertive foreign policy grew after the global financial crisis, when the weakness of the US and European economies was laid bare. Yet, after some vacillation, Hu Jintao's administration officially stuck with Deng's "bide and hide" dictum. In September 2011, the government released a "White Paper on Peaceful Development", which reiterated that "the central goal of China's diplomacy is to create a peaceful and stable international environment for its development".[7]

The old tenets of foreign policy began to unravel after the leadership transition in 2012–13. At a Party work conference in October 2013 dedicated to regional diplomacy, Xi Jinping made a speech titled "Let the Sense of Community of Common Destiny Take Deep Root in Neighbouring Countries".[8] Following Deng's line, he said that foreign relations must secure "good external conditions for China's reform, development and stability", but added that China must also foster a sense of "common destiny" in Asia. Implicitly rejecting Deng's advice to lie low, he declared that China's regional diplomacy should instead be *fenfa youwei*—an expression often translated as "enthusiastic" but better rendered as "proactive". Foreign Minister Wang Yi used a similar term to describe the overall direction of foreign policy at his inaugural parliamentary press conference in March 2014.[9]

In November that year, two weeks after the APEC meeting, Xi chaired a rare Central Work Conference on Foreign Relations. This was the first such high-level meeting since 2006, when a restrained President Hu Jintao had called for China to take its place in a "harmonious world". Xi presented a more muscular vision: China should carry out "diplomacy as a great power", he said, and consolidate its leadership in Asia. Reiterating a line used by previous leaders, he said that a benign external security environment gave China a "period of strategic opportunity" to concentrate on internal development through 2020. But for the first time, he implied that maintaining the favourable environment depended less on good fortune than on China's own diplomatic efforts. Finally, he explicitly linked the nation's resurgence as a great power to the "Chinese Dream" of national rejuvenation.[10]

Deciphering China's rapidly evolving diplomacy under Xi Jinping is tricky: smiles have frequently turned into snarls, especially in Southeast Asia. But his two work conference speeches give us a baseline to start from. Under the banner of the "Chinese Dream", Xi Jinping is pursuing a newly assertive foreign policy that prioritizes China's economic leadership in Asia. Simultaneously, he is seeking a "new type of great power relationship" with the US, demanding that China be treated as an equal. These ambitions have implications for global institutions: at a Politburo study session on developing a Free Trade Area for Asia-Pacific in December 2014, Xi said that Beijing should "participate and lead, make China's voice heard, and inject more Chinese elements into international rules".[11] China has long pressed for a "multipolar" world, but President

Xi is the first Chinese leader in at least two generations to try to make this happen.

This ambition is underpinned by ever growing economic might. China's economy may be slowing, but even 5% annual growth adds the equivalent of a mid-sized economy like Argentina to its gross domestic product every year. China already accounts for nearly half of Asian GDP, is by far the region's largest trading partner, and is challenging Japan to become its largest investor. Beijing believes its financial resources and engineering prowess will prove irresistible, especially in countries lacking the capacity to finance and construct their own infrastructure. With the Belt and Road Initiative, it is effectively dangling a vast economic carrot before its neighbours. China's leaders judge that few countries are in a position not to bite, especially weaker states that cannot provide basic services for their citizens.

Yet China will struggle to convince its neighbours to embrace a new regional order centred on Beijing, precisely because they fear its immense economic power. No one wants to become a Chinese vassal. Beijing's pursuit of a "community of common destiny" is seen across the region to be as much of a threat as an opportunity—especially in the South China Sea. Here there is little doubt that China's "win–win" diplomacy, a formula repeated ad nauseam by Chinese diplomats, is designed to serve China's interests first. Even among countries with a friendly relationship with China, fear of economic overdependence is widespread. Like the blue skies enjoyed by delegates during the APEC meeting in Beijing, China's fine words about mutual prosperity seem too good to be true.

CHAPTER 1

BELT AND ROAD INITIATIVE

The centrepiece of Xi Jinping's "proactive" foreign policy is the Belt and Road Initiative. Stretching from the South China Sea across the Eurasian land mass, it is arguably the most ambitious development plan ever conceived. Taking its inspiration from the ancient Silk Road that ran from China to Europe via central Asia, it envisages building roads, railways and industrial corridors across some of the wildest terrain on earth, and linking these to upgraded ports in Asia, Africa, the Middle East and Europe. Beijing says the initiative will dismantle investment barriers, create new trade routes, improve international logistics, and deepen regional financial integration. It even grandly claims that it will promote "world peace".[12]

The initiative runs under a confusion of different monikers. President Xi first proposed building a "Silk Road Economic Belt"—a land route through central Asia and the Middle East to Europe—at a speech in Kazakhstan in September 2013.[13] A month later, in a speech to the Indonesian parliament, he proposed creating a "21st Century Maritime Silk Road"— a web of sea lanes through the South China Sea and Indian Ocean.[14] First called the New Silk Road, the scheme was later dubbed "One Belt, One Road" (*yidai yilu*), which sounds less clunky in Chinese than in English. After much internal debate, it is now officially translated as the "Belt and Road Initiative". Beijing is adamant that it should not be called a "plan" or a "strategy", lest it be interpreted as a ruse to build a vast economic empire. China claims no ownership over the initiative, which it says is about "mutual trust, equality, inclusiveness and mutual learning, and win–win cooperation"—though, in reality, it is very much a Chinese project.[15]

Beijing claims the initiative will run through sixty-seven countries, and Chinese media have published a number of maps purporting to show its route. In fact, there is no clearly defined Belt or Road: Chinese firms will help to lay new roads and railway tracks, linking them to new ports, wherever they can find willing partners. Some routes, such as the rail lines that lead from China to Europe via Kazakhstan and Russia, already exist; others are on the drawing board and may never leave it. For example, a potential southern route of the Silk Road Economic Belt through Iran and Turkey may or may not cross Kyrgyzstan, and may or may not have spurs through the troubled states of Iraq and Syria. Much like the ancient Silk Road, the Belt and Road will form a network of trading routes influenced by the competing demands of geography, commerce and geopolitics.

The initiative is motivated by a number of sweeping goals. In the first place, it aims to protect national security. China wants to create a network of economic dependency that will consolidate its regional leadership, enable it to hedge against the United States' alliance structure in Asia, and diversify energy supplies. Beijing has few friends in Asia, but it is serious about helping its neighbours if they return the favour. This is a departure from the past, when Beijing did not try to cultivate close diplomatic relations, other than with the rogue states of North Korea and Myanmar.

Equally important are economic motivations. Beijing's great hope is that state commodity producers, engineering firms and capital goods makers will find a lucrative new source of growth. The Belt and Road will require billions of tonnes of steel and cement, hundreds of thousands of workers, thousands of cranes and diggers, and dozens of new dams, power stations and electricity grids. Beijing views the initiative as a lifeline for indebted firms suffering from weak demand at home and looking to export their overcapacity. The scheme is China's second big overseas investment push, following the "Go Out" policy launched by Jiang Zemin in 1999. Then, the goal was for Chinese state-owned enterprises to acquire overseas energy and mining assets. The updated policy is broader and more ambitious, and includes an important domestic element: Beijing calculates that better connectivity will help its under-developed border regions become viable trade zones.

There are also financial considerations. In March 2015, Beijing released a policy document entitled "Vision and Actions on Jointly Building Silk Road Economic Belt and 21st-Century Maritime Silk Road".[16] In addition to outlining plans to improve connectivity and create new trade routes on land and sea, it called for greater financial cooperation and integration of cross-border markets, proposing an increased use of the renminbi for trade settlement. This would serve the long-term ambition of making the renminbi an international currency, taking its place alongside the dollar and the euro. In addition, Beijing wants to nurture an alternative investment channel for its massive foreign exchange reserves, which stood at over US$3 trillion in 2016 even after significant outflows in 2015. Rather than investing these in low-yielding US treasury bonds, it would do better to finance foreign infrastructure projects at an interest rate of 5-6%—especially if this proves to the advantage of Chinese exporters and construction firms.

Although too broad and vague to amount to an operational roadmap, the Belt and Road policy document is Beijing's most comprehensive articulation of the initiative. In essence, it lays out a strategic vision for turning China into the primary global engine of economic development, rooted in the understanding that China's security interests are best served by tying other countries into ever closer trade and investment relationships. "China is committed to shouldering more responsibilities and obligations within its capabilities," the document states in carefully diplomatic language, reassuring that its chief aim is to deliver "common development" and "mutual prosperity".[17] Yang Jiechi, China's most senior diplomat, told Southeast Asian nations on the day of its release that the initiative is "by no means a tool for any country to seek geopolitical advantages".[18] After a number of diplomatic setbacks across the world, not least in Africa, Beijing is painfully aware that it is not trusted.

At home, however, the master narrative is different. Leaders continue to reiterate that China must play a bigger role in the world commensurate with its economic might, and that China will not be pushed around. There is little doubt that President Xi sees the Belt and Road as a practical step towards realizing the strategic goal of national rejuvenation—the "Chinese Dream"—and thereby securing his own political legacy. He is said to divide the Chinese reform process into three periods, each lasting roughly thirty years. In the first period, beginning with the founding of the People's Republic in 1949, Mao Zedong consolidated the power of the Communist Party and strengthened China after years of foreign humiliation. In the second period, from the beginning of Reform and Opening in 1978, Deng Xiaoping set China on course to become a great economic power. And in the third period, beginning with Xi's own coronation as Party chief in 2012, China will finally take its rightful place as a world power. Hu Jintao and Jiang Zemin are but historical footnotes.[19]

Xi claims ownership of the Belt and Road Initiative, even if much of the thinking behind it is not original. "Unlike Greek mythology's description of Athena emerging fully formed from Zeus' head, it should not be viewed as the comprehensive brainchild of President Xi and his close advisers," says Christopher Johnson, the Freeman Chair in China Studies at the Center for Strategic and International Studies (CSIS) in Washington, DC.[20] The Asian Development Bank (ADB) has been funding better connectivity across Asia for many decades. Work on a "Eurasian land bridge" between China and Europe began long before Xi Jinping took office, for example. But President Xi has cleverly folded a number of existing or planned schemes into the grand narrative of the "Chinese Dream", and made the Belt and Road crucial components of his geopolitical push to build a Sino-centric order in Asia.

ASIAN INFRASTRUCTURE INVESTMENT BANK

China's ambitions are built on economic power. The most potent symbol of this is the AIIB, which is closely associated with the Belt and Road Initiative. In fact, Xi Jinping first proposed that China set up its own multilateral development bank during the same speech, in Jakarta in October 2013, in which he announced plans to build a Maritime Silk Road. The rapid success of the venture surprised everyone, not least Beijing: within just eighteen months, fifty-seven countries had agreed to become founder members of the new bank. These included most Asian and many European countries; even states with which China has a difficult relationship, such as the Philippines and Vietnam, were among them. When the AIIB's articles of agreement entered into force on 31 December 2015, the only two noticeable absentees were the US and Japan.[21]

The "Chinese bank", as nervous ADB officials initially called it, has probably garnered more headlines than any regional multilateral development lender in history.[22] For this, Beijing largely has Washington to thank: the world would have paid little attention had the US not foolishly tried to dissuade its allies from joining. US officials claim today they never actually lobbied against the bank, but this is disingenuous. The US took a clear position, and such countries as Australia, South Korea and Indonesia were reluctant to defy it. But when the United Kingdom unexpectedly announced that it would join, many others followed, including Europe's other big three economies, in addition to Australia, South Korea and Indonesia. Even geopolitical rivals of China, like India, decided it would be foolish to look a gift horse in the mouth.

The foundation of the AIIB reflects a shift in tactics for China. Over the past three decades, it joined most of the big international organizations, and occasionally found them useful—but it generally preferred to exercise its economic muscle in bilateral negotiations where it had more leverage. Across Asia, China's willingness to build and finance infrastructure is designed to win friends. But these efforts often have the opposite effect, as local people resent the presence of Chinese workers or fear for their economic livelihoods. Bilateralism has its limits, because smaller states do not want to be reduced to Chinese clients. So Beijing has learned that it pays to play a less obtrusive role within multilateral organizations, such as the World Bank or ADB.[23]

The big problem for China is that it has struggled to gain enough influence in these US-sponsored institutions to serve its full purposes. China's share of voting rights within the International Bank for Reconstruction and Development (IBRD), the World Bank arm responsible for non-concessional loans, is just 5%. The US's share is 15%, and a full 45% of votes are controlled by the US, Japan and European countries. Until December 2015, China's voting share in the International Monetary Fund was an even more paltry 3.8%; the IMF agreed to raise this to 6% in 2010, but its implementation was held up by Republicans in the US Congress. Even under the new system, the US maintains a share of 16.5%, reflecting its pre-eminent position in the global economic system. Finally, in the ADB, Japan and the US contribute 31% of the capital stock and control 26% of the votes. For years China pushed for greater representation on the ADB board and to increase its shareholding of 5%, but it was blocked by the US and Japan.

In 2013 Beijing's patience finally wore out: rather than fruitlessly seeking to increase its representation in existing institutions, it would set up its own. In so doing, it took a leaf out of its rival's copybook: Japan founded the ADB in 1966 to advance its own regional interests, initially by making infrastructure loans to its trading partners. Today the ADB stresses poverty reduction, but it remains a useful conduit of Japanese capital to Asia—especially as Prime Minister Abe encourages Japanese firms to hedge their bets in China by investing elsewhere. The ADB's Japanese president Takehiko Nakao publicly welcomed the AIIB, which China says will not interfere with the ADB's work.[24] After all, Asia's infrastructure needs are so huge that there is plenty of room for other financiers. But, in private, ADB officials worried the AIIB would compete for the same projects, only with lower standards, and threaten its role as "Asia's bank".

Washington saw an even bigger threat. China, it feared, was trying to provide an alternative to the US-dominated system of global development finance, enshrined at Bretton Woods, which could reshape the economic architecture of Asia. This was more than paranoia: the AIIB was specifically conceived as an arm of China's economic diplomacy. The Belt and Road Initiative's founding document clearly states that the AIIB would be used as a channel for government support.[25] Understandably, Washington viewed the AIIB as a potential competitor to the ADB and World Bank, and was genuinely concerned about its commitment to adhere to rules of good governance, responsible lending and environmental protection. But its attempts to undermine an institution that could improve lives across Asia were petty and short-sighted. Far from trying to dissuade its friends from joining an institution it did not trust, shrewder diplomacy would have welcomed their ability to influence it from the inside.[26]

Yet Washington was right about one thing: the AIIB is part of Beijing's attempt to redress the inequities in the Bretton Woods system. At its signing ceremony in June 2015, China's finance minister Lou Jiwei said the AIIB represented "an important move on the part of China to fulfil its growing international responsibilities, and to improve and complement the existing international order".[27] The following month saw the establishment of the New Development Bank (NDB), a global development bank set up by the five BRICS countries—Brazil, Russia, India, China and South Africa—to "mobilize resources for infrastructure and sustainable development projects" across all emerging economies.[28] Headquartered in Shanghai, the NDB has been called the AIIB's sister institution. Both banks operate in a similar space to the ADB and World Bank.

It is therefore no surprise that elements within the US government believe that China is trying to replace the existing global economic architecture. Yet this view overestimates the impact of China's economic institution building: rather than seeking to build an alternative to the US-sponsored system of development finance, China is instead attempting to remould and augment it. Jin Liqun, the AIIB's urbane president and a fluent English speaker, is himself a former vice president of the ADB. He has worked hard to reassure sceptics that the AIIB will not seek to overturn the tenets of multilateral development finance. The bank, he says, will be "lean, clean and green": managerially efficient, intolerant of corruption and environmentally friendly.[29] The AIIB's website promises that the bank will put in place "strong policies on governance, accountability, financial procurement and environmental and social frameworks".[30] It has busily recruited international consultants to help it achieve these aims, including high-ranking Western diplomats and senior staff from the World Bank.

The AIIB's success in attracting so many shareholders means that China's control over it is limited. China naturally exercises significant leadership and is the AIIB's largest shareholder, based on its US$29.8 billon stake. In addition, its voting share of 26% gives it an effective veto, since a "super-majority" of 75% is needed to make significant decisions. But this share will almost certainly fall as a further thirty economies prepare to join, with Hong Kong one of the first on the list. With so many countries having a stake in the outcome, the AIIB has to respect international lending standards.

It is also in Beijing's longer-term interest to ensure the AIIB is well run. It knows that advancing China's influence requires it to project a friendlier, more multilateral face. The AIIB's first steps turned out to be gestures of cooperation: in three of its first four projects, it is contributing additional funds to projects already arranged by the World Bank, the ADB and the European Bank for Reconstruction and Development. The AIIB "will complement and supplement the efforts of our MDB [multilateral development bank] partners", Finance Minister Lou Jiwei told attendees at its first annual meeting in June 2016.[31] Rather than maximizing the dollar value of contracts for its own firms, Beijing has chosen to maximize

China's global prestige by turning the AIIB into a truly multi-lateral organization.[32]

In any case, the AIIB is only a minor weapon in China's financial arsenal.[33] It will help support projects along the Belt and Road, among other things; but it plans to lend no more than US$2 billion per year for its first five years of operation—significantly less than other multilateral development banks, and a puny amount compared to the vast loans routinely issued by China's giant policy banks. The AIIB has authorized capital of US$100 billion, but its paid-in working capital is much smaller. Authorized capital almost always exceeds working capital at multilateral development banks, mainly to reassure ratings agencies and buyers of bonds that there is backup cash available. This enables development banks to borrow huge amounts at very low rates, despite their razor-thin margins.

By 2020, the AIIB will have roughly US$20 billion of usable equity, similar to that of the ADB. The established development banks—the World Bank, the ADB, the Inter-American Development Bank and the African Development Bank—disbursed amounts equal to 40–50% of their equity in 2014. The newer CAF Development Bank of Latin America, with which AIIB shares some characteristics, disbursed an impressive 70%. If the AIIB and the NDB disburse a plausible 45–70% of their equity, together they could lend in the region of US$15–20 billion per year by the early 2020s—roughly as much as the World Bank's non-concessional arm loaned in 2014, and two to three times as much as the ADB. Assuming that annual disbursements at all other multilateral development banks rise by 10% between now and then, the two new Chinese-backed banks could account for as much as quarter of non-concessional development lending by multilaterals. This is significant, but hardly earth-shattering.

Another pool of capital will come from the Silk Road Fund, largely funded from China's foreign exchange reserves. This is a private equity fund specifically set up to provide anchor financing for Belt and Road projects. But like the AIIB, there is a significant disparity between its authorized capital of US$40 billion and its paid-in capital of US$10 billion. Even if the Silk Road Fund invests all its available funds by 2020, it will only amount to US$2 billion per year. A much bigger potential source of financing is China's commercial banks. Bank of China has indicated it will lend US$100 billion in 2016–18 on Belt and Road projects, while CITIC Bank has pledged total lending of US$113 billion over an unspecified time frame. But these promises should be taken with a pinch of salt, as any loans made to companies with interests overseas can be labelled under "Belt and Road" by savvy executives looking to impress their political masters.

Instead, the real money to support China's ambitions overseas will come from its big policy banks, China Development Bank (CDB) and China Exim Bank. CDB's original mandate was to support domestic infrastructure, but since 2008 it has also funded foreign resource acquisitions by state-owned firms. In addition to financing China's push across Africa, it helped to grease big state-to-state oil deals with Venezuela, Russia and Brazil. Its portfolio of international loans rose from nearly zero in 2007 to US$187 billion in

2013, though its net lending fell back a little in 2014.[34] Chinese press reports suggest that CDB has been instructed to concentrate more on domestic development, and it is hard to know how much cash it will have for supporting foreign adventures. But its average annual net international lending exceeded any of the multilateral development banks in 2008–14.

That leaves the really big beast of economic diplomacy: China Exim Bank. Traditionally a supplier of trade credits to facilitate exports and imports, since 2010 Exim Bank has become a major financier overseas. In 2014, it disbursed US$151 billion, equivalent to the entire GDP of Bangladesh. Its accounts are rather opaque, but in 2014 its total non-trade-related disbursements amounted to US$80 billion—more than the combined lending of all the seven major multilateral development banks. Some of this was spent in China in the form of loans to engineering firms and materials companies selling goods and services abroad, but Exim Bank probably ranks as the world's single biggest financier of overseas development. Exim's contribution to China's international development schemes, including the Belt and Road, may already exceed the contribution that AIIB and NDB are likely to make even a decade from now.

In sum, China's financial power really resides in its policy banks, which will not work on a multilateral basis. They will happily support projects, such as coal-fired power stations, that multilateral development banks would not touch. But the relatively modest scale of the China-led AIIB and NDB repudiates US fears that China is building a credible alternative to the Bretton Woods institutions. The salient point is that China has plenty of money to support its infrastructure diplomacy, even if the AIIB is only a minor source of it.

ASIA'S INFRASTRUCTURE ARMS RACE

Despite fears about economic dependence and China's growing sphere of influence, Asian countries have generally welcomed the promise of investment in much-needed infrastructure. Developed Asia has some of the best infrastructure in the world, but the continent's poorer countries have some of the worst. Laos, Cambodia, Mongolia, Kyrgyzstan, Pakistan, Tajikistan, Bangladesh, Nepal, Timor-Leste and Myanmar rank within the bottom forty countries for the quality of their infrastructure, alongside countries in sub-Saharan Africa, according to the World Economic Forum. All come below India, whose infrastructure deficiencies are infamous. In these impoverished parts of Asia, crumbling roads are swept away by summer rains, electricity is patchy, and mobile phone signals are often non-existent.[35]

The logic of the Belt and Road Initiative is founded on China's own experience that investment in infrastructure promotes economic growth and reduces poverty. The challenge is greatest in inland areas far from seaports, such as landlocked central Asia. Even in coastal areas, rapid economic and population growth is putting enormous strain on existing infrastructure, particularly transport and energy. An oft-cited study by the ADB estimated that US$8 trillion investment in new infrastructure in the decade to 2020 would produce real income gains of around $13 trillion.[36] Even with Chinese largesse, this scale of investment is pie in the sky. But the ADB was on solid ground when it concluded that "building roads, railways, bridges, power stations, and pipelines across the region should be a priority for the region's policymakers".

Nowhere is this truer than in Cambodia, Southeast Asia's poorest country on a per-capita basis. Here China and Japan are engaged in an infrastructure-financing war, armed with chequebooks and construction equipment.[37] In Phnom Penh, the capital, twin bridges soar over a tributary of the mighty Mekong River. The first bridge was built in 1966 as a gift from Japan. A parallel structure, built by the China Bridge and Road Corporation with a soft loan from China Exim Bank, opened in 2014. As China cranks up the Belt and Road Initiative, Japan and its multilateral allies are responding by pumping out more development finance of their own. In April 2015, a spectacular new bridge opened 60 km downriver from Phnom Penh—built and financed by Japan, with the support of the ADB.

China, no doubt, will soon respond. Japan invested US$56 billion in ASEAN countries in 2011–13, more than twice China's US$22 billion. EU members invested still more, at US$75 billion. But in certain Asian countries, including Cambodia, China is already by far the biggest outside investor. Over the next decade or so, as the Belt and Road Initiative gains momentum, Beijing hopes its influence will spread. To this end, it is also stepping up aid—grants and loans made at minimal interest rates. In Southeast Asia, Japan is the most lavish donor, viewing aid as a crucial means of maintaining its regional sphere of influence. China remains some way behind, but its contribution is growing rapidly. In 2013, it disbursed US$7 billion in aid globally, ranking sixth, according to the OECD (Organisation for Economic Co-operation and Development).[38]

Worried by China's financial muscle flexing, Tokyo is fighting back. A new "Development Cooperation Charter", released in February 2015, states that aid must be targeted at protecting Japan's national interest. For the first time, it must also seek to establish the "rule of law" and "democratization".[39] It was followed by a report on foreign aid, which explicitly stated that Japan should build stronger ties with ASEAN to ensure national security in the face of China's growing regional influence.[40] Finally, in May 2015, Prime Minister Shinzo Abe announced that Japan would provide a whopping US$110 billion over five years for "high quality" Asian infrastructure projects—a pointed response to the establishment of the AIIB, which critics fear will finance shoddy Chinese construction.[41] Half of Japan's funds will be disbursed bilaterally, and half in collaboration with the ADB.

Japan's promise to deliver "high quality" infrastructure is no idle boast. An hour east of Phnom Penh, located on the busy highway to Ho Chi Minh City, the magnificent Neak Loeung Bridge shows how the finance battle between China and Japan can benefit underdeveloped Asia. Gliding over the Mekong, the 2 km-long structure opened just six months after China's more modest bridge in Cambodia's capital. Built with a US$130 million grant from Japan, it eliminates a ferry crossing that had become a bottleneck for vehicles travelling between the two cities. On busy days, vehicles had to queue for as long as seven to eight hours, more than doubling the journey time. The ADB views the bridge as a vital link in building a "southern economic corridor" between Thailand and Vietnam—a key part of its Greater Mekong Subregion development programme.[42]

The competition between China and Japan is spreading across Southeast Asia. In Hanoi, 1,500 km north of Phnom Penh, China Railway Group is building part of the city's new urban rail system. Both China and Japan are helping to finance the project. Vietnam's capital city is already home to a gleaming new US$1 billion airport terminal, connected to the city by a sleek six-lane expressway and 9-km bridge over the Red River—all built partly with Japanese aid. For a country at Vietnam's still lowly level of development, the quality of Hanoi's infrastructure is stunning.

In Vietnam, Cambodia and beyond, regional leaders are keen to borrow cheap money. In May 2015, speaking at the "Future in Asia" conference in Tokyo, Cambodia's minister of commerce appealed to the World Bank and ADB not to "penalize" his country for joining the AIIB. "It doesn't matter where the money comes from," Minister Sun Chanthol explained; "we need money to finance infrastructure to improve connectivity."[43] Back in Phnom Penh, one of his advisers put it more bluntly. "We need power stations and highways," Dr Sok Siphana, who led the negotiations for Cambodia's accession to the World Trade Organization, told me. "This is mostly coming from two places: China and Japan. The rest—the UN, World Bank, ADB—are a joke."[44]

There are signs, however, that China's ambitions are stirring the traditional multilateral lenders into action. In 2015, after the establishment of the AIIB, the World Bank offered Indonesia US$11 billion in new loans for infrastructure projects. Meanwhile, the ADB expanded its lending capacity by 50%. "The AIIB is a big deal for Cambodia," says Dr Sok. "Competition is good, because now we can shop around." He added that Cambodia would prefer to borrow from a multilateral organization like the AIIB than on a bilateral basis: "That is better because we won't owe any single country."

Whether the AIIB will prove a rival or a partner for the World Bank and ADB remains to be seen. But it has already succeeded in bringing a new pot of cash to the table and in provoking a positive response from Japan and other multilateral lenders. Add in the bigger funds promised by China's policy banks to support the Belt and Road Initiative and it seems that Asia stands on the verge of an unprecedented infrastructure boom.

The only big uncertainty is whether all these financiers can find bankable projects. Experts in development finance say this, not a lack of funds, is the root cause of Asia's infrastructure deficit. The optimum level of infrastructure investment for any country depends on a combination of its potential growth rate, structure of growth and quality of governance, not to mention commodity prices. History is littered with examples of over-optimistic projections of future needs. Although China has plenty of cash, it may struggle to find worthwhile projects to invest in. One fear is that no-strings-attached aid will simply become a source of graft for local elites, more than a source of economic benefit. Parts of Asia are desperately short of infrastructure, but not all infrastructure is economically productive—as China's own experience of overinvestment shows only too well.

Another fear is that Chinese enterprises will overreach themselves searching for viable projects. Planners envisage Belt and Road investments in such volatile states as Syria, Iraq, Afghanistan, Pakistan, Yemen, Egypt and Ukraine. Significant funds will no doubt be channelled into strategic projects with little chance of making a return. Some investments will bolster China's economic security or bring much-needed development to impoverished areas; others will be about little more than geopolitical bribery. Moreover, for its investments to succeed in troubled parts of the world, Beijing needs to rethink its policy of offering loans to corrupt regimes. From Zambia to Liberia, South Sudan to Myanmar, China's policy of working with unsavoury governments has backfired.

亚洲梦

China portrays the Belt and Road Initiative as an international project, designed to create new trade routes and economic linkages across borders. But there is also a significant domestic component: every province in China has its own Belt and Road investment plan. For local governments looking to stimulate flagging growth, it makes sense to jump on the investment bandwagon. Nationally, policy makers talk up the initiative's potential to create new demand for construction firms and capital goods makers. China's transition to an exporter of high-value capital goods has stalled since the global financial crisis of 2008, dampened by fierce competition and weak global demand. Growth in overseas engineering revenues

halved between 2010 and 2015. Part of the economic rationale behind the Belt and Road Initiative is to arrest this spiral.[45]

In January 2015, the State Council called for "using overseas
construction projects and foreign investment to strengthen
exports of equipment". It has tasked the AIIB, Silk Road Fund
and Chinese policy banks with enabling Chinese firms to
finance seaports, pipelines, power grids, logistics centres, roads
and railways. In turn this should create demand for cement, steel
and capital goods, such as diggers, power turbines and cranes.
Because China's policy banks lend to their own, the biggest
beneficiaries will be Chinese state-owned construction firms.[46]

Unfortunately, the official rhetoric emanating from
Beijing exaggerates the potential of the Belt and Road Initia-
tive to absorb China's industrial overcapacity and revive global
commodity demand. It is plausible that China could finance
US$50–100 billion of overseas Belt and Road projects per year.
Of this the policy banks would provide US$30–80 billion and
the AIIB and Silk Road Fund together a further US$20 billion.
In addition, individual enterprises will be able to borrow from
commercial banks and dip into their own savings. But with
China's domestic infrastructure spending running at some
US$150 billion per month in 2015, a full year of spending on
foreign projects along the Belt and Road is unlikely to match
even a single month's spending at home.

Take steel, which China was accused in 2016 of dumping
onto world markets at below the cost of production. In
2015, China had around 170 million metric tonnes of excess
steel capacity. If the Belt and Road generated new overseas
spending of US$100 billion a year, of which US$15 billion

wound up in the pockets of Chinese steel makers, the impact on steel demand would only be marginal. At late 2015 prices, US$15 billion bought 28 million tonnes of steel—just 16% of China's excess capacity. That does not come close to solving the problem. Of course, not all Belt and Road spending is occurring abroad. The National Development and Reform Commission's (NDRC) first list of successful investments included long-planned projects, such as new air freight hubs in Chengdu and Xiamen, which had been hastily rebranded under the Belt and Road moniker. But since these would have been built anyway, they did not add to the total demand.[47]

The Belt and Road Initiative is a long-term project that will need time to gain traction. So far, there have been hits and misses among projects listed by the NDRC. The biggest investments, such as the "land bridge" from western China to Europe and the development of Pakistan's Arabian Sea port of Gwadar, are noteworthy. The opening of cement factories in Indonesia and Myanmar are exactly the kind of outward corporate investments that Beijing wants to encourage. Another interesting project is a "port alliance" between ten Chinese ports and six Malaysian ports, which are working together to reduce bottlenecks and boost trade. China is investing US$10 billion in a deep-sea port and commercial marina project in Malacca.[48] But many projects, such as Xinjiang's plan to develop integrated cotton production in Tajikistan, sound like pretty small beer. Others, such as Zhengzhou Airport's costly attempt to become a freight hub along the Belt and Road, are nonsensical: located in central China, Zhengzhou is far from the core of either the Belt or the Road. Here the initiative is yet another excuse for regional investment.

In fact, many Chinese "investments" are no such thing. The Belt and Road Initiative is as much about securing engineering contracts for state-owned construction firms, often from foreign governments themselves investing borrowed Chinese funds, as it is about building and subsequently owning assets. China's Ministry of Commerce claims that Chinese firms made direct investments worth US$14.8 billion in 49 countries along the Belt and Road in 2015; the biggest recipients were Singapore, Kazakhstan, Laos, Indonesia, Russia and Thailand. But they also signed nearly 4,000 engineering, procurement and construction projects in 60 countries, worth a much larger US$92.6 billion.[49] It is unclear how many of these projects were truly products of the Belt and Road, and how many would have happened anyway. Either way, Chinese ministries are cranking up the propaganda to support President Xi's grand initiative.

Both at home and abroad, sceptics fear that the Belt and Road Initiative will become an excuse for wasteful spending. "There will be successes and failures," says one doubter with links to the government. "To be very blunt, when people mention the Belt and Road I think back to the Great Leap Forward," he added darkly, referring to China's disastrous policy to transform its economy in 1958–61.[50] Most countries will be happy to take China's money, but they remain wary of its strategic intentions and certainly do not share its vision of a Sino-centric Asia. Geopolitical constraints mean that the Belt and Road could deliver less than promised. "I am sceptical of China's capacity to sell the notion of 'common destiny' to the international community," says Zha Daojiong, professor of International Political Economy at Peking University.[51]

Nevertheless, the Belt and Road Initiative is a bold project that must be taken seriously. It shows how China's evolving foreign policy could make a material difference to economic welfare in Asia and beyond. It should help deliver a much-needed investment stimulus to emerging markets, whether directly or indirectly by encouraging competitive lending. And it will provide work for Chinese engineering firms and new opportunities for capital goods exporters—even if claims that the initiative can slay the ghost of overcapacity are much exaggerated. Xi Jinping sees greater regional integration as part of his legacy, and is determined to make it happen. But to have a chance of succeeding, China will have to convince its neighbours that its grand initiative does not amount to a strategic push for regional hegemony.

CHAPTER 2

MARCHING
WEST

THE ECONOMICS OF
POWER IN CENTRAL ASIA

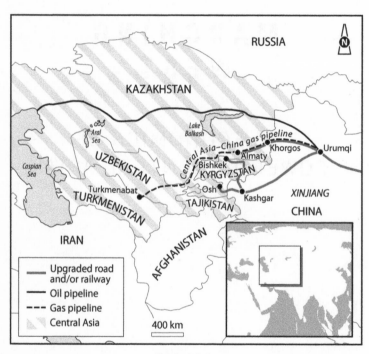

Central Asia

Two decades ago, Astana was just a small Soviet railway town in the middle of nowhere. When, in 1995, Kazakhstan's first (and so far only) president announced that the capital would be moved there from Almaty, diplomats were appalled. With its leafy streets, pavement cafes and ornate Russian buildings painted in marshmallow hues, Almaty has an air of Eastern European sophistication. In Astana, which literally means "capital" in Kazakh, winter temperatures have been known to sink below minus 50°C. But the construction of a new capital for a newly independent nation went ahead, financed by oil drilled from the depths of the Caspian Sea.

Kazakhstan's new capital is still windswept and freezing, but it has been transformed by twenty years of vast oil profits. Designer skyscrapers, bizarre monuments and sparkling mosques jostle for attention beside the city's most futuristic structure—a huge shopping mall resembling nothing so much as a giant, tilting teepee.[1] Amid the jumble of weird and wonderful buildings, two palaces dominate the skyline. One is the blue-domed and golden-spired Presidential Palace: the grand home of Nursultan Nazarbayev, Kazakhstan's all-powerful leader. The other is a twenty-five-storey hotel owned by China's national oil company, CNPC. With its ornate gateway and eaved roof set on vermilion pillars, the Peking Palace is the hotel of choice for Chinese dignitaries visiting Central Asia's dominant economic state.

The Peking Palace symbolizes China's growing might in Central Asia. China is the region's biggest trade and investment partner, and its biggest financier. CNPC alone controls one-quarter of Kazakhstan's oil production.[2] When China's finance minister Lou Jiwei wined and dined Asian leaders in May 2014, explaining Beijing's plan to set up what would become the Asian Infrastructure Investment Bank, he did so at the Peking Palace's Great Wall restaurant. In Central Asia, as across Asia, the balance of power is shifting towards China.

It was also in Astana, at Nazarbayev University in September 2013, that Xi Jinping first announced the intention to build a "Silk Road Economic Belt", stretching from western China across Central Asia to Europe.[3] Chinese work on a "Eurasian land bridge" began long before President Xi took office, but he has wrapped the scheme into his grand narrative of national rejuvenation: the Belt and Road Initiative is Xi's signature project. The vision is about more than building new export corridors and importing yet more oil, gas and minerals. In addition to creating a regional network of economic dependency, Beijing calculates that better connectivity will help its underdeveloped border regions become viable trade zones. It also wants to establish a security cordon in Central Asia that will enable it to keep a lid on ethnic tensions between the native Muslim populace and Han Chinese immigrants in its northwestern region of Xinjiang.

The diplomatic endgame, whether planned or not, is to bind Central Asia to China. Even as Vladimir Putin pushes his alternative vision of a Eurasian Economic Union rising from the ashes of the Soviet Union, China is busy filling the economic vacuum left by Moscow's retreat from the region. Russia retains a strategic interest in the five Central Asian states, and Beijing is careful to portray its regional initiatives as purely commercial, not a bid to extend political influence. But as it boosts investment and offers financial assistance to the fragile regimes over its borders, China's influence is strengthening at Russia's expense. Its growing economic clout will soon make its position in Central Asia unassailable. China's "march westwards" has drawn far less attention than the US's "pivot to Asia", but it may prove more significant.

XINJIANG

China has a long history of influence in the sparsely populated steppe and deserts to its west. During the Tang Dynasty (618–907), when the Chinese Empire extended far along the Silk Road, khanates in present-day Uzbekistan and Turkmenistan sent tribute by camel to the imperial capital in Chang'an. In the 18th century, the Qianlong Emperor captured the eastern half of central Asia, which was eventually renamed Xinjiang—"new territory". Foreigners continued to refer exotically to "East Turkestan", a name that would be revived by Uyghur nationalists in the 1930s. By the end of the 19th century the larger western chunk of central Asia was in Russian hands. Under the Soviet Union, China had little interaction with the republics on its western border, especially after diplomatic relations were broken off in 1960.[4]

When Kazakhstan, Kyrgyzstan, Tajikistan, Uzbekistan and Turkmenistan gained independence in 1991—collectively dubbed Central Asia, with a big "C"—Beijing's first priority was to demarcate its borders and ensure the security of Xinjiang. In 1996 it created the Shanghai Five Forum, a regional security association consisting of China, Russia, Kazakhstan, Kyrgyzstan and Tajikistan. After adding Uzbekistan in 2001, the Shanghai Five was renamed the Shanghai Cooperation Organization (SCO). In 2015, after a decade of deadlock over its expansion, both India and Pakistan were invited to become full members. The SCO's charter requires members to combat the "three evils" of terrorism, separatism and religious extremism, but China also views it as a vehicle for economic cooperation.[5]

The establishment of the Shanghai Five in the mid-1990s coincided with China's growing recognition of the economic and strategic potential of Central Asia. The region is rich in natural resources, with untapped oil and gas fields, deep uranium reserves, and lots of potential for hydro power. Beijing views stability in Central Asia as essential for the prosperity of landlocked Xinjiang, with which it shares a 2,800-km border. By building roads, railways and pipelines connecting the regions, Beijing's strategists believe cross-border trade will flourish. Modernization and economic development, they hope, will help integrate Xinjiang into the region and keep its restive separatists in check.

In 2012 former premier Wen Jiabao announced plans to transform Xinjiang's capital city Urumqi into the "gateway to Eurasia", with a new airport and roads to Kyrgyzstan and

Tajikistan.[6] Wen's speech echoed the vision of Wang Jisi, dean of the School of International Studies at Peking University and one of China's foremost foreign policy thinkers. In an article published in October that year, Wang advocated building "a new Silk Road extending from China's eastern ports, through the centre of Asia and Europe, to the eastern banks of the Atlantic Ocean and the Mediterranean coastal countries in the west". Rather than focusing on the troublesome East and South China Seas, he contended, China should "march westwards".[7]

In his 2013 speech at Nazarbayev University, President Xi put flesh on the bones. He spoke of the ancient trade links between East and West, when silk and other Chinese goods made their way from the imperial capital at Chang'an (now known as Xi'an) across Central Asia to Turkey and the Mediterranean Sea. "Looking back on that epoch," Xi said wistfully, "I can hear the camel bells echoing in the mountains and see the wisps of smoke rising from the desert." A year later, Xi returned to Central Asia to attend the 14th Summit of the SCO, held in Tajikistan. But this time security concerns were at the top of his agenda: Xi called for an agreement to help curb Islamic extremism and urged the SCO's anti-terrorism agency to play a greater role in drug trafficking.

The SCO was founded long before President Xi started to wax lyrical about building a New Silk Road. But the two China-led initiatives are connected: China's leaders believe that economic development will help to deliver greater regional stability, both in Xinjiang and in the fragile states over its western frontiers. Beijing has ploughed billions of dollars into investments across Xinjiang, where it is attempting to placate restive Uyghur nationalists. And it has extended its largesse to the five post-Soviet states of Central Asia, helping them to rebuild crumbling infrastructure, partly in return for access to oil and gas.

China's security concerns are real, despite its inaccurate habit of portraying Uyghur nationalism as religious extremism. Yet its move into Central Asia is about more than ensuring regional stability or grabbing natural resources, important as they are. It also signals a shift in Beijing's geopolitical gaze—long focused on China's eastern seaboard—over its land borders. The "New Silk Road" concept marks Beijing's rediscovery of its traditional continental ambition. Central Asia watchers have noted, persuasively, that China's growing presence in the region over the past decade amounted to building an "inadvertent empire".[8] But Xi Jinping's determination to keep "marching westwards" suggests that China is now actively seeking to establish itself as the central economic power in Eurasia.

Beijing's ambitions focus on trade and investment, which it sees as part of the solution to the security problem in Xinjiang. China's leaders have long encouraged Han Chinese to migrate to this distant corner of the empire, whose native population is mainly Turkic-speaking Muslims. Before China's Communist revolution in 1949, the Muslim Uyghur minority comprised more than 90% of Xinjiang's population; today it accounts for just 40% of its 22 million inhabitants. Beijing has channelled vast sums into updating the transport network and developing the oil and gas industries, which dominate Xinjiang's economy. But most of this wealth has flowed back to Beijing or into the pockets of Han immigrants, fuelling resentment and protests among the native Uyghur minority. In 2009, vicious Uyghur-led riots in Urumqi killed 197 people and injured nearly 2,000.[9]

In 2013, violence spread beyond Xinjiang. That October, a jeep driven by a Uyghur protester crashed through a crowd of pedestrians on the edge of Beijing's Tiananmen Square and burst into flames, killing five people. Then, in March 2014, eight knife-wielding Uyghurs rampaged through a packed railway station in Kunming in southwest China, killing 29 people and wounding more than 140 others—a massacre described by national media as "China's 9/11". A month later, two suicide bombers detonated explosives at a railway station in Urumqi—the first bombing in the city for seventeen years. And, in July, ethnic rioting in southern Xinjiang county of Shache left an official death toll of 96. The reported body count in 2014 was around 400, though the actual number was probably considerably higher.[10]

Beijing blames these attacks on separatism fuelled by radical Islam. It maintains that terrorists are attempting to create an independent Islamic state in Xinjiang, directed by hostile foreign forces aligned with al-Qaeda and the Taliban. Since the World Trade Center attacks in New York in 2001, it has explicitly linked its crackdown in Xinjiang to the US's Global War on Terror, portraying China as a fellow "victim of international terrorism". Specifically, it blames a shadowy and nebulous organization known as the East Turkestan Islamic Movement (ETIM) of masterminding terrorist attacks from abroad.

Terrorism experts disagree over the role of the ETIM; some even dispute its very existence. Either way, there is little evidence that the ETIM or any other "terrorist" organization was responsible for the attacks in Beijing and Kunming. In his book *China's Forgotten People*, former Xinjiang resident Nick Holdstock contends there is actually little organized Islamic terrorism in the region. Instead, he argues that the spiralling violence witnessed over the past few years is a desperate act of resistance to the very policies Beijing has put in place to control "terrorism"—a self-fulfilling prophecy that is, tragically, now inciting the real thing. In the name of "security", the authorities have turned much of the region into a police state, raiding homes and banning symbols of religious devotion. In response, small groups of militant Uyghurs have begun to target civilians for political ends.

Whatever the reality, Beijing's fear of growing Islamism in Xinjiang is not unjustified. In early 2016, a defector from Islamic State (IS) leaked more than 3,500 foreign-fighter registration forms collected between mid-2013 and mid-2014. Analysis by the New America Foundation, a Washington-based think tank, found that 118 of the fighters came from China—114 of them from Xinjiang.[11] In 2015, IS released a recruitment video in Mandarin accusing Beijing of persecuting Uyghurs, and encouraging more Chinese Muslims to join the global jihad. According to reports from northern Syria, several thousand Chinese Uyghurs from Xinjiang have settled in military camps there. They are described as members of the al-Qaeda-affiliated Turkistan Islamic Party, a new incarnation of the ETIM.[12]

On August 30 3016, a suicide bombing at the Chinese embassy in Bishkek, the capital of Kyrgyzstan, strengthened Beijing's case against the ETIM. A car crashed into the embassy gate and detonated, shattering windows and injuring three local employees inside.[13] Kyrgyzstani state security said the attack had been ordered by militant Uyghurs active in Syria and carried out by an ethnic Uyghur from Tajikistan, who belonged to the terrorist group. "[The ETIM] have blood all over their hands," China's foreign ministry spokesperson responded. "We will firmly strike against them and safeguard the safety of the Chinese people in foreign countries."[14] Such attacks only make it easier for Beijing to justify clamping down on Islamic practices at home.

Nevertheless, the authorities continue to believe that Uyghur resentment in Xinjiang can be contained by developing the local economy and improving livelihoods. It has poured money into the region since 2010, building new roads, railways and markets. But tension remains high. At Beijing airport, passengers travelling to Xinjiang go through a special security check and are herded along a caged walkway to the departure lounge. At Urumqi, hand luggage is swabbed for explosives on the gangplank leading into the plane. So far, economic development and the lure of wealth are failing to satisfy a colonized people craving political, cultural and religious freedom.

亚洲梦

Two centuries ago, Urumqi was possibly the most remote place on earth. Located at the very centre of the Eurasian landmass, it is surrounded by endless steppe, desert and mountains.

"Urumqi" translates as "beautiful pasture" in the language of the Dzungars, the Mongolian tribes who ruled the area until they were obliterated by the Qianlong Emperor's military campaigns in the mid-18th century. Today it is the largest city in greater central Asia and the nucleus of Beijing's effort to build the Silk Road Economic Belt. Urumqi is located farther from an ocean than any other city on earth, but it is on its way to becoming a regional transport and financial hub.

Since 2011, Urumqi has staged a giant China–Eurasia Expo to encourage regional trade. In 2014, when I visited, the theme was explicitly "Building the Silk Road Economic Belt". Held in a gargantuan exhibition hall, which resembled a silver flying saucer of extra-terrestrial proportions, the venue was protected by marching People's Armed Police and SWAT teams in armoured personnel carriers. It attracted regional leaders, traders from Asia and beyond, and jostling crowds of locals snapping up foreign handicrafts and edible delicacies.

The most illuminating displays were in the central pavilion. Here a giant map projected how the new Silk Road Economic Belt would recreate but ultimately dwarf the ancient Silk Road, turning a landlocked region into a virtual ocean for trains and trucks—modern "ships of the desert". It was accompanied by a film which showed the origins of the Silk Road more than 2,000 years ago, when the Han Dynasty envoy Zhang Qian first crossed central Asia to establish trade routes between China and the lands to the west. That history, the film explained, is inspiring China to push its vast domestic transport networks over its borders, as it gears up to dominate trade and investment across Asia and into Europe. This will be to the "mutual benefit" of the entire region, delivering peace and economic development in Eurasia—but most importantly, it will help to realize Xi Jinping's dream of "the great rejuvenation of the Chinese people".

Other displays showed how Chinese enterprises are prudently placing their own activities in the grand Silk Road narrative. The pavilion was awash with corporate infrastructure porn—expressways cutting through jungle and desert; tunnels rammed through mountains; trains racing across the permafrost of the Tibetan plateau—demonstrating the ability of China's road and rail companies to bring efficient transport links to the wildest regions on earth. Outside the exhibition hall, a display of giant cranes, loaders and earthmovers left one in no doubt about China's engineering power to tame the inhospitable terrain of central Asia.

The goal of the Silk Road Economic Belt, which runs from northwest China to Europe, is to create a land transport network that will lop thousands of miles off the traditional sea routes from China's east coast. It is also a transport route for imports of oil, gas and other natural resources. In the last few years, Beijing has connected Urumqi to the rest of China with a high-speed passenger railway, and it has built a new freight rail line and expressway running 700 km from Urumqi to the border with Kazakhstan. From there, it is financing upgraded roads and railways to Russia and Europe. Improved transport links are already enabling high-end goods to travel from inland China in a fraction of the time it takes by sea. Road and rail transport may be more expensive, but it is cost effective for time-sensitive consumer goods and components.

On the border with Kazakhstan, Beijing's planners want to turn the small town of Khorgos into one of the biggest distribution hubs in Central Asia—a "dry port" with acres of warehouses and an industrial park.[15] A new railway from Urumqi passes through Khorgos, where rows of cranes transfer containers from China's standard gauge wagons to the broad gauge used across the former Soviet states. The line then loops into the old Soviet network at Almaty, while a new line will serve the Caspian seaport and oil town of Aktau. The first transcontinental services to Germany began in 2012 and take fifteen days to make the 10,000-km journey, thirty days quicker than by sea. HP, Acer and Foxconn use the route to export computers from their manufacturing bases in Chongqing; Volkswagen, Audi and BMW use it to ship parts from Germany to their factories in inland China.[16] From its global base in Chengdu, Dell sends all its laptops for the European market by transcontinental train. Bulkier desktops, on the other hand, tend to go by sea. Other services to Europe run from the inland cities of Wuhan, Changsha, Chengdu, Xi'an and Zhengzhou.

The railway is also opening up emerging Asian markets. Since 2016, a service to Tehran has delivered Chinese-made clothes, bags and shoes via Kazakhstan and Turkmenistan. In addition, an intermodal freight centre at the port of Lianyun-gang, 200 km south of Qingdao, in theory provides land access to Central Asia and Europe from South Korea and Japan. DHL Global Forwarding has opened a service from Lianyungang to Istanbul, transiting through Kazakhstan, Azerbaijan and Georgia. The company expects volumes on its Asia–Europe rail services to double or triple by 2020.[17]

When I visited Khorgos in late 2014, Kazakh middlemen told me the new infrastructure had helped considerably. "Business these days is very good," one grinning trader told me, explaining that the new border crossing between China and Kazakhstan provided enhanced facilities for trucks. His family firm, based over the border from Khorgos in the dusty trucking town of Zharkent, sends up to fifteen lorries a day on to Moscow. A new expressway to Almaty connects with roads running north to Russia, west to Uzbekistan and south to Kyrgyzstan—transport corridors part-financed by the Asian Development Banks' Central Asia Regional Economic Cooperation (CAREC) programme.[18] China has skilfully used this multilateral umbrella to build crucial sections of the Silk Road Economic Belt, even persuading the ADB to locate its new regional headquarters in Urumqi.[19]

Some success has been made in facilitating trade, perhaps a tougher challenge than building the infrastructure itself. On the old rail route from Xinjiang to Russia, which crosses into Kazakhstan a few hundred kilometres to the north, trains spent an average of seventeen days at the border in 2012. By comparison, the rapid service through Khorgos to Germany, which enjoys simplified border formalities, shows what is possible with high-level support. Goods these days pass quite efficiently through the Kazakhstani border into the Eurasian Customs Union. Yet some European businesses complain that the route is too expensive to be economical. The boss of a large petrochemical company told me the only reason his firm exported over the land bridge was to keep both central and local officials happy.[20]

In addition to a transport and logistics hub, Beijing is trying to transform Khorgos from a sandy outpost into a centre for business and commerce. These plans date back to an agreement signed by Presidents Hu and Nazarbayev during a meeting of the SCO in 2005, well before any talk of a Silk Road Economic Belt. New apartment blocks are rising in the scrubby desert, and traders across China have been drawn to Khorgos by tax breaks and cut-price rents. They work in a giant glorified bazaar straddling the border, officially known as the Border Cooperation Centre. In the entrance hall, crowds of Uyghurs, Kazakhs and Hui apply for permits to cross into the special zone, where they are allowed to stay visa free for thirty days. The women, dressed in bright dresses and headscarves, flash smiles with gold teeth.

The border zone is designed to push local economic development by encouraging trade, with storage depots, bonded warehouses and plans for export processing. The reality is that most visitors simply come for tax-free shopping. The Chinese side is already reasonably developed, with several large wholesale markets and tall new office buildings. Busloads of shoppers arrive from Almaty to buy fur coats, clothes and shoes; most store names are written in Russian rather than Chinese. But the Kazakhstani side is smaller than a village bazaar—just a few old shipping containers-cum-shops selling Kazakh groceries and camel milk to Uyghur grandmothers. It hardly looks like a commercial hub in the making.

Khorgos' biggest drawback is that the region is so sparsely populated; the nearest big cities are Almaty, 360 km to the west, and Urumqi, 670 km to the east. Chinese traders in the bazaar grumble that they were deceived into moving to the middle of nowhere. Sales slumped after the devaluation of the Kazakhstani currency in August 2015, when the tenge lost more than a quarter of its value in a single day, reducing customers' spending power. "The area is still quite poor: it's not like selling goods back home," complained Mr Zuo, a shoe trader from Guangdong province. "It was a mistake to come here."[21]

亚洲梦

A thousand miles southwest of Urumqi lie the fabled bazaars of Kashgar, one of the most important stops on the old Silk Road. China's most westerly city, Kashgar borders Kyrgyzstan, Tajikistan, Afghanistan and Pakistan. It is famous for its heaving Sunday Market, actually open daily. Most of the customers are local and, despite a few signs in English pointing towards "tourist souvenirs", the Sunday Market mainly sells everyday items—bright textiles for ladies' dresses, embroidered skull caps, furs and leathers for the cold winters, TVs toys and fridges. There are bulging sacks of walnuts, raisins and sweets, street stalls offering glasses of iced curd, and smoky restaurants where men grill skewers of fatty lamb over charcoal braziers. Both culturally and geographically, Kashgar is as close to Turkey as it is to the Chinese heartland.

Away from the wide roads and tower blocks of the modern city, where the city's Han Chinese residents live, Kashgar remains resolutely Uyghur. The streets are filled with women wearing voluminous dresses and bright headscarves; a few even cover their entire head with a rough brown shawl, peering out through the stitching. Some working men, in flat caps and faces grizzled with stubble, are so Western-looking they could be Turkish or even Sicilian. Older men, dressed in flowing white robes and embroidered skullcaps, sport a magnificent array of beards—long and wispy, flowingly luxuriant or carefully cropped. With deep-set eyes and high noses, they look quite distinct from their Mongoloid neighbours in China proper and across the central Asian steppe.

Much of Kashgar's old town has been destroyed and rebuilt over the past decade. The narrow lanes outside the famous Id Kah Mosque were flattened to make way for a large public square, deemed essential in any modern Chinese city. Old mud and timber homes are being replaced by brick and cement houses and apartment blocks. Across the road from People's Square, which has become a parking lot for the armoured vans of the People's Armed Police, a young man in an embroidered skullcap vented his frustration to me about the Han invaders: "The Chinese have no faith; all they worship is money," he sneered. "But I am Uyghur—Turkic. We are different." Other Uyghurs, however, show a begrudging acceptance of their Han colonizers. "I have Han friends and most of us get on fine," Hadicha, a middle-aged woman in a shapeless blue dress, told me in broken Mandarin. She said the city government pays every resident 200 yuan per month, about US$30, to help keep the peace.[22]

Money and power are what Beijing understands best. At Kashgar airport travellers are greeted by armed police and a poster declaring "Realize the dream of the Kashgar Special Zone!" In 2010, Kashgar was classified as the first new SEZ in fifteen years, supposedly following the model that was so successful in Shenzhen.[23] Kashgar, of course, does not enjoy

Shenzhen's prime advantage: its coastal location next to Hong Kong. But policy makers have unveiled favourable tax policies and instructed Guangdong province to invest US$1.5 billion in the city, part of a broader policy of forcing wealthier parts of China to subsidize development across Xinjiang. The aim is to re-establish Kashgar as gateway to Central and South Asia, with ambitious rail projects planned to connect the city with neighbouring Kyrgyzstan and Pakistan, and beyond.

Guangdong has funnelled its investments into "Guangzhou New City", which sprawls across a dusty plain a few kilometres out of town. Few of the planned residential blocks had been completed when I visited, but a series of large, low-rise wholesale markets had opened amid a grid of wide roads fronted by vacant lots. In its organized emptiness, it was the opposite of the thriving but chaotic Sunday Market. As yet, there is little economic rationale for such a large development in this remote, under-populated corner of the country. At a clothes market I found shopkeepers lured 5,000 km from their homes in coastal Zhejiang province by three years of free housing and knockdown rents. "We came here because we heard it would be a big international market," one trader told me, "but so far it's very quiet."

Down the road, foreign merchants in the shiny new Eight Country Shopping Mall were a little more optimistic. They too receive subsidized shop rents and three years of free accommodation, as the government attempts to get the project off the ground. Habdul Razzaq, a native of Faisalabad in Pakistan, estimated that around 150 of the 1,000 traders who work between Islamabad and Kashgar had moved into the new mall. They truck their goods over the Karakoram Highway, which winds its way to Xinjiang through the mountains of Kashmir. "When the road is impassable in winter I'll have to fly my goods in, but that'll be expensive. I hope they do build a new railway to Islamabad," he said, referring to plans to build a transport corridor from Kashgar to the Arabian Sea.

In the Uzbekistan section of the mall I met Firuza Nadirova, whose complicated family history makes a mockery of the national borders that artificially divide the region. An ethnic Uzbek from Kyrgyzstan, she is married to a Kyrgyzstani Uyghur; their daughter attends a bilingual Chinese–Uyghur school in Kashgar. Sporting a striking monobrow thickened with black paste, she showed me her bright-blue Kyrgyzstani passport filled with Chinese visas, which she renews in Kashgar. My translator was Nurbiya, a young Uyghur trader who spoke fluent Kyrgyz. In perfect Mandarin—rare among Uyghurs—she told me she went to a Chinese school and just returned from teaching students at the Chinese government-sponsored Confucius Institute in Bishkek.

It is too early to say whether Guangzhou New City—and other developments associated with the Silk Road Economic Belt—will realize policy makers' ambitious plans of fostering new trade hubs. Yet they are already creating economic opportunities for women like Nadirova and Nurbiya. This will hardly satisfy the millions of Uyghurs who crave religious freedom and resent speaking a foreign language in their own land. But by building up trade links with neighbouring countries, Beijing is offering the potential of a more prosperous future—though only to those who are willing to play the political game.[24]

CENTRAL ASIA

Liu Yazhou, an outspoken general in the People's Liberation Army, once called Central Asia "the richest gift bestowed on the Chinese people by the heavens".[25] For China, Central Asia offers an abundance of natural resources. Kazakhstan has large reserves of oil and uranium, Turkmenistan supplies nearly half of China's imported gas, and there is enormous potential to boost regional mineral extraction. Central Asia accounts for only around 1% of Chinese trade, but its geostrategic value is considerably greater than raw numbers indicate.

Over the past decade, CNPC has outmuscled Russia's own state firms to become Central Asia's energy giant. Kazakhstan claims the world's tenth largest oil reserves, but a decade ago Chinese oil companies owned only one major asset there. Its three big oil fields—Tengiz, Karachaganak and Kashagan—were controlled by Western majors, with two pipelines running through Russia to Europe. China's penetration of the market has been rapid and aggressive. In 2005, CNPC outbid India's Oil and Natural Gas Corporation (ONGC) to buy Canadian oil company PetroKazakhstan for US$4.2 billion, turning Kazakhstan into its second-largest foreign production base overnight. In 2006, China and Kazakhstan opened a 3,000-km oil pipeline, stretching from the Caspian Sea to Xinjiang. And when the financial crisis hit in 2009, CNPC bought up local producers suffering from the crash in global commodity prices. By 2010, it had majority stakes in fifteen Kazakhstani energy companies.[26]

CNPC pumps most of its Kazakhstani oil to Europe, but is feeding a rising share into the Central Asia–China pipeline.

With deliveries expected to rise to 20 million tons by 2020, Kazakhstan's president has raised the prospect of building a second pipeline. His confidence is based on projected flows from the giant Kashagan oil field, in which CNPC secured an 8.3% stake in 2013—the first fruit of its "strategic partnership" with KazMunaiGas, the national oil company, in which China's sovereign wealth fund holds an 11% stake. ConocoPhilips, the former owner, had agreed to sell its stake in Kashagan to India's ONGC; but the Kazakhstani government used its right of first refusal to acquire it instead, selling it on to CNPC for US$5 billion. Not for the first time, India's oil major lost out to its deeper-pocketed Chinese competitor.

So far, Kashagan has not proven the enormous boon that CNPC expected. The Caspian oilfield is the industry's biggest discovery for forty years, with recoverable reserves estimated at 13 billion barrels—but it is also one of the costliest. After years of overruns worth an estimated US$50 billion, production finally began in 2013, just four days after CNPC secured its stake. But a series of gas leaks caused by stress cracks in the pipeline rapidly brought production to a halt. Full-scale resumption is not expected till 2017, a delay that will cost billions more. Nevertheless, CNPC's stake in Kashagan means that China has muscled its way to the top table. Far from playing catch-up in Kazakhstan's growing oil market, it is now one of the leading foreign presences there.

It is a similar story in Turkmenistan, the other natural resources power in the region. Once a stronghold of Russian gas major Gazprom, the balance of power shifted firmly towards China in 2009, when CNPC opened a gas pipeline running from Turkmenistan, through Uzbekistan and Kazakhstan, to Xinjiang. Russia did itself no favours. Since Soviet-era pipelines only ran to Russia, Gazprom was able to exploit its monopoly position. It bought gas at below-market prices, re-exporting it to Europe at a hefty mark-up. Keen to end this costly dependence, Turkmenistan did a deal with CNPC. Turkmenistan now exports more gas to China than it sells to Gazprom. The tables have turned so decisively that the government in Ashgabat is now highly dependent on exports to China.

Russia's big four energy companies—Gazprom, Lukoil, Transneft and Rosneft—continue to pump large amounts of oil and gas from Kazakhstan to Europe via Russia. Rosneft even pumps Russian oil to China via Kazakhstan, which earns Astana useful transit dollars. So Russia retains considerable economic leverage in Central Asia. But China's talons dig deeper: it has built power plants, refineries and transmission lines in addition to gas infrastructure, mostly to the detriment of Russian firms, which are unable to compete with their Chinese competitors' easy funding and rapid construction. CNPC is building an alternative route for Turkmenistani gas through Kyrgyzstan, with spurs to energy-poor parts of the region. And the Xinjiang arm of the State Grid Corporation of China is preparing to pour further billions into a new electricity grid—inevitably labelled the "Power Silk Road"—linking Central Asia to Xinjiang.

亚洲梦

Economically, China—not Russia—is now top dog in Central Asia. For Kazakhstan and Turkmenistan, it is a vital energy partner and an important source of cheap loans. But for the region's minnows, Tajikistan and Kyrgyzstan, it is an economic lifeline. Their leaders are dependent on Chinese firms to construct national transport and power networks, mainly funded by cheap loans from China's own policy banks. Chinese firms have built two new highways from Kashgar to Kyrgyzstan, together with a road that will connect the north and south of that country. The ADB is helping to finance the projects, but the bulk of the loans come from China Exim Bank. Few other financiers have either the funds or the inclination to lend to fragile states that have yet to secure an official credit rating.

One of the most important new roads is designed to boost trade between Kashgar and Osh, two of the ancient Silk Road's biggest trading hubs. Chinese traders have carried goods between the market towns, over the Irkeshtam Pass in the foothills of the Pamir Mountains, for more than 2,000 years. The volume quintupled over the past decade, as Kyrgyzstan transformed itself into a regional wholesale market. A full two-thirds of its imports officially come from China—household goods, toys, shoes, clothes and electrical products—and the true figure is more if contraband is taken into account. Until the new highway opened, they were trucked along a potholed road that suffered from frequent landslides. Most are re-exported, primarily to Uzbekistan and Kazakhstan: Kyrgyzstan's bazaar economy would collapse without Chinese shuttle trade.

The new highway, I was told by local traders, had halved the twenty-four-hour journey time between Kashgar and Osh. I decided to test it for myself, leaving Kashgar after breakfast. My driver was Osman, a Uyghur with heavily stubbled cheeks and a thick black moustache. Driving west along the expressway, we cut through a moonscape of eroded sandstone, past craggy dun cliffs flecked with red rock. The road passed through a desert punctuated with tumbledown farmhouses of mud-baked bricks, decorated with carved wooden doors. Scrawny sheep grazed on an unappetizing diet of scrubby grass and sand. Chinese customs control was located in a small bleak town populated mainly by Kyrgyz, still 135 km from the actual border. We bypassed the smattering of trucks waiting to clear the modern customs building and set off on the new highway for the Irkeshtam Pass.

Here the barren landscape grew starker—all desert scree and jagged rocks, rising to biscuit-coloured mountains. My new driver, an ethnic Kyrgyz but a Chinese national, hooked up a video display in his ramshackle Geely, a cheap Chinese car. Women in fur hats warbled to an accordion. Fluttering on the Geely's dashboard were two miniature red flags, representing the Chinese state and the Chinese Communist Party.[27] From the clean asphalt of the new highway we caught glimpses of the winding and corrugated old road. Bridges cut through sheer rock, and new radio masts ensured perfect mobile coverage in one of the remotest spots on earth.[28] Ulugqat, the last village in China, was an ugly grid of brick bungalows with walls covered in Chinese development propaganda painted in Arabic script. But in the fields beyond, felt-hatted farmers swept the mountain grass with sickles, the snow-capped Pamirs rising gloriously behind them.

At the Chinese border a soldier glanced at my passport and waved me into no-man's land, where I counted a line of more than a hundred lorries waiting to pass into China. At the Kyrgyzstani border, thickset troops with rifles slung over their shoulders barked at me in Russian. *"Narkotiki?"* a customs guard asked with a big belly laugh, waving me through.[29] On the other side, the road ascended rapidly to 3,600 metres along desolate, rolling steppe. Horses and sheep grazed on the grass, which was scattered with yurts and trailers that looked like rundown gypsy caravans. By the roadside, children with burnished faces hawked fermented mare's milk in plastic bottles. Then the road zigzagged down a steep mountain pass following a rushing river flecked with ice-melt. Finally we entered the fertile Ferghana Valley, arriving in Osh in time for an early supper—a journey of ten hours.

The road trip showed how Chinese engineering is altering the landscape of Central Asia. In Soviet times, Kyrgyzstan's roads mainly led northwards to Kazakhstan and Russia. China proper remains remote, but it is now perfectly feasible to truck in goods from factories on the east coast. If Chinese strategists have their way, the road from Kashgar to Osh will be accompanied by a railway leading on to the larger markets of Uzbekistan, Iran and Turkey. This would allow Chinese goods to bypass Kyrgyzstan, which has at times threatened to ban Chinese trucks from entering the country. The final section of the Kazakhstan–Turkmenistan–Iran railway opened in 2014; Turkmenistan is working on a new line through Afghanistan and Tajikistan, while Uzbekistan is also laying 129 km of new track. A Chinese-built railway through Kyrgyzstan, on which former prime minister Temir Sariyev said work would begin in 2016, would link into this regional network.

Osh was once an important trading town on the section of the Silk Road running between Kashgar and Samarkand. Today it is a crumbling relic of the Soviet Empire, rundown and ramshackle, plagued by congested roads and unreliable plumbing. More than any other city in Kyrgyzstan, its economy runs on re-exporting imports of Chinese goods. The trade is centred on the Kara-Suu market, almost on the Uzbekistani border. Like the other great regional bazaars in Bishkek and Almaty, it is built of thousands of double-stacked shipping containers, and is chaotic and crowded, filled with cheap clothes, shoes, electronics and tat. Porters with boxes stacked on metal carts rush through the crowds shouting *push, push!*—"watch out, watch out!"

Chinese traders, mostly from the southeast coastal province of Fujian, began to arrive in Kara-Suu a little over a decade ago. When violence flared between local Kyrgyz and Uzbeks in 2010, there were around 2,000 Chinese in the bazaar, mainly serving wholesale merchants from Uzbekistan. But much of that business has dried up, and around half have returned to China. "The Uzbeks are too scared to come," explained Zuo Ya, a trader from Fujian who has worked in Kara-Suu for ten years. "It's also much tougher to move goods across the border now; they are often grabbed by customs." Bribing border officials is simply part of doing business in Central Asia, but many Chinese traders have had enough. "Business is terrible," said another Fujian native, dressed in a tiny miniskirt. "I'm definitely going home."[30]

One of the biggest complaints in Kara-Suu is that Uzbekistani traders are sourcing goods directly in Guangzhou, and arranging for them to be trucked via Urumqi to Tashkent. They employ the services of Abu-Sahiy, a logistics company owned by the family of Islam Karimov, who ruled Uzbekistan with an iron fist from its independence in 1991 till his death in 2016. A short drive from the bazaar, I found Abu-Sahiy's trucking depot in a dusty carpark ringed by graffiti-covered walls. It was staffed by Uyghurs, who act as middlemen between Central Asia and China. One of the managers, a swarthy man called Alijan, confirmed their trucks never have trouble at the border. "Our business", he said with a grin, "is thriving."

In central Osh, the Chinese-run Taatan market sells essentials to Chinese investors. I spoke to Mr Yu in his industrial hardware store. Originally from the coastal city of Nantong near Shanghai, he moved to Osh in 2007 to supply Chinese entrepreneurs buying up cement factories and steel plants. His wife lives in Urumqi, where she organizes shipments of hardhats, cement mixers, industrial fans and machine parts. Most go via Kashgar by truck; some are shipped by train via Kazakhstan. CNPC and the state-owned China Road and Bridge Company both have a presence in Osh, which is also becoming a hub for private Chinese investment in mining—gold, coal and crystals. In 2014, China opened a consulate in the city to support the growing Chinese community there. As money flows along the Silk Road Economic Belt, more men like Mr Yu will arrive to try their luck.

亚洲梦

As China bankrolls development across Central Asia, ordinary people fear being swallowed by their neighbour. In Kyrgyzstan, the metaphor has become reality: locals even joke about Chinese labourers feasting on their donkeys. Most view Beijing's plan to build a railway across their tiny country as more a threat than a potential boon. The challenge for regional leaders is to balance public opinion with economic reality. "We should not fear China's expansion and fence it out," Kyrgyzstan's president, Almazbek Atambaev, urged his people. "We should use to our advantage the fact that China is our neighbour. Even if we do not build the railway, the Chinese will still come to us."[31]

Fed for years by anti-Chinese Soviet propaganda, China's economic influence is viewed as inevitable but pernicious. "China is a huge magnet attracting all the small countries around it," Chubak, a bull-headed shoe salesman, told me in Osh market. "We need them for economic growth—but if we're not careful, we could lose our nation." Warming to his theme, he moved onto a common complaint. "What really annoys me is that Chinese companies win every government tender for new roads, but then they never employ local workers," he said, banging a porky fist into his palm. China Road and Bridge Company, which built the highway I took through the Irkeshtam Pass, imports most of its workers. Later that day I passed Chinese labourers in fluorescent orange bibs resurfacing a road on the edge of town.

The historical fear of "yellow peril" remains alive in Central Asia, especially in black humour about Chinese immigrants pouring over the border. "In 2030 we'll all wake up and find ourselves speaking Chinese," runs a common saying. "Everyone has seen the videos of the Chinese army training—a billion people acting as one," Nurbala Amiebayera, a software engineering student, told me over a tasty dinner of horse kebabs in Almaty. "It scares us to death. When we study our history we learn that tribes close to China invaded us."[32] In Kyrgyzstan, where the media is rife with exaggerated stories about Chinese incomers marrying local women, populist politicians have even made outlandish speeches about Chinese blood weakening the national gene pool.[33]

Firm migration data do not exist, but reports about hundreds of thousands of Chinese immigrants pouring into Central Asia are certainly exaggerated—particularly in Kazakhstan, which maintains tight visa controls. Tens of thousands is a better estimate. Many migrants do not have a happy time: Chinese communities are the victims of petty theft or extortion by criminal gangs, often with police protection, so they tend to keep a low profile. In December 2013, the Beijing-based *Global Times* newspaper reported a "wave" of attacks on Chinese entrepreneurs and students in and around Bishkek. In the summer of 2015, the Chinese owner of a chain of spectacles stores in the Kyrgzstani capital was beaten unconscious and died in hospital after a disagreement with a police chief.[34] Yet most anti-Chinese sentiment is fed by a lack of contact, not too much. Outside of the bazaar, few ordinary Kyrgzstanis meet Chinese people. Road builders imported from the Chinese countryside are usually herded into camps far from locals, feeding rumours that they are actually convicts performing forced labour.

Few Chinese migrants put down roots in Central Asia: they see themselves as transitory traders, earning some cash before they return to China. This is quite different from many other parts of the world—even Africa, which tens of thousands of Chinese migrants have made their home.[35] At the Taatan market in Bishkek they stared listlessly at Chinese TV shows on their phones. The traders I spoke to were from Xinjiang and Fujian, but they said people came from all over China. "Are you used to life here?" I asked one young man from Fujian, who had worked in the market for seven years. He shrugged, miserably. I saw no Chinese restaurants targeted at the immigrant community, and even the money changers in Bishkek advertised every regional currency except Chinese renminbi. China's presence felt skin-deep.[36]

In Kazakhstan, most Chinese arrive on short-term business visas. On weekdays, the pavement outside its embassy in Beijing is crowded with practical-looking men, mostly in their thirties and forties, clutching forms. In the visa office, officials bark questions at them in Russian-accented Chinese: "Why do you want to go to Kazakhstan? What training do you have? Where will you stay and when will you return to China?" The Kazakhstani authorities are keen to milk China for investment and expertise, but they are careful to limit the flow of Chinese into their country to skilled workers. The applicants are oilmen destined for the rigs and pipelines of the Caspian Sea, machinery operators engaged in Chinese-funded infrastructure projects, or technicians attending equipment fairs—all carrying invitation letters, stamped with their company seal.

When I visited to collect my visa, other applicants were more speculative. Professor Wang from Jilin Agricultural University wanted to attend a deer farming forum in the eastern city of Ust-Kamenogorsk. Chinese investors are interested in buying into Kazakhstan's deer farms, he explained, because antlers are used to make Chinese health tonics. A middle-aged man from Dalian, a coastal city in northeast China, was hoping to set up a brick factory. "I haven't been to Kazakhstan before, but I'll see what it's like when I get there," he said.[37] This is the sort of speculative entrepreneurialism that has enabled Chinese investors to overrun Laos, Myanmar and much of Africa. Wherever there's a chance of profit, they'll give it a shot. So far, however, the Kazakhstani government has done a good job of keeping Chinese immigration to a minimum: workers fly in and out, but they do not stay.

In most cases, Chinese migrants benefit local economies—but the perception of China's malign influence is as important as reality. Take the Chatkal region of Kyrgyzstan, where locals accuse Chinese gold miners of turning forest into desert, working secretly at night, and bribing tax officials. Much of the resentment stems from before 2010, when the law allowed dozens of Chinese firms to snap up mining licences for no more than the cost of the paperwork—less than US$10 per time. There is an overwhelming belief among ordinary people that money-grubbing officials allow China and its firms to behave with impunity.

The people of Central Asia increasingly believe their own governments are also in China's pocket. The truth, as the elites Kyrgyzstan and Tajikistan know only too well, is that they need China just to keep the lights on. Beijing is playing a shrewd game, investing in projects—from new electricity grids to oil refineries—that bring it few obvious commercial benefits. During a trip to Tajikistan in 2014, President Xi attended a ground-breaking ceremony of Line D of the Central Asia–China gas pipeline, which will run from Turkmenistan to China via both Tajikistan and Kyrgyzstan. Neither has its own gas supply. Shorter, easier routes were available; but this goodwill gesture showed how Beijing is carefully buying political leverage.

Central Asia badly needs the economic growth that trade and investment with China can bring. On the outskirts of Bishkek, rural migrants live in mud huts with plastic sheeting for windows. The city itself is pockmarked with rusting old factories. Yet it is doubtful whether the region's corrupt governments are capable of exploiting China's rise for the public good. In fact, by keeping the weakest economies from collapse, China's largesse may also be keeping the dictators in power.[38]

RUSSIA

China's rise in Central Asia is viewed with trepidation in Moscow, which has long regarded the region as its own turf. Across the post-Soviet space, as the old Soviet Union is known today, Vladimir Putin laments Russia's waning influence. Like Xi Jinping, President Putin is a nationalist seeking the rejuvenation of his humiliated country. His grand scheme to achieve this end is the formation of a Eurasian Union, stretching from Ukraine, across the Caucasus and Central Asia, to the Russian Far East. Critics call it a "Soviet Union-lite".[39]

Putin's dream moved closer to reality on 1 January 2015 with the establishment of the Eurasian Economic Union (EEU), which grew out of an existing customs union between Russia, Belarus and Kazakhstan. So far the EEU has five members, with Armenia and Kygyzstan joining the original three. The Kremlin put enormous pressure on Kyrgyzstan to join, and is leaning heavily on tiny Tajikistan to follow. Like the European Union, the EEU's primary aim is to ensure the free movement of goods, capital, services and people across an integrated single market. But Putin's long-term goal is grander: to create a supranational political union that can form a bridge between Europe and Asia to rival the EU and China. In short, it is Russia's bold attempt to preserve its sphere of influence across the whole of Eurasia—including Central Asia.

The EEU, then, is as much about preventing China's "march west" as it is about preventing the expansion of the EU in Eastern Europe. There are good economic reasons, however, to believe that it will not thrive. In the first place, it is fundamentally inward-looking and protectionist. Higher external tariffs have damaged trade with non-customs union members, notably shuttle trade between China and Kyrgyzstan. Although the union has boosted overall trade volumes within the region, it has mainly done so to Russia's advantage. Kazakhstan's trade deficit has widened with its neighbours; yet Russia has insisted on retaining exemptions on internal energy tariffs, worth US$40 billion per year, until 2025.

The biggest stumbling block, however, is political. The idea of a Eurasian Union was first mooted in 1994 by President Nazarbayev of Kazakhstan. But his vision extended only as far as a common trading bloc—not the political union he fears is Putin's true goal. At his insistence, the Eurasian Union was renamed the Eurasian *Economic* Union. Russia's irredentist ambitions are a perennial concern in Astana. At a pro-Kremlin youth camp held at Lake Seliger near Moscow in August 2014, Putin declared that "Kazakhs had never had statehood" and that Kazakhstan was ultimately part of the *Russki mir*—"Russian world". "Kazakhstan will not be part of organizations that pose a threat to our independence," Nazarbayev retorted, angrily, on state television.[40]

But it was Russia's annexation of Crimea in 2014 that really caused jitters in Astana. Kazakhstan has much in common with Ukraine: 22% of its people are ethnically Russian, rising to more than 40% in the cities along its northern border with Russia. Many Russians basically view northern Kazakhstan as Russian territory, just as they do Crimea and parts of eastern Ukraine. In a rare show of public defiance ahead of the EEU treaty negotiations, 500 protesters marched through the leafy streets of Almaty appealing against membership. After more than a century of being ruled from Moscow, the people of Kazakhstan—like their former comrades in western Ukraine—guard their independence fiercely.

Political analysts in Kazakhstan believe that Russia's aggressive attempt to enlarge its sphere of influence has handed the geopolitical initiative to Beijing. "Crimea has weakened Russia," says Nargis Kassenova, director of the Central Asian Studies Centre at Almaty's KIMEP University. "We were afraid of China, but it looks a better bet than Russia. The Chinese do not interfere in domestic issues; they show respect, and they do not impose political conditions."[41] Aidar Azer-bayev, an academic at Almaty's Institute for World Economics and Politics, agrees. "Ukraine strengthens Xi Jinping's hand," he told me over dinner in a local restaurant. "China can loosen Russia's embrace in Central Asia and present its vision of a new Silk Road as a more open alternative."[42]

President Nazarbayev made Kazakhstan's position quite clear at the EEU treaty signing, in comments clearly directed at Putin: "We see the EEU as an open economic community, organically plugged into global communications and as a reliable bridge between Europe and growing Asia." Kazakh-stan is positioning itself as the crossroads of Eurasia, where it is determined to balance competing external interests. "We are landlocked and remote from world markets, so we need better connectivity," Timur Zhaxylykov, vice minister of economy and budget planning, told me on the sidelines of the ADB's 2014 annual meeting, held in Astana. "Roads, rail links and pipelines mean we can have direct access to China, the second-biggest and fastest-growing market in the world," he added, almost singing from Beijing's hymnbook.[43]

So if Putin's dream of Eurasian integration is likely to fail, how much space does that leave for China to push its own agenda in Central Asia? On a hot morning in Bishkek, I put this question to Talant Sultanov, then the head of the national strategic studies think tank. "China has considerable economic power, but it does not want to annoy Russia," he told me in a dingy Soviet-era building on Kiev Street. "Their leaders' message is this: 'We want our neighbours to be stable and prosperous, and that will be good for China. If we grow together, it will be beneficial for both sides. But we have no ambition to take over.'" If Kyrgyzstan thought it was becoming too assertive, he added, "Beijing knows we would go running back to Moscow."[44]

Central Asian countries are in a delicate position—economically reliant on China, but militarily dependent on Russia. Russia remains the only credible security force in the region: its troops provided stability in the wake of interethnic violence in Kyrgyzstan and they patrol Tajikistan's porous border with Afghanistan, a hotbed of Islamic extremism and a haven for drug trafficking. The Moscow-driven Common Security Treaty Organization (CSTO) has proven a much more effective security organization than the Beijing-backed SCO, which has few resources and limited relevance.

Culturally, too, Central Asia is much closer to Russia. This is true even at the eastern-most fringe of the old Soviet Union. Just thirty minutes from the Chinese border at Khorgos, the Kakakhstani town of Zharkent owes its relative prosperity to trade with the giant economy next door: its streets are lined with trucks and its bazaar filled with goods from China. Every morning, residents stream to the border to process shipments or work in the customs department. Yet even here, I could find no one who spoke Chinese. As they do across most towns in Central Asia, people spoke Russian in addition to their ethnic tongue. Kazakhs, Uyghurs and Slavs all share a Russified culture alongside their individual ethnic identities. One lesson from Zharkent is that Russia's cultural tentacles run deeper in Central Asia than do China's in large parts of Xinjiang, where few Uyghurs ever master the Chinese language.

For all China's growing economic muscle, its soft power remains minimal. Beijing has opened Confucius Institutes across Central Asia and offered thousands of scholarships to its universities. In Osh, I visited the local Confucius Institute, housed on the top floor of a handsome, pillared Soviet-era building at Osh State University. It has 170 students, who file past a bronze bust of China's ancient sage and through a red doorway decorated with red Chinese lanterns. But the proportion of Chinese speakers in Central Asia is still tiny. For more than 99% of its people, China and its language are entirely alien. This will take many decades to change, if indeed it changes at all.

Russia, then, is not about to cede its traditional influence in Central Asia. Yet there are signs that it is finally accepting the reality of China's economic predominance. The evidence was a summit in Moscow in May 2015, when Putin and Xi signed a joint declaration to coordinate the development of EEU and the Silk Road Economic Belt. Rather than setting out two competing visions, they agreed to build a "common economic space" in Eurasia that included a free trade agreement between the EEU and China.[45] The new thinking in Moscow and Beijing is that the two projects should be viewed as complementary. For Chinese exporters, the existence of a single trade bloc running from the Chinese border all the way to the EU will save time and money along the Silk Road Economic Belt. For its part, Russia will look to China to help upgrade and finance its own infrastructure, starting with a 770-km high-speed rail line between Moscow and the southern city of Kazan. The project, which is expected to cost more than US$15 billion, will cut the journey time between the two cities from 12 hours to three and a half hours. Beijing is reportedly ready to back the line with a US$6 billion loan.[46]

What Russia's change of heart really shows is a new geopolitical reality: that, post-Ukraine, it needs China far more than China needs it. When Moscow signed a long-delayed US$400 billion deal to deliver Russian gas to Chinese consumers in 2014, it did so because it needed to find an alternative market to Europe. With its economy tottering under the pressure of Western sanctions, it was forced to look east for energy deals and political alliances. But the very public "friendship" between President Xi and President Putin is a tactical alignment based on mutual pragmatism, nothing more: China and Russia play up their common interests in public, but their "strategic partnership" is still pervaded by mistrust and rivalry. A former Kazakhstani diplomat, interviewed by the International Crisis Group, colourfully described the relationship between China and Russia in the SCO as a "dance of the mongoose and the cobra".[47]

The question now is how long China can maintain its policy of non-interference in Central Asia. At a bilateral summit in Astana in October 2015, China and Kazakhstan agreed to expand inter-military cooperation on common security concerns, such as combating terrorism. Kazakhstan's defence minister told his Chinese counterpart that they shared a common desire to ensure stability in Central Asia. This was an intriguing development, because the bilateral relationship had previously only been about economic linkages. What it suggests is that Kazakhstan remains wary of Russia's political ambitions, and is willing to upgrade its political relationship with China to hedge against further Eurasian integration.

China's expansion into Central Asia over the past decade was primarily driven by economic opportunism rather than by diplomatic strategy—by the promise of oil, gas and new markets for Chinese goods. But Xi Jinping's vision of a Silk Road Economic Belt marks a diplomatic step-change: China is now actively seeking to increase its clout over its western borders. In time, it is logical that China's deepening economic presence will translate into greater political leverage, whether Russia likes it or not. This will surely test the China–Russia relationship, which Beijing's ambassador in Moscow claims is now "as close as lips and teeth"—a phrase once used by Chairman Mao to describe China's relationship with North Korea.[48]

There is one caveat to this conclusion. Beijing's position among the ruling elites of Central Asia is solid, but Chinese firms and the immigrants they bring with them are deeply unpopular—a state of affairs that recalls China's position in Myanmar a few years ago. Until 2011, Beijing and state-owned enterprises were happy to work closely with Myanmar's generals, and Chinese firms were set to build new roads, railways and power lines. But when the military junta was dissolved, popular protest was rapidly redirected at Chinese firms. With several major infrastructure projects cancelled or on hold, Beijing has yet to regain its footing in its former client state. In Central Asia, too, it must beware popular blowback. If Beijing's authoritarian friends were ever replaced by populist regimes, China's inexorable march westwards could grind to a halt.

CHAPTER 3

IN THE HEAT OF THE SUN[1]

ADVANCING DOWN THE MEKONG

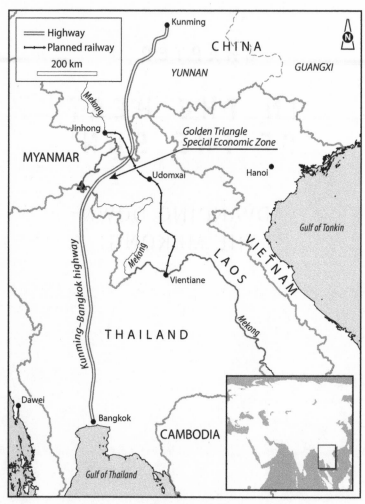

Mekong River Basin

The city of Jinghong, located 3,000 km from Beijing on a bend in the Mekong River, is one of the remotest places in China. Back in 2001, when I first visited this southern frontier of Yunnan province, it was still possible to stay in traditional wooden stilted houses with palm-thatched roofs. It was a sleepy town with a handful of hotels and two cafes catering to backpackers hopping between China, Laos and Thailand. A few Burmese gem traders, dressed in sarongs, had crossed the border from Myanmar to sell to the first wave of domestic tourists.[2] But business was slow: they spent their afternoons dozing in the shade of their shop fronts. Aside from a sprinkling of brothels, Jinghong's only evening entertainment was a riverside night market where men with loudhailers pestered passers-by to try rickety fairground rides.

Since then, domestic tourist dollars have transformed this sultry backwater. The last stilted houses have been cleared for blocks of flats, and high-rise hotels have sprouted like weeds along the bank of the Mekong, here known as the Lancang River. The city's palm-shaded streets resemble a giant jade bazaar, lined with glass-cased showrooms offering milky green trinkets to tourists dressed in Hawaiian shirts. Other stores sell packaged discs of local Pu'er tea, which is said to aid weight loss, or decorative elephants carved in tropical rosewood. A less chaotic version of the old night market survives, but it competes with an expensive bar street and neon-lit karaoke parlours. The roads rumble with diesel-belching trucks hauling exotic fruits across China, smudging the blue sky grey with smog.

Jinghong's newfound prosperity is built on massive investment in transport infrastructure. Until a new expressway more than halved the journey time, it was a fifteen-hour drive south from Kunming, the provincial capital, along twisting roads. I remember a torturous journey in the spring of 2003, when I fled from Beijing to Yunnan during the outbreak of Severe Acute Respiratory Syndrome (SARS), which killed hundreds of people in the capital. Early in the morning, after an uncomfortable night on a sleeper bus, hospital staff wearing medical space suits floated on board to check our temperatures and spray disinfectant. In those days, travelling by bus was easier than flying, as flights were few and far between. Today, the city airport is served by forty daily flights from the provincial capital of Kunming: Jinghong no longer feels like an isolated outpost on the forgotten edge of the Chinese empire.

In fact, for most of its history Jinghong barely belonged to China at all. The capital of Xishuangbanna prefecture, it is home to an ethnic Tai people, called Dai in Chinese. For centuries, Xishuangbanna was an important stop on the Ancient Tea Horse Road, a network of mule caravan paths that wound their way through the mountains of Yunnan and Burma. This "Southern Silk Road" led north into Tibet and the foothills of the Himalayas, west to Bengal and India, and south into Indochina. To the north, China is attempting to revive this trade route by building an "economic corridor" from Kunming through Myanmar, Bangladesh and India. Jinghong is looking to the southern stretch of the old route for its future—to Laos, Thailand and beyond.

Planners believe that improving connectivity with mainland Southeast Asia, with which Yunnan shares a 4,000-km border, will foster new markets and bring mutual prosperity. China's expansion into the Mekong River Basin, as in Central Asia, is based on a broadly successful policy at home. Back in 2000, China began a huge development push in its then-impoverished central and western regions. The "Go West" policy focused on building an efficient transport network across a remote and often inhospitable region that remained cut off from the rest of the country. The goal was to open up the interior to domestic trade, connecting it to the much wealthier eastern seaboard. Today China's western provinces are knitted together with roads and railways; domestic trade is booming.[3]

Yunnan has made tremendous progress in improving its connections to the rest of China, especially in the past five years. In 2012, a vast new airport opened just outside Kunming, its capital city. In 2015 it was the country's seventh busiest, serving nearly 38 million passengers, many of them domestic tourists seeking some of China's most beautiful scenery. To put that in perspective, more passengers passed through Kunming Airport that year than through Berlin or Newark.[4] Doubtless still more tourists will flock to Yunnan's natural wonders, which run from snow-capped peaks to tropical jungle, when a 2,000-km high-speed railway from Shanghai to Kunming opens. Yet Yunnan still remains hampered by its land-locked location: the closest major domestic seaport is Shenzhen, some 1,500 km away over often difficult terrain.

Yunnan is China's second-poorest province, giving it a national status akin to Romania within the EU or West Virginia in the US. But it is still far more developed than its neighbours: in dollar terms, the average Yunnan resident is around three times better off than his counterparts in Laos or Cambodia. Because its neighbours' poverty is holding back Yunnan's own development, Beijing's planners want to expand the "Go West" policy over its borders. In 2011, they designated Yunnan a "bridgehead" (*qiaotoubao*) for pushing development into Southeast Asia.[5] "Bridgehead" is a military term referring to a fortress controlling the frontline, but Beijing's strategists have adopted it to describe a regional gateway or geostrategic hub. The term frequently appears in government reports, but is not directly translated into foreign languages, suggesting the planners are aware of its unsettling connotations.

The "bridgehead" strategy dovetails with the Belt and Road Initiative and the earlier call by former president Jiang Zemin for state enterprises to find new markets overseas. Beijing's vision is that Yunnan's efforts to build hard infrastructure over its borders will benefit its own economy. If they can turn Yunnan into a viable trade zone, it will lift the whole region towards greater development. This is partly what China's leaders mean when they talk about "win–win" diplomacy and "shared destiny". For a tiny country like Laos, China's development push will be hard to resist: Yunnan's economy alone is nearly twenty times larger.

The risk for Laos and Cambodia is that they will become economic vassals. Both are already heavily reliant on China for trade, investment and financial assistance. As the Chinese sun burns ever hotter, they are on the road to becoming satellites within the Chinese solar system. In Laos, senior members of the ruling Lao People's Revolutionary Party work closely with their Communist cousins to the north. Cambodia is nominally democratic, but its unsavoury government relies on Beijing for vital political support, shielding it from UN-sponsored attempts to seek justice for the victims of the murderous Khmer Rouge. Cambodia's willingness to return the favour has provoked accusations that it is a Chinese client state. As China strengthens its economic grip in the Mekong Basin, the geopolitical implications are ever more troubling.

LAOS[6]

Laos is one of the most diplomatically inoffensive countries on earth, but its recent history has been blighted by foreign interference.[7] In the late 19th century, the ancient city of Luang Prabang was ransacked by Chinese bandits, known as the Black Flag Army. Rescued by France, Laos was rapidly absorbed into French Indochina. The colonial government introduced the *corvée*, a system of forced work that required every male Laotian to contribute ten days of manual labour per year. After independence in 1953, parts of Laos were invaded and occupied by North Vietnam for use as a supply route to the South during the Vietnam War. From 1964 to 1973, raids by American B52s killed up to 350,000 civilians and gave

Laos the unenviable title of "the most heavily bombed country on earth". Incredibly, more bombs fell on Laos than on all of Europe during World War II.

Since 1975, Laos has been ruled by a Communist government that has been accused of committing genocide against the Hmong minority, among other human rights abuses. It is one of the most corrupt countries on earth, and its people suffer from high levels of malnutrition. As the only landlocked country in Southeast Asia, its economy has struggled, despite being rich in minerals and blessed with enormous hydropower potential and fertile farmland. Of course it is this bounty that interests Chinese investors, not Laos's failings of governance. China has maintained good relations with the Lao People's Revolutionary Party, becoming the country's largest investor and second-largest trade partner.[8]

Yunnan's companies have responded enthusiastically to Beijing's call to carry development over its borders. To get to Laos, streams of investors drive down the new US$4 billion highway from Kunming, which skirts Jinghong and passes through the north of the country on its way to Bangkok— part of a longer route known as "Asian Highway 3". On the Chinese side, the road cuts through green hills forested with rosewood and mahogany. All available farmland is intensively cultivated, with neat rows of vegetables growing under black mesh and regimented lines of banana trees. I saw plenty of trucks carrying fruit and vegetables, some with licence plates registered 4,000 km away in the frigid northeast. At Mengla, the last town before the border, the Yunnan government is building a 4,500 square km economic zone that it plans to turn into a "comprehensive transport hub" for the Mekong region, complete with a new airport.[9]

I hitched a lift into Laos on a truck belonging to Yunnan Hydropower, which operates a dam in the north of the country. Chinese financiers and developers have interests in at least half of the more than seventy proposed hydropower schemes on the Mekong and its tributaries. Other Chinese investments range from construction and infrastructure to agriculture and mining: Laos has large deposits of gold, copper, bauxite, iron, lead, zinc ores and potash. Much of this mineral wealth has yet to be mapped, and Laos is seeking help from China's state-owned miners to conduct detailed surveys. China's big mining companies all have a foothold there: Aluminum Corporation of China (Chalco) and China Minmetals Corp both operate copper mines; China Nonferrous Metals has a bauxite project.

Although Beijing has provided much of the funding for the Kunming–Bangkok Highway, the Laos section is part-managed by the Asian Development Bank (ADB). Its Greater Mekong Subregion Programme (GMS) is designed to promote intra-regional trade by upgrading transport connectivity and establishing "economic corridors" between the major cities of the Mekong Basin. Yunnan and neighbouring Guangxi are members, together with Laos, Cambodia, Myanmar, Thailand and Vietnam.[10] The ADB's road-building programme is enthusiastically supported by Beijing as it will in theory give container trucks from Yunnan access to Thailand and the port of Bangkok. Another road heading southeast will connect to Hanoi and the port of Haiphong, in northern Vietnam. The ADB's involvement has helped China extend its regional influence.

From the border, the highway winds its way south past simple wooden homesteads housing both people and pigs—a familiar scene in Yunnan until just a decade or two ago. Roads in Laos are typically rutted tracks that turn to mud when the monsoon arrives, yet we drove along a smooth highway lined with deep concrete ditches to drain away rainwater.[11] That evening, in the town of Udomxai, I discovered why. Looking for a bite to eat, I followed a peal of raucous laughter to a restaurant filled with Chinese road engineers enjoying a boozy dinner. "We built the road from here to the border," explained Wang Xiao, an engineer at Yunnan Sunny Road & Bridge Co., over mouthfuls of salted fish and smoked duck. "Without us, Laos couldn't develop—they simply don't have the money. We build their roads and their government borrows money from our banks at a favourable interest rate."[12]

Wang Xiao and his team had been in Laos for four years, after stints in Pakistan and Ethiopia. "This country is like Africa," he told me, as his red-faced colleagues downed glasses of Yunnan rice spirit. "We offer the locals good money to work, but they are so slow. They don't work hard like we Chinese do, so we hire mainly Chinese workers. Chinese are willing to work in difficult conditions because they want to make better lives for their families." Their next task, he said, was to rebuild the potholed road that runs to Luang Prabang, the holy Buddhist town famed for its glittering monasteries, perched on the banks of the Mekong River. I doubted whether Luang Prabang's monks, already deluged by noisy Chinese tourists and unwashed Western backpackers, would welcome the development.

Eventually, it will be possible to drive the 1,000 km from Kunming to Vientiane in a day. Chinese businesses are already busily remaking the skyline of Laos's once-sleepy capital with investments in shopping complexes and hotels; they even control the city's funerary services.[13] For the moment, however, the best road in Laos forks west to the border with Thailand. Until December 2013, this section of the Kunming to Bangkok Highway came to an abrupt stop at the Mekong River, which forms the border with Thailand. Trucks had to unload their containers onto boats, which was costly and time-consuming. But a new 500-metre bridge, part financed by Beijing, has created a viable transit route. "The bridge is the missing link," declared Stephen Groff, the ADB's vice president, at the opening ceremony. "With all of the infrastructure in place, the potential for this corridor to become a driver of regional trade, tourism and investment can be realized."[14]

That is the plan—yet when I visited a few months after the bridge opened, I did not see a single truck pass through the sleek new customs point.[15] China's own experience of development means it has enormous faith in investment-led growth; but the philosophy of "build in and they will come" may not prove so effective over its borders, especially in areas that are sparsely populated. The highway opens up opportunities for trade with Thailand, but few Chinese trucks will travel the full 1,800 km from Kunming to Bangkok—even if they are ever allowed to cross into Thailand, which they currently are not. For regional road trade to take off, the GMS countries will need to simplify customs procedures and unify logistics standards. Until that software is in place, the infrastructure hardware will remain underutilized.

China's regional ambitions extend well beyond roads: it wants to build a "high-speed" railway running down the spine of mainland Southeast Asia, connecting Kunming to Singapore. The Laos section alone is projected to cost up to US$7 billion, around half the country's annual economic output. The 417-km line from the Chinese border to Vientiane will have 154 bridges and 76 tunnels, and could require 50,000 workers—most of them to be imported from China. Beijing is keen to build the railway because of the improved access it would offer to the consumer markets of Thailand and Malaysia. From Bangkok, there is also potential for an onward link to the Thai-invested deep-sea port at Dawei in southern Myanmar. For its part, the Lao government believes the railway will bring trade, investment and economic development to the impoverished nation—not to mention a white bullet of sleek modernity.

First agreed in 2009, the Laos section of the project was delayed in 2011. When former railway minister Liu Zhijun was arrested for corruption that year, China re-examined all aspects of railway policy—especially high-speed rail, which was Liu's pet project. The Chinese state-owned developers doubted whether it was commercially viable. Meanwhile, the deal was held up in the Lao parliament over the massive cost of repayment and fears that the project would do little to benefit ordinary people. Opponents pointed out that Laos would inevitably have to use untapped minerals as collateral for Chinese loans. If repayments were made by ceding mining rights to

Chinese companies, the railway could prove a conveyor belt for shipping wealth out of the country.

With Beijing offering strong support, these fears have been put to one side. The railway was finally given the green light in November 2015, and construction began the following month. Under the finalized deal, 70% of the investment will come from China with most of the financing provided by China Exim Bank. The line will be built, with a target completion date of 2020, by a consortium of Chinese companies led by China Railway Corporation. With GDP per head below US$2,000 and 80% of its 6.8 million population employed in subsistence agriculture, it was clearly difficult for Laos to turn down China's offer—even if it risks tying itself financially to China for decades to come. Future growth, the Lao government believes, hinges on becoming a transit zone within the Mekong region.[16]

The line will connect with a separate China-built railway from Vientiane to Bangkok. This deal, part of larger US$10 billion package to build 867 km of railway in Thailand, was finally signed in December 2015 after years of wrangling over financing costs.[17] Chinese firms will provide all the rolling stock on the line, which will be funded mainly by bank loans. As in Laos, passenger trains will run at average speeds of around 160 km per hour, with freight trains restricted to 120 km per hour—so the line can only be described as "medium speed" at best. If it is linked to Singapore, trains will take the best part of a day to get there from Kunming.

China's rollout of hard infrastructure could have far-reaching consequences for the geopolitics of Southeast Asia.

"Driven by the high-speed rail networks, new roads and tele-communication facilities centring on Kunming, together with China's burgeoning economic engagement with the Greater Mekong area, mainland Southeast Asia is in the process of disconnecting from maritime Southeast Asia," says Geoff Wade at Australian National University. The railway, he predicts, could even create a fault line through ASEAN.[18] This argument probably goes too far, but there is no doubt that China's grip on the region is tightening.

This is clear on the ground, where the number of Chinese investors continues to grow. In Udomxai, the biggest town in northern Laos, Chinese residents make up around 15% of the population. The first Chinese traders arrived in 2000, but their numbers have swelled since the new road from Yunnan opened. When I visited shortly after Chinese New Year in 2014, many of the biggest houses had traditional red stickers pasted over their doorways. The central market was divided into two sections—one filled with local vendors slurping soup-noodles with spoons, the other with Chinese traders eating with chopsticks. Next door, the biggest supermarket in town was run by a couple from the east coast city of Wenzhou. "Life at home wasn't good," the shopkeeper told me in the sibilant accent of Zhejiang, sitting in front of shelves stacked with Chinese goods. "Business is easier here because there's less competition."

Up the road, past markets selling Chinese scooters, the Sichuan-Udomxai Hotel is the plushest in town. I chatted to the owner in front of a glass cabinet filled with Chinese Double Happiness cigarettes. Wang Xinming explained how he moved his family here on the advice of a friend working in one of Laos's Chinese motorbike factories. "It's more expensive to invest in Laos than back home because most of the building materials need to be shipped in from China," he said. "But we're doing really well—the hotel's nearly full." A growing number of guests are middle-class urbanites on driving holidays. Visitors to Luang Prabang complain about the car horns as Chinese SUVs blare their way through its narrow streets.

Wang is an eager proponent of the railway, which he said will bring more tourists. "The road to the border is too slow and windy," he explained. "The railway will be much quicker and more convenient. It'll be great for business!" But critics say the huge cost has the potential to cripple the economy, while the environmental impact is unknown. Chinese companies are keen to develop land along the railway, where illegal logging is already a serious problem. Hills along the main highway in northern Laos have been stripped of their dense tropical plumage and replaced with spindly rubber trees—many of them owned by Chinese rubber barons. At the Laos–China border, a customs photo board shows smugglers squatting, head bowed, next to trucks filled with secret stashes of mahogany and rosewood. Laos is trying to tighten up on the timber trade, but tropical wood is easy to buy. "All of my hotel furniture is made of the finest mahogany," Wang, the hotelier, told me with pride.

For many private Chinese investors, Laos's big draw is its cheap and fertile land. Guests at the Sichuan-Udomxai Hotel included a group from Sichuan scouting for business opportunities. "I read an article about Laos online," said Mr Yu. "We're thinking of investing in agriculture—growing watermelons or vegetables, or perhaps raising chickens. We have a meeting with the provincial government this afternoon. They're very friendly to Chinese investors." Ordinary Laotians feel less kindly about Chinese investors: this is exactly the kind of entrepreneurial spirit that scares people across Asia. Chinese investors bring valuable capital, skills and technology—but they also bring competition.

Chinese farmers see a clear opportunity in Laos. "Renting 1 *mu* of land costs just a few hundred yuan a year," a watermelon farmer from Shaanxi told me in the immigration queue, grinning through tobacco-stained teeth.[19] He said his partner, a man with a scraggly moustache, trucked the produce back home to northwest China. Farmers like this one bring many things that Laos lacks—irrigation systems, fertilizer, pesticides and agricultural management—and employ plenty of local people. But large investors prefer to take land concessions, only hiring a small number of locals. When the product is ready to harvest, it is packaged on site and trucked over the border to Yunnan, where the bulk of the profits are collected. Not all investment is equally welcome.

Small investors typically sell their produce to trading companies, which ship it to markets across China. They contact men like Fei Xiaodong, who I met on a bus from Jinghong to the China–Laos border. Fei was a beefy man with a shaven head and pot belly, carrying a wad of cash in a crocodile-skin bag with the baby croc's head still attached. He worked for a logistics company with offices in Ruili, on the Myanmar border, and Urumqi, thousands of kilometres north in Xinjiang. In the guttural burr of northeast China, he barked a stream of numbers and place names down his iPhone: "Xiamen, Hangzhou, Shenyang, Beijing … I'll ask how much in Kunming, but it'll cost a few thousand." He was picked up by a colleague in a four-wheel drive bearing the licence plate of Heilongjiang province. "We go over the border all the time," he said.

Several hours' drive from the border, at the infamous meeting point of Laos, Thailand and Myanmar known as the "Golden Triangle", I found Chinese investors growing bananas. The area is better known for illegal poppy cultivation, but the legal plantations here are on an industrial scale. The swaying palms were dotted with patches of unnatural blue—protective plastic wraps used by Chinese farmers to keep off pests and encourage the fruit to ripen. They were watered by a network of pipes and divided into sections with signs written in Chinese characters. If any confirmation of ownership was needed, the SUV parked beside the trees had a Yunnan number plate.

In fact, nowhere is China's growing clout in Laos more evident than in the Golden Triangle, where a different kind of investor has carved out a little piece of China far from the border. The Golden Triangle Special Economic Zone occupies 103 square km of land on the banks of the Mekong, across the river from Thailand and Myanmar. Although still officially Lao territory, it is held on a ninety-nine-year lease and operates tax free. Its centrepiece is the Kings Romans casino, a columned temple with a golden dome and a giant neon crown. Everything in the zone is imported from China, from the paving stones to the officious security force. Kings Romans shipped building materials down the Mekong from Jinghong on 400-tonne barges, docking at the zone's private wharf. Only Chinese currency is accepted in the hotels and restaurants, and the cell-phone network is provided by China Mobile. The zone runs on Chinese time, meaning that its workers must rise an hour before locals.[20]

There are plenty of other casinos in the Golden Triangle serving Chinese and Thai punters, who cannot gamble legally at home. But Kings Romans is the biggest and glitziest, nick-named "Macau on the Mekong". Within its marble halls, gamblers throw Chinese yuan and Thai baht onto the green baize tables. Most Chinese guests cross over the Mekong from Thailand on holiday tours, but a rising number drive from Yunnan along the new highway. Kings Romans Group is registered in Hong Kong under its Lao name, Dok Ngiewk Kam, but little is known about this shady company.[21] The group operates another casino in Mongla, a Chinese-domi-nated border town in Myanmar's Shan State, which is ruled independently by the United State Wa Army, a rebel group. Other casinos in the Golden Triangle region have a reputation for laundering drugs money, not to mention "disappearing" punters who cannot pay their gambling losses. Kings Romans claims its Laos casino is a legitimate business, and in 2015 it presented the Lao government with US$6.3 million of taxes owed for the previous five years.[22]

Zhao Wei, the chairman of Kings Romans Group and a native of northeast China, wants to create more than a gambling den in the jungle. The SEZ contains a Chinatown with supermarkets and noodle bars, a new "Lao–China Friendship School" to teach employees' children, and a Chinese temple staffed with monks flown in from mystical Wutai Mountain. "Eventually there will be thirty of us here," said an elderly monk dressed in ochre robes.[23] But I found the complex a typically Chinese mix of enormous ambition and half-hearted follow through. The "traditional" buildings in the Chinatown were made of concrete and surfaced with fake bricks. The karaoke hall, which looked like an emperor's palace, was guarded by a brigade of discoloured terracotta warriors in worse shape than their real, 2,000-year-old brethren. On the bank of the Mekong, Mongolian yurts had been erected under brown-leaved palm trees strung with dusty Chinese lanterns. The complex felt like a rundown holiday camp, only with a flashy casino attached.

Even the working girls are imported from China. Around the corner from the temple, I found a whole building of massage parlours called "Street of a Hundred Flowers"—an old Chinese euphemism for prostitutes. Strictly in the interests of research, I chatted with the girls in "Fire Phoenix" and "Blue Moon". "We can give you a massage—or anything you like," said one helpful young employee from Guangxi province, preparing her makeup for the night ahead. A dark-skinned girl from Yunnan looked Burmese but declared herself "pure Chinese". She belonged to the Jingpo minority, known in Myanmar as Kachin. "I can come to your room for 100 yuan (US$15)," she offered, brightly. I imagined a night in the hotel, mildewed and mosquito-ridden, was preferable to bunking up in a shabby shared dormitory. "Isn't that rather cheap?"

I asked. "It's expensive compared to Ruili," she replied, in reference to Yunnan's infamously louche border town.

Leaving the zone, I passed a garage full of cars for visiting "VIPs": Hummers, a Bentley and two stretched limos. They are used to pick up guests in Jinghong or from the local airport at Huayxai, an hour to the south. But if Zhao Wei gets his way, that will be a thing of the past. The brains behind the SEZ believes there is so much potential demand from Chinese gamblers that he is building an international airport to fly them into the SEZ from Kunming and Shanghai. "It'll be the biggest airport in Laos," a Kings Romans employee told me, pointing towards a pair of diggers flattening scrubland to create a runway. The airport is the final part of Zhao's grand plan to create a mini-Chinese colony with up to 50,000 residents.

How concerned should Laos be about China's rapidly growing influence? China's economic embrace is barely more than a decade old, but its tentacles are rapidly growing longer and thicker. Vietnam and Thailand have traditionally been the biggest investors in Laos, but China overtook them in 2013. Lao government data state that China's total accumulated investment surpassed US$6 billion in 2015, but the true figure is surely much higher.[24] Laos is both underdeveloped and underpopulated, so there is plenty of scope for Chinese investment and controlled immigration. If the Lao government ensures that Chinese capital, technology and expertise benefit the local economy, they could prove Laos's ticket out of poverty. But there is a very real danger, too, that Chinese companies will suck the country dry—grabbing its minerals, wrecking its landscape and dominating its trade.

The Lao government has been exceptionally welcoming of Chinese investment, but that might change if local resentment becomes politically destabilizing. There are signs that the Lao People's Revolutionary Party is already reassessing its relationship with Beijing. A reshuffle in January 2016 saw the removal of senior officials deemed close to China, including the Party secretary-general and a deputy prime minister who had overseen the Laos–China railway project. "There has been a palpable anxiety within the public as well as among Party members that the ousted leaders had made Laos grow too dependent on China in recent years," says Murray Hiebert, a Senior Fellow at the Center for Strategic and International Studies think tank in Washington, DC. He believes that Laos may now be tilting back towards Vietnam, its traditional sponsor.[25] In 2016, Barack Obama also became the first US president to visit the country, as Washington stepped up its charm offensive across Southeast Asia.

Beijing's economic leverage with its neighbours is growing, but it must tread carefully to maintain friendly relations. That is why, for all the military connotations of its "bridgehead" strategy, it is trying harder to emphasize "good neighbourliness". The language of diplomacy that Beijing employs across its southwestern land borders is far more emollient than the often belligerent tone directed across the South China Sea. If this strategy succeeds, the centre of gravity in mainland Southeast Asia will continue to shift northwards. But as China's economic empire expands, Laos risks being swallowed up.

CAMBODIA

Cambodia does not share a border with China, but it too has been sucked into its sphere of influence.[26] Beijing's diplomatic leverage is so great in this small kingdom of 15 million people that critics have labelled it a Chinese proxy. Cambodia relies on China for one-third of its imports and, like Laos, to build roads, bridges and dams. Yet China's influence is not benign: it backs Prime Minister Hun Sen's refusal to arrest leaders accused by the UN of massacring civilians under Pol Pot, and its companies readily work with Cambodia's corrupt business elite. This sort of diplomacy can be effective in authoritarian states dominated by government cronies, where civil society is weak or non-existent. But it will hardly convince more liberal states that China is truly interested in building a "community of common destiny" across Asia.

Beijing has long been a powerful presence in Phnom Penh, Cambodia's steamy capital, but the extent of its influence did not become apparent until 2012. Chairing that year's ASEAN summit, Cambodia refused to back other member states in condemning Beijing for its far-reaching territorial claims in the South China Sea. When negotiations broke down and ASEAN failed to issue a joint communiqué for the first time in its history, critics labelled Cambodia a Chinese puppet. "China bought the chair, simple as that", stated one regional diplomat.[27] Hun Sen, Cambodia's long-term leader, angrily denied the charge. Earlier, he declared that Cambodia was "not going to be bought by anyone".[28]

The reality is that Cambodia is heavily reliant on Chinese cash. Accumulated foreign direct investment from China surpassed US$10 billion in 2015, one-third of the total and at least double that of South Korea, the next biggest investor.[29] Chinese factories dominate Cambodia's garment and footwear industries, one in three roads are said to be Chinese built, and Chinese firms have spent nearly US$2 billion constructing six dams. In 2013 China Exim Bank lent US$1.7 billion to Sinopec and Cambodian Petrochemical to build the country's first oil refinery.[30] Chinese companies also have extensive investments in banking and finance, agriculture, tourism, mining, real estate, transport and telecommunications. Unsurprisingly, the billboard on the road exiting Phnom Penh airport advertises Bank of China.

China's biggest potential investment remains on the drawing board. In 2012, China Railway Group signed a US$9.6 billion deal to build a 405-km railway and seaport.[31] Its partner, a mysterious company called Cambodia Iron and Steel Mining Industry Group, is registered to three Chinese brothers. CISMIG chairman Zhang Chuanli said the railway would connect the port to a new steel mill, to be built at a further cost of US$1.6 billion. This would enable Cambodia to exploit its untapped iron ore resources and export steel. China Railway Group made no mention of the project in recent annual reports but, if it goes ahead, it would represent one of the biggest infrastructure projects ever undertaken by a Chinese firm overseas.

As Chinese money rolls in, Chinese culture is becoming pervasive. Cambodia has a long-established community of

Chinese immigrants, but a new wave of entrepreneurs are being lured by opportunities in what is probably Southeast Asia's most open economy. Shop, hotel, business and even street signs in Phnom Penh are written in Chinese. Chinese schools are proliferating, teaching native Khmer speakers in Mandarin beside their Chinese-speaking classmates. Chinese New Year is not an official holiday, but the capital effectively shuts down during the celebrations. I found doorways across the city pasted with good-luck couplets written in Chinese calligraphy.

There is plenty of good will for immigrants, say recent arrivals from China—though many ordinary Khmers are actually less happy than the Chinese incomers realize. "We're not treated as foreigners here, because we Chinese have made such a big contribution to the country by building roads and dams," explained Mr Ying, who runs a supermarket on a busy strip of Chinese shops and restaurants in Phnom Penh. He told me the city is home to 60,000 Chinese Cambodians, mainly third-generation immigrants, plus 50,000 mainlanders who have arrived in the past decade or so. "I know the numbers because we often have meetings at the embassy," he said, standing beside a shelf of rice wine and puffing hard on a Chinese cigarette. "There are 3,000 people from my home county in Zhejiang province alone."[32]

Beijing has smoothed the way for Chinese immigrants such as Mr Ying by financing and building desperately needed infrastructure. At a paltry US$1,168 in 2015, Cambodia's GDP per capita was the lowest in ASEAN, even outranked by Myanmar.[33] China is Cambodia's most generous aid donor, disbursing grants and concessional loans worth nearly US$1.5 billion in 2009–13—more than the UN, World Bank, ADB and other multilateral financiers put together.[34] While Western donors and development banks sometimes withhold funds, citing human rights abuses and endemic corruption, China keeps pumping in money. As far back as 2006 Hun Sen lauded China's approach: "China talks less but does a lot," he said upon pocketing a US$600 million pledge from Beijing.[35]

This is a common sentiment, even among Western-educated Cambodians with little natural sympathy for the Chinese way of doing business. David Van Vichet was born in Phnom Penh but fled a week before Pol Pot's forces captured the city. His father, then the head of military police, feared the worst and got his family out. He stayed on and was killed—one of an estimated 1–3 million people who were slaughtered during Pol Pot's four years as prime minister of Democratic Kampuchea, as the country was renamed. Van Vichet lived in France for ten years as a refugee, before moving to Singapore and eventually working for the UN; today he advises the Cambodian Ministry of Commerce. We met for dinner at La Residence, an expensive French restaurant housed in a grand villa that suffered heavy artillery fire during the coup d'état in 1997, when Hun Sen ousted his co-premier, Norodom Ranariddh.

Van Vichet had just returned from a tour of the US with government ministers and businessmen. He explained how Cambodia was keen to seek investment from the US, but said President Obama's administration had failed to respond. He recounted how in 2014, when Hun Sen visited Washington with a simple message of "Cambodia wants to be friends", he received little more than criticism of Cambodia's flawed democracy and appalling record on human rights. Human Rights Watch's Southeast Asian director, David Roberts, has described Cambodia's government as a "vaguely communist free-market state with a relatively authoritarian coalition ruling over a superficial democracy".[36] This, of course, does not bother China at all. "When China comes it brings a big chequebook, but Westerners come with a lot of conditionality attached," Van Vichet told me over smoked salmon served in sugarcane bark. "If you were in the Cambodian government, you would find it a no-brainer."

I heard a similar opinion from Dr Sok Siphana, a US-trained lawyer who once worked for the UN and led the negotiations for Cambodia's accession to the WTO in 2004. I found him in the offices of his law firm in uptown Phnom Penh, extravagantly dressed in a paisley bowtie, stripy braces and heavy silver cufflinks. "I'm a US citizen and people here say I'm too Americanized with my bowties and suspenders," he told me in a rapid-fire interview.

> But I'm very critical of the US. I used to be a fervent defender of the US's democratic cause, but now I realize growth and jobs must come first. I went through the killing fields. The last thing I want is a goddamn revolution here. That's not what I want for my children.

Working closely with China, he continued, was simply in Cambodia's national interest. He explained how the government was fed up with being bullied by critics in Washington who do not understand that it must prioritize growth above all else. Beijing, on the other hand, understands perfectly. "The harsh reality is that we need to secure 300,000 jobs a year for young people entering the marketplace, which requires investment in transport infrastructure, power stations and factories," he said.

Where's this coming from? It's mostly coming from two places: China and Japan. The rest is a joke—all blah, blah, blah reports from agencies that no one reads. The UN, World Bank, ADB—you name it. We're tired of cut and paste consultancy reports that bring no additional value.

Far from being a Chinese stooge, he added, Cambodia was simply acting with expediency: "We need friends—and China happens to be a friend with money."

Yet there are less enlightened reasons why the Cambodian elite is so keen on working with China. Cambodia's authoritarian, patronage-infused economy is fuelled by crony capitalism. Even Western aid is often funnelled in via the military, and powerful families retain close links to the government. The ruling Cambodian People's Party hands out commercial licences, land concessions and government positions to business tycoons and investors, who channel funds back to their sponsors. Cambodia was ranked the most corrupt country in Southeast Asia in 2015 on Transparency International's Corruption Perceptions Index. It placed 150th worldwide out of 168 countries, tied with Zimbabwe and Burundi. Chinese investors, however, are perfectly happy to play the game.[37]

It helps that many of Cambodia's tycoons, like so many across Southeast Asia, have Chinese origins. Take Kith Meng, Cambodia's richest man, described by the chairman of the Cambodia Mekong Bank as a "ruthless gangster".[38] As chairman of The Royal Group—a conglomerate with interests in telecoms, media, banking, insurance, resorts, education, property, trading and agriculture—he enjoys a close relationship with Chinese bankers. In 2010, The Royal Group pocketed a US$591 million loan from Bank of China, enabling it to repay a smaller loan that had previously financed the acquisition of CamGSM, the country's leading mobile phone operator.[39] CamGSM then signed a US$500 million partnership with Shenzhen-based Huawei Technologies for the supply of equipment and services.[40] The Royal Group is also partnering Chinese firm HydroLancang on a controversial US$800 million dam in northeastern Cambodia. Opponents claim 5,000 people will be evicted from their villages when the reservoir fills, and 40,000 living on the banks of the Sesan and Srepok rivers will lose much of the fish they rely on for food.[41]

The symbiotic relationship between China and Cambodia is expressed in mutual political support. Beijing has backed Hun Sen's refusal to press ahead with the next stage of the UN-sponsored Khmer Rouge Tribunal. It is no accident that China, which supported Pol Pot's genocidal regime, does not want to see the chief perpetrators brought to trial. Sophal Ear, a US-based academic who fled the Khmer Rouge as a child, argues that Beijing's money has retarded the country's development: "When Cambodia falls under pressure from international bodies to reform its human rights abuses, corruption, oppression of its people, or misuse of power, it turns to the Chinese for financial support."[42] But Hun Sen, who once described China as "the root of everything that is evil" because of its support for the Khmer Rouge, now calls China "our most trustworthy friend".[43]

Cambodia has reciprocated with its own diplomatic backing, unhesitatingly supporting Beijing's line over its core interests of Taiwan, Tibet, Xinjiang and the South China Sea. In 2009 it sent home twenty-two Uyghur asylum seekers who fled China to avoid prosecution for their alleged involvement in violent protests in Xinjiang. It was rewarded with a US$1.2 billion package of grants and soft loans delivered in person by the then vice president, Xi Jinping. So it was no big surprise when, at the ASEAN meeting in 2012, Cambodia fended off demands from Vietnam and the Philippines to condemn China's assertive policies in the South China Sea. Phnom Penh continues to echo Beijing's contention that territorial disputes should be solved bilaterally rather than through international arbitration.

Even Sam Rainsy, the pro-Western leader of the opposition Cambodia National Rescue Party (CNRP) supports a close relationship with China. In a television interview in January 2014 he bluntly declared his party to be "an ally of China". "CNRP fully supports China in the assertion of her sovereignty over [the] Xisha and Nansha islands in the South China Sea," Rainsy said, probably influenced by the Khmers' own long history of territorial disputes with the Vietnamese.[44]

We are not allying with the US because it supports Vietnam. The presence of China is necessary to counterbalance against the influence of Vietnam [in Cambodia]. Now,

Vietnam has many allies—the US and Japan—in order to
confront with China. But CNRP stands with China.[45]

Later that year, anti-Vietnamese feeling erupted in street
protests in Phnom Penh, forcing Vietnamese workers to flee as
a man was beaten to death and businesses looted.

Despite its close relationship with China, Cambodia does
not want to be bound to it. Following the infamous ASEAN
meeting in 2012, it was condemned by international critics
as China's "stalking horse", "proxy", "client" and "satellite"—
accusations that rankled in a country with a long and bitter
history of colonialism.[46] Over the past couple of years Cambodia
has upgraded its relationship with Japan to a "strategic partnership" and Hun Sen has repeatedly made friendly noises to
the US. Washington has responded warily, but Phnom Penh is
hopeful that the US will write off US$400 million of its debts.
As a small and impoverished country, Cambodia needs all the
friends it can get: it is simply not in its best interest to be wholly
reliant on China. "If the US came to us tomorrow, we'd be
hugging and kissing them," admitted Dr Siphana.

The government also fears rising criticism at home. Strong
anti-Chinese sentiment is less common in Cambodia than in
many other Southeast Asian countries, notably Myanmar and
Vietnam. But there is resentment at land lost to Chinese investors, who own more than half the 8 million hectares granted
to foreign firms in 1994–2012. "Cambodia has painted itself
into the Chinese corner," laments analyst Lao Mong Hay.[47]
"They behave more and more like the colonialists of the past."
Son Chhay, a parliamentarian with the opposition CNRP, has
accused China of exploiting Cambodia: "They are willing to

supply loans for roads, bridges and hydro dams, but they must go through Chinese companies, who multiply the real cost so they can make huge profits."[48]

Popular concern over Chinese land grabs and environmental degradation helped the opposition gain an unexpected number of seats in the 2013 election, despite Hun Sen's best efforts to rig the result. By one estimate, more than 500,000 Cambodians have lost their land since 2000.[49] In 2014, representatives of a Tianjin firm working on a tourism resort in Koh Kung were accused, along with Cambodian soldiers, of destroying crops and burning down the homes of 29 families.[50]

A Chinese dam project in the densely forested southwest was suspended in 2015 after sustained protests by locals and a social media campaign that spread among urban youth. With a stronger opposition, it is not in the government's interests to rouse discontent by giving China an ever greater slice of the pie. "The risk of domestic blowback is one of the prime reasons why small states have disincentives to become identified as clients," says John Ciorciari of the University of Michigan's Ford School of Public Policy.[51]

Nevertheless, China continues to offer valuable support that other countries cannot match. During Hun Sen's visit to China in 2015, Beijing agreed to build a new hospital and granted 1 billion yuan towards a massive sports and entertainment complex in Phnom Penh. The two sides also agreed to boost tourism: half a million Chinese tourists visited Cambodia in 2014, and the Cambodian authorities want that to rise to 2 million by 2020.[52] They went on to announce closer military ties, which have already strengthened in recent years. Beijing has provided military assistance and equipment, including trucks, helicopters and aircraft, and built military training and medical facilities. In 2014 China agreed to provide over 400 training scholarships for Cambodian officers, which it hopes will cement friendly long-term relations between the two militaries.

Unsurprisingly, Prime Minister Hun Sen has enthusiastically endorsed Xi Jinping's Belt and Road Initiative, which government advisers hope presages yet more Chinese investment. "The New Silk Road is positive, because it will help to bring roads, ports and industrial zones," said Dr Siphana. "We have a list of projects, and this is just what we need." The big question is whether the next wave of Chinese money will be invested responsibly or siphoned off into the pockets of government cronies. The role of the Asian Infrastructure Investment Bank, which will need to adhere to international financing norms, can only help. Yet without a fundamental change in culture, both at the government and corporate levels, some of the money will inevitably be misused.

For the moment, Chinese and Cambodian elites are happy to work hand in glove. Yet, as Beijing pushes the Belt and Road Initiative, it must beware repeating the diplomatic errors it has already made in Sri Lanka and Myanmar. There its close association with corrupt former regimes has weakened its geopolitical position. Cambodia is a democracy, imperfect though it may be, and its government must respond to public opinion. Hun Sen has been in power for more than twenty-five years; he cannot remain there for ever. China also knows that drawing closer to one country may alienate others. Its leverage in Cambodia, for example, is keenly resented in Vietnam. As China attempts to expand its sphere of influence, the international politics will be fiendishly difficult to manage.

CHAPTER 4

CALIFORNIA DREAMIN'

HOW CHINA "LOST" MYANMAR

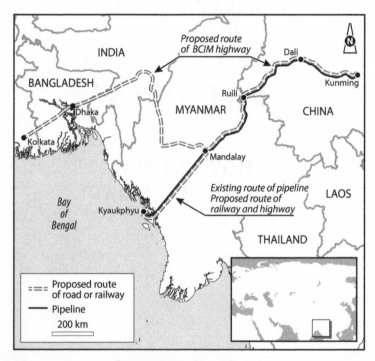

Gateway to the Bay of Bengal

In late 2012, an anonymous text message went viral across Myanmar, formerly known as Burma.[1] "Chinese get out," it said. "We're not afraid of you."[2] This low-level protest followed a string of anti-Chinese demonstrations that erupted after Myanmar's military junta, which had ruled for nearly five decades, dissolved itself in 2011. The major targets were investments by Chinese state firms in a giant dam, a copper mine, and twin oil and gas pipelines. The firms were accused of failing to compensate farmers adequately for lost land, wrecking the environment, and ransacking the country's natural resources. China's much-heralded *paukpaw* relationship with Myanmar, based on "brotherly" affection between two authoritarian states, was starting to crumble.[3]

For two decades, China had been the pariah state's only friend. Beijing provided the bulk of its foreign investment and arms imports, propping up Myanmar's military government while the West punished it with economic and financial sanctions. Beijing consistently defended its client state from international censure at the UN Security Council, just as it did Mahinda Rajapaksa's murderous regime in Sri Lanka. Yet after the 2010 general election, when the military regime embarked on a series of liberalizing reforms, the relationship rapidly soured. Myanmar's sudden and remarkable transition to democracy brought greater freedom of expression, unleashing a wave of popular nationalism and anti-Chinese feeling across this beautiful, but brutalized, land. Keen to loosen its dependence on China, Myanmar's new quasi-civilian government turned its back on Beijing for better relations with the United States and the West. When the new president suspended work on the US$3.6 billion Myitsone Dam in the country's north, Chinese analysts began to talk openly about the "loss of Myanmar".[4]

At the time, China feared that its erstwhile ally was falling into the US's embrace. For Beijing's analysts, visits by Secretary of State Hillary Clinton in 2011 and President Obama in 2012 confirmed that the US "pivot" to Asia, a fresh initiative under the new Democratic administration, was designed to contain China in its own backyard.[5] Some even argued that Myanmar's transition from military dictatorship to incipient democracy was actually a ploy to curtail China's outsized influence. There was an element of truth in this: Myanmar's generals no longer wanted to be shackled to Beijing. But their overriding reason to initiate the reform process was to save their skins at home, not to cosy up to Washington. Either way, China lost its privileged position just as it was inching closer to building a crucial new transit route from southwest China to the Bay of Bengal—a long-held ambition to create a proxy west coast and turn Myanmar into "China's California".[6]

Today, Beijing's relationship with the government in Naypyidaw remains frosty—yet Myanmar's geostrategic importance to China has not diminished.[7] In the wake of the

National League for Democracy's (NLD) landslide election victory in November 2015, which brought to power the country's first fully civilian government for fifty years, that leaves one big question. If icy relations could develop under a government led by ex-military officers with whom it had worked closely for two decades, how can Beijing expect to claw back influence with a government led by Aung San Suu Kyi, a world-renowned democracy activist?

On the eve of the election, China's *Global Times* newspaper fired a warning shot. "No observer deems that Myanmar will completely tilt toward the US, as such a witless move would ruin the strategic space and resources it can obtain from China's amicable policies," it wrote in a blunt editorial. Myanmar's ties with China, it added, had moved from "special to normal".[8] The *Global Times* is a sister paper of the *People's Daily*, the mouthpiece of the Chinese Communist Party. It is strongly nationalistic and likes to court controversy, but it does not represent official opinion. Nevertheless, Beijing allows it to play "bad cop" in the bland world of Chinese diplomacy, saying what mealy-mouthed diplomats cannot. In an interview with Xinhua after her victory, Aung San Suu Kyi responded with a straight bat. Her government, she told China's official news agency, would adopt a friendly foreign policy with all countries, including China. Praising Xi Jinping's Belt and Road Initiative, she added that Myanmar would welcome Chinese investment.[9]

How that works on the ground will depend on a number of factors, not least the willingness of Myanmar's people to accept the presence of China and its engineering firms. For as China's star ascends over Southeast Asia, anti-Chinese sentiment is deepening. The government worries the country could become a satellite within the Chinese solar system, like Laos and Cambodia, as China pursues its Asian dream of regional pre-eminence. Ordinary people fret less about the geopolitics and more about losing their land and livelihoods to savvy Chinese businessmen. It will take many generations before they forgive China for working so closely with the hated generals. For Beijing, the loss of Myanmar is a cautionary tale of how easy it is to lose both hearts and minds. [10]

亚洲梦

Anti-Chinese feeling in Myanmar is hardly new: the relationship between China and Myanmar is ancient and complex, characterized by an ambivalent sense of fraternal enmity. For centuries the Burmese court in Mandalay paid tribute to the Chinese emperor, and Myanmar has long viewed China as both its closest ally and its greatest threat.

Ordinary citizens, especially, have good reason to be fearful. After the country's rulers ditched socialism for crony capitalism in 1988, China worked closely with the military leaders who made their lives a misery. Myanmar's generals allowed Chinese bounty-hunters to rifle through the country's natural treasures, damming rivers, felling forests and mining gemstones. Working with the military conglomerates that dominated business in Myanmar, Chinese companies threw farmers off their land and plundered local resources. After the US and European Union imposed sanctions on investments in the late 1990s, Chinese businessmen faced little competition—

but they also made enemies. Plenty of Burmese blame China for helping to prop up the military junta.

Chinese investors, including state giants directly under Beijing's control, funnelled vast wealth into the hands of the people's oppressors. The most egregious example was the huge Mytisone Dam, the largest of a series of seven dams to be constructed by state-owned developer China Power Investment at the confluence of the Mali and N'mai rivers near the Yunnan border. Rumour has it that several generals, who became members of the new parliament under President Thein Sein's civilian-led government, received kickbacks of US$20–30 million each for giving the go-ahead to 140-metre-high structure. After construction began in 2007, the dam became a focus of local protests. Not only would it deliver 90% of the power it generated to China—it would flood an area of the Irrawaddy River regarded by Burmans, the country's ethnic Burmese majority, as the cradle of their civilization.[11] Activists also said the dam would submerge historic temples and churches of the local Kachin people, in addition to washing nearly 12,000 people out of their homes.[12]

Until 2011, executives at China Power simply shrugged off these concerns—just as Chinese officials ignored the underlying tide of anti-Chinese anger rising across the country. To the Chinese, it was unfeasible to call off a project designed to produce 100 billion kilowatt-hours of power per year, on a par with the Three Gorges Dam. But as the civilian government relaxed its grip on censorship, popular discontent crystallized around Myitsone. With the support of local media, protesters appealed to nationalist sentiment, making the dams a symbol of civilian defiance. As far away as Yangon, formerly known as Rangoon, car bumper stickers declared, "We love Irrawaddy". On 30 September 2011, President Thein Sein suspended work on the main dam. This was a genuine turning point: it showed the new civilian-led government would neither ignore public grievances nor tolerate corrupt deals with Chinese enterprises. Today the dam construction site is empty and desolate, guarded by a handful of bored security guards.[13]

For China, it was shocking to see how quickly a free media could bring down such a giant project. Until that moment, Chinese firms in Myanmar had always been insulated from public opinion. Yet popular resentment in foreign climes is hardly a new experience for state-backed Chinese firms. From Gabon to Papua New Guinea, irresponsible business practices have provoked anti-Chinese backlashes. Nonetheless, the misstep in Myanmar, a neighbouring country where China has stronger geopolitical interests, is far more serious. Until 2011, China viewed Myanmar as its strategic corridor to the Indian Ocean and its puppet in the Association of Southeast Asian Nations (ASEAN). The dream that Myanmar can become a proxy Chinese province giving unimpeded access to a western seaboard now looks a fantasy. Ordinary Burmese citizens, emboldened by freedom of speech and egged on by an uncensored media, will not let it happen.

China has found that the biggest threat to its once-favoured position in Myanmar is not the US but the power of public opinion. The Mytisone Dam is not the only example. In 2012, protesters targeted the US$1.1 billion Letpadaung copper mine owned by a subsidiary of Norinco, a state-owned

Chinese arms manufacturer. Activists and monks occupied the mine for several months before police cleared them away with tear gas and water cannon. The furious demonstrations forced a national inquiry chaired by Aung San Suu Kyi. "There was a shift in popular sentiment," says Yangon resident Wong Yit Fan, a former chief economist at Standard Chartered. "Anger at the military moderated and was retargeted at China." With little experience of civil society at home, Chinese companies responded clumsily. China Power exacerbated the tension in Myitsone when it set up a website spewing self-serving propaganda.[14]

Grassroots anger is widespread. "Most of the Burmese people hate the Chinese," says Khin Tun, an investment consultant hired by Chinese companies to communicate with irate locals. This feeling is not shared by most government officials, who know that Myanmar has no option but to maintain good relations with the superpower on its doorstep, not to mention its biggest investor and trading partner. But one former dissident, who returned to advise President Thein Sein after years in exile in the jungles of Thailand, told me China had to address the resentment created by its cooperation with the military. And he warned that Myanmar would no longer allow China to monopolize its foreign policy:

China needs to understand that the geopolitical system has changed. We still want to be friendly with China, but we want to be friendly with everyone else, too, including the US and Russia. There is no reason why we should have to choose between countries.[15]

Chinese analysts initially viewed "the loss of Myanmar" as a US conspiracy. "Many Chinese policy intellectuals saw the improvement of US–Myanmar relations, the reform process in Myanmar, and problems for Chinese projects there as part of a US-directed plot to contain China," says Josh Gordon, an expert on China–Myanmar relations at Yale University.[16] Over the past few years, however, China has learned that it is not the sun around which Myanmar revolves. "The idea that the democratic transition had anything to do with China is nonsense," says the presidential adviser. The truth, he says, is that the military always planned to return power to the people, but needed to design a political system in which they retained a large slice of power. The failed uprising by monks in 2007, known as the Saffron Revolution, showed the generals that they were living on borrowed time; they rushed to ratify a new constitution for a civilian government with a significant military presence. In short, the generals believed the regime would fall without radical reform—so they put in place changes they hoped would assure their own survival. China, in his view, was not a significant factor.

In the intervening years, Beijing has begun to understand how its mighty economy and geopolitical ambitions are seen as a threat across much of Southeast Asia. Myanmar is far from the only country seeking to extract itself from China's immense gravitational pull. One aim of the Belt and Road Initiative, launched two years after the postponement of the Myitsone Dam, is to persuade China's neighbours of the mutual benefits of working with it. Beijing also recognizes that Chinese companies must be brought to heel. These firms have begun to understand that investing vast sums of money does not allow them to behave with impunity, and that they must do a better job of working alongside local communities. Big state-owned enterprises have stepped up corporate social responsibility programmes and are making progress on engaging with public opinion. One former high-ranking British diplomat in Myanmar says China Power now runs one of the most sophisticated operations by a Chinese company in the country.[17]

Significantly, China is also attempting to play a more positive diplomatic role. On a flight to Yangon in January 2013, I sat a few rows behind Fu Ying, China's vice-minister of foreign affairs and the former ambassador to the UK. The elegant lady with curly grey hair and expensive jewellery, seated in 1A, looked vaguely familiar. I confirmed her identity by surreptitiously looking over the shoulder of the delegate in the seat in front of mine, who was reading preparatory documents for the trip. Madam Fu was met at Yangon by uniformed generals with medals dangling from their chests. She was whisked off to meet President Thein Sein to discuss bilateral relations, led by the fighting between the government and ethnic rebels in northeastern Kachin State. Two months after that meeting China appointed former deputy foreign minister Wang Yingfan as China's first special envoy for Asian affairs, with a focus on Myanmar—clear evidence that Beijing was taking its diplomatic task there seriously.

Madam Fu's visit came just after China had coordinated peace talks between the Myanmar government and the Kachin Independence Army (KIA), actively mediating between the two sides. "China [had] never before played such a public role in an internal conflict between the central government and a local rebel group of another sovereign nation," says Sun Yun, a non-resident fellow at the Brookings Institution.[18] Although the exact nature of China's involvement in various border disputes is hazy, it seems that Beijing refrained from seeking leverage against the Myanmar government by supporting the KIA—against the advice of its more hawkish analysts. And when the separate Kokang ethnic insurgency erupted in 2015, sending an estimated 40,000–50,000 refugees over the border into China, Beijing ignored calls by its own citizens to aid a people who identify as ethnically Chinese. It even failed to react strongly when a Burmese military aircraft strayed over the border, dropping a bomb that killed four Chinese civilians.[19]

亚洲梦

It is important not to exaggerate China's demise in Myanmar. Its star may have waned in recent years, but it is still Myanmar's biggest investor and most important bilateral partner. Its companies maintain a sizeable presence in hydropower, mining, oil and gas, and often lead the way in telecoms equipment and real estate. The reality is that China has deeper roots in Myanmar than any other country and can provide much of what it needs: capital, infrastructure and cheap goods. It also offers a large and convenient export market. The lifting of most Western embargoes has allowed foreign access to much of the economy; but Chinese expertise will still be needed in power generation, oil and gas projects, manufacturing and telecommunications in coming years.

When I visited Yangon in early 2013, Myanmar's sweltering capital initially felt far from China. It is a beguiling city of smiling, burgundy-robed monks, men wrapped in sarongs (here known as *longyi*) sipping tea by the roadside, and women with faces smeared with *thanaka*, a chalky paste made from tree bark.[20] But Chinese communities have settled in Myanmar for centuries and Yangon is a cultural melting pot: Chinese temples intermingle with shining golden pagodas, Hindu shrines, Muslim mosques and the decaying edifices of the Raj. Under British rule in the early 20th century, the city then known as Rangoon was the world's top immigration destination—busier than New York or Shanghai. In addition to millions of Indians, boatloads of Chinese from the coastal provinces of Guangdong and Fujian arrived to make a new home there.

Chinese influence, then, has a long history—but there have always been tensions. In the 1960s, the brutal military leader Ne Win prohibited foreigners—including many resident Chinese—from owning land and holding business licences, and deliberately stoked racial animosity. When anti-Chinese riots broke out in Rangoon in 1967, Chinese shops were looted and set on fire; horribly, girls in a Chinese school were burnt alive. After bilateral relations broke down, China openly intervened in Burma's civil war. Discrimination and anti-Chinese riots continued to flare in the 1970s, with the covert support of the Burmese government. And when a new law in 1982 further restricted Burmese citizenship for ethnic Chinese, it accelerated an ongoing exodus of Burmese Chinese out of the country.

When the first military regime was thrown out by rebel generals in a coup in 1988, the situation improved dramatically.

The State Law and Order Restoration Council, as the new military government named itself, loosened the state's grip on the economy, encouraging private sector growth and foreign investment. Ethnic Chinese businesses have flourished: look around Yangon or Mandalay today and much of what you see will be owned by businessmen with Chinese connections. Locals grumble that the grip of Burmese-Chinese entrepreneurs is tightening. "Chinatown is spreading far beyond its traditional borders," said Judy Ko, who runs a Yangon-based trading company. "Chinese businessmen are taking over market stalls, food joints and medicine shops across the city." Relatives of second- or third-generation Burmese Chinese, she told me, were pouring in from China and Taiwan. "They pay off immigration officials or marry locals, so they can legally buy property. The influx of Chinese investors is pumping up prices to crazy levels and pushing locals out of the market," she complained. Even if this account is exaggerated, the perception of an influx of Chinese people and money is widespread.

Indeed, critics say that official Chinese investment—which hit an accumulated total of US$15 billion in 2015, although annual inflows have fallen sharply since 2011—is just the tip of the iceberg.[21] Many nominally "Burmese" companies are really financed via mainland Chinese shell companies, sometimes representing the interests of ethnic Wa drugs smugglers. Other companies belong to long-term Chinese immigrants—most infamously Asia World, Myanmar's largest conglomerate, founded by convicted heroin trafficker Lo Hsing Han. Asia World is closely associated with the United Wa State Army, which independently controls territory near the Chinese border. It is also one of China Power's local joint venture partners on the Myitsone Dam.

Most Burmese Chinese were born in Myanmar and are as "Chinese" as their fellow immigrants in other parts of Southeast Asia. Ethnic ties help oil the wheels of commerce in Myanmar, as they do across Southeast Asia; but there is a considerable cultural gap between local Burmese Chinese and mainland investors, which is probably underestimated by other Burmese. In Yangon, many local Chinese belong to the Chinese Myanmar Chamber of Commerce. "We've been here for a hundred years," the Chamber manager told me. "We have no contact with outsiders coming from China. We keep our Chinese customs, but we speak Burmese and are Burmese."

Culturally, Yangon's Burmese-Chinese residents are closer to their cousins in Southeast Asia than to those in mainland China—and it is questionable how welcoming they would be to a new wave of Chinese immigrants. But within the Burmese-Chinese community itself, ethnic ties run deep. In the Chinese Chamber—located in a big, dusty building over-looking the wharfs along the Yangon River—there is a wall displaying donors. Prominent on the list is Asia World, which presented 5 million yuan (then worth about US$750,000) to the chamber in 2010. Burmese resentment of the role played by Chinese firms, whatever their origin, is not hard to understand.

Tensions began to rise when overland trade with China was reopened in 1988. Anxiety over the influx of Chinese money is most keenly felt in the north, especially the areas bordering China. According to one estimate, 300,000 people migrated from Yunnan to Mandalay in the 1990s alone, and

Chinese people make up roughly one-third of the city's population. Yet Chinese associations in the city say the population is stable at just 5,000 families—nearer to 50,000 people. Establishing how many Chinese people really live in Mandalay is an impossible task, especially as mixed marriages make it difficult to define exactly what "Chinese" means. Popular estimates are almost certainly exaggerated, says Roman Caillaud, an investment consultant who has studied border trade and immigration in northern Myanmar.

Locals complain that Mandalay—the cultural home of ethnic Burmans, who make up two-thirds of Myanmar's population—has been inundated with Chinese immigrants. They talk about an influx of traders flooding the market with shoddy goods, and blame Chinese investors for pillaging their land. Mandalay, they say, has become a "Chinese city". Local folk singer Lin Lin confronts the issue in his most popular song, "Death of Mandalay", which has 100,000 views on Youtube. "Who are they in this city? / Neighbours that arrive from northeast," he laments, plucking a guitar. "I close both my ears in utter shame / Messed up with strangers / The death of our dear Mandalay."[22]

Thirty years ago, Mandalay was famed for its traditional wooden buildings, twisting backstreets and glittering golden stupas. Today, after twenty years of Chinese investment, it looks like a typical Chinese city: wide roads and ugly concrete houses laid out on a monotonous grid. Its once cultured streets are congested with honking trucks and choked with exhaust fumes. But for a city in Southeast Asia's poorest country, Mandalay is surprisingly prosperous: one survey in 2012 found an average household owned three scooters or motor-bikes. Few people used to drink alcohol, but now there are "beer stations" on every street corner. Late in the evening, men slump over tables crowded with bottles of Myanmar Beer and Grand Royal whisky.

With a population of around 1 million, Mandalay is just one-fifth the size of Yangon—but it felt considerably richer when I visited. Most of the vehicles on the roads were new and the streets hummed with commerce. The reason for Manda-lay's wealth is simple: trade with China. The city is a ten-hour drive down the Burma Road from the frontier towns of Muse and Ruili, the major distribution centre for goods streaming over the border. Bilateral trade topped US$9 billion in the first ten months of the 2015–16 fiscal year, almost all of it overland, according to Chinese statistics.[23] But the real total is signifi-cantly higher, as many goods—including exports of illegal jade, timber, opium and methamphetamines—are smuggled across the border.

Global Witness, a London-based environmental watchdog, estimates Myanmar's jade trade was worth an incredible US$31 billion in 2014 alone, almost half of the country's GDP. "The jade business is a significant driver of Myanmar's most serious armed conflict, between the central government and the Kachin Independence Army/Kachin Independence Organization," it concluded in a report.[24] Very little of this income benefited the state, instead finding its way into the pockets of military elites and drug lords. Mining deaths are common, and drugs and prostitution feed off the trade. Those who stand in the way of the miners face land grabs and intimidation at gunpoint.

Ordinary Burmese do profit from commerce with China, but they resent being so economically dependent on it. One of the biggest complaints, from Mandalay to Yangon, is that China exports trash: fake drugs, contaminated food, products that fall to pieces. Until Western trade sanctions were repealed, little else was available; but Mandalay's shops and markets remain piled high with cheap Chinese goods. Many of the brand names on Mandalay's streets are Chinese: Zoomlion construction equipment, Zongshen motorbikes, Haima cars, Midea white goods, Huawei phones, Haier fridges. A giant billboard at a busy intersection even advertises the services of one Dr Yun, a plastic surgeon across the border in Ruili.

Resentment of Chinese encroachment is strong. Tin Soe, the manager of a downtown hotel, told me most of his guests are mainlanders. Some are supervisors on China National Petroleum Corporation's (CNPC) oil and gas pipelines, which pass through the Mandalay area on their way to the Chinese border. Others are in jade mining: Mandalay is famous for its gemstones markets, and the hotel makes a useful base for scouting investment opportunities. "We Burmese do not like the Chinese: they smile with their faces, but are crooked in their heart," he said. Chinese immigrants, he added dolefully, are taking over the city: "Chinese traders in Ruili bribe immigration officials to allow them to settle over the border in Muse. Once they have Burmese nationality, they move down the Burma Road and buy up property in Mandalay."

Ethnic Chinese are estimated to make up no more than 4% of Myanmar's population—up to 2 million people out of a total population of roughly 52 million. The situation is further complicated by locals' failure to differentiate between established Burmese Chinese and more recent arrivals—even those who are not strictly Chinese at all. In the 1990s, drug and jade barons from the Wa and Kokang minorities invested their ill-gotten gains in Mandalay, building fancy villas and shopping centres. The Kokang (unlike the Wa) are ethnically Han Chinese, but have lived in Myanmar for centuries. Yet many Burmese consider any minorities from the border area to be "Chinese".

Chinese migrants from Yunnan first settled in northern Myanmar in the late 19th century. The next wave came in the 1930s, as the Japanese army marched through Yunnan, and in the 1940s, when nationalist Kuomintang troops fled the victorious Communists. These long-term migrants retain many of their Chinese customs, and tend to stick together. In Mandalay's Chinatown, local Burmese-Chinese families gather at the Yunnan Exhibition Hall and Chinese temple, built in 1953. The traditional eaved gate, topped with golden dancing dragons, has been renovated with money from the Yunnan provincial government—so old connections remain intact. But these Burmese Chinese are generally integrated into the local community and speak the local language.

Their presence, however, has become far more influential since overland border trade with China restarted. Resentment is stirred by the obvious wealth of Chinese families in Mandalay. "It is true that many of us are richer than local Burmese," admitted a Burmese-Chinese girl working in her family pearl store in downtown Mandalay. "But we have worked hard for our success. My grandparents came here seventy years ago without a penny in their pocket," she told me in southern-inflected Mandarin. Burmese Chinese are not afraid to flaunt that wealth: they drive Japanese SUVs to pricy Yunnan restaurants and throw flashy wedding parties for hundreds, even thousands, of guests. Two weeks before Chinese New Year, many of the best houses in town had festive greetings stuck above the front door—a sure sign their owners were ethnically Chinese.

Much of this wealth comes from helping mainlanders negotiate Myanmar's investment climate. Language barriers must be overcome and investment regulations are strict—even if they can be circumvented by greasing the right palms. Burmese Chinese work as fixers, setting up meetings and managing informal inflows of capital. Mr Long, a lead miner from the central Chinese province of Hunan, told me doing business in Myanmar would be impossible without Burmese-Chinese middlemen. "If you want to make an investment, you have to go through them," he explained. "They have all the local connections and can act as translators." A jade miner from Yunnan province agreed: "To do anything here, you have to work with locals. And to work with locals, you need to work with Burmese Chinese."

Trade is dominated by local Chinese families, not mainlanders. Trucks from as far as Guangdong and Fujian arrive at Ruili, but all goods must be reloaded onto Myanmar-registered trucks to cross the border. Traders belonging to ethnic minority groups found on both sides of the border, such as the Kachin (known as Jingpo in China) and Shan (known as Dai), cross easily. But restrictions are tighter for ordinary Chinese traders. Mr Shao, a trader in Ruili who imports machinery, jade and textiles, told me his visa allowed him to travel over the border but not to cross back. Instead he had to fly from Mandalay to Kunming, and then back to Ruili—a long, expensive and circuitous route. "I do whatever I need to do to put food on the table," he said, with a glint in his eye.

Myanmar is full of tales of Chinese immigrants buying up forged identity papers of dead Burmese to become naturalized citizens. No doubt this practice goes on. But some mainland traders buy Myanmar citizenship cards on the black market simply to lubricate business and make cross-border travel easier, with no intention of settling in Myanmar. Investors in logging, mining and agriculture typically fly back and forth between Mandalay and Kunming, which is served by daily flights. When I took a flight out of Mandalay ten days before Chinese New Year, it was packed with Chinese businessman returning home for the holiday.

亚洲梦

If there is one place to look for evidence of a "Chinese invasion" in northern Myanmar, it is Lashio. The biggest town between Mandalay and Ruili, Lashio was the starting point of the famous Burma Road. Built by Burmese and Chinese labourers under British direction, it helped keep the Chinese government supplied with goods, arms and food during the initial years of the war with Japan in 1937–45. These days most of the trade goes in the other direction: just 100 km over the border from Ruli, Lashio is the first major stop for goods flowing in from China. It is also an obvious base for border traders transporting goods up and down the modern Burma Road.

With a population of around 130,000, similar in size to Exeter in England, Lashio is very ethnically mixed. Around one-third of its residents are of Chinese origin, almost entirely from neighbouring Yunnan. But the town is also home to native Burmans and a large ethnic Tai population (known as Shan in Myanmar and Dai in Yunnan). Indian Sikhs, Muslims and Hindus form another visible minority, and a large mosque looms over the town centre. Assorted hill tribes—belonging to some of the 135 minority groups recognized by the Myanmar government—walk into Lashio every day to sell beans and tomatoes at the roadside.

Lashio is dominated by a huge concrete market that spills out into the surrounding roads and alleyways, where stall-holders sit below nylon tarpaulins strung out on bamboo poles. They sell a vast array of fruits and vegetables, dried fish, chilies, mysterious powders, medicines and toiletries, clothes, shoes and bags—as well as gold, jade and diamonds. In the run-up to Chinese New Year, stalls pop up selling shiny red and gold decorations—lanterns bearing the Chinese character for "prosperity", door stickers to bring luck to guests, and fire crackers to ring in the new year and scare away malingering ghosts.

Aside from their own local dialect, a variant of Yunnanese, Lashio's Chinese residents typically speak Burmese and Mandarin. Most also know Shan, the local language. Several stallholders told me their families came from Tengchong, a former stage on the Southern Silk Road on the Chinese side of the Myanmar–Yunnan border, with its own history of ethnic mixing. Lashio's ethnic Chinese population belongs to a long tradition of border trade that has produced complex, multiple identities.

Many came to Lashio as victims of history. Mr Zhong, a seventy-year-old who sells traditional Chinese medicines such as dried lizards and deer antlers, left Yunnan's Dali in 1949 aged just two. His father, who had fought with the nationalist Kuomintang army, fled with his family when the Communists swept into power. Mrs Duan, selling Chinese lanterns auspiciously inscribed with double goldfish, arrived as a baby twenty years later, when her parents fled the Cultural Revolution. Others were less certain. "We've been here a long time," one stallholder explained in passable Mandarin. "At least 100 years—maybe 300. Who knows?"

I found newer arrivals hard to find, despite all the hysteria in Yangon and Mandalay about a flood of Chinese settlers inundating northern Myanmar. In fact there is little obvious modern Chinese influence in Lashio, aside from the traded goods themselves. Signs and labels in Chinese are invariably written in the traditional characters used before the Communists introduced a simplified writing system in the 1950s and 1960s. Had there been a big influx of mainland settlers since the Burma Road reopened in the late 1980s, these people would surely have brought the new writing system with them. Nor was there much sign of Chinese food. Instead there were Burmese staples: barbequed meat and vegetables, and dubious piles of greasy pre-cooked stews, swimming in a pool of oil, accompanied by raw vegetables and Indian-style pickles. If the Chinese had really taken over, the town's restaurants and street stalls would sell noodles. No doubt much of the investment in Lashio is of Chinese origin—but the evidence of a Chinese invasion was thin on the ground.

Resentment of China's economic invasion in Mandalay and northern Myanmar confuses the influx of businessmen from the mainland with the growing wealth of the Burmese-Chinese citizens who serve them. Fears that a flood of Chinese investors from over the border are "taking over" Mandalay and turning the towns along the Burma Road into outposts of China are overdone. Mandalay still feels Burmese: street signs are in Burmese or English, restaurants and street stalls serve Burmese food, and most people are ethnically Burman. Mandalay is less "foreign" than many cities in the developed world with large immigrant populations.

The truth is that Myanmar does not need to fear being overrun by Chinese people, but it should worry about Chinese money. Myanmar's problem is less one of outsiders arriving and taking over than one of outsiders taking what they want and then leaving. The majority of mainlanders come to Myanmar to do business, not to settle in an alien country. As Myanmar democratizes and public opinion becomes a growing force in domestic politics, anger should not be directed at long-established immigrants. It should be directed instead at the corrupt Burmese elites who allow Chinese investors to plunder the country's natural resources at the expense of local people.

GATEWAY TO THE BAY OF BENGAL

A few years ago, one focus of such resentment was the construction of twin Chinese oil and gas pipelines from the port of Kyaukphyu on Myanmar's west coast, through Mandalay and Lashio, to the Yunnan border town of Ruili.

CNPC provided compensation to farmers who lost their land, but some complained they had nowhere left to grow crops, while others accused CNPC of damaging the environment. Armed ethnic groups fought with government troops sent to protect the pipeline, forcing people to flee their homes.

The protests died down after the completion of the pipelines in 2013. That year, searching for the pipeline along the Burma Road, I caught glimpses of narrow strips of freshly dug farmland, scattered with white marking posts. Underneath the deep-red earth lay twin tubes of shiny steel, each about a metre in diameter. The Myanmar section of the US$2.5 billion project stretches for nearly 800 km, and then for a further 1,600 km through Yunnan province. From Kunming, the provincial capital, an extension pipeline pumps gas eastwards to the provinces of Guizhou and Guangxi. Another will send oil northwards to Chongqing, home to 30 million people, where China is building a second refinery.

CNPC began to pump natural gas from Myanmar's offshore Shwe gasfield in 2013, under a thirty-year purchase deal that will deliver tens of billions of dollars to the Burmese government. The pipeline's annual capacity is 12 billion cubic metres a year, though the actual flow reportedly fell far short of that in 2014 and 2015. The first oil was pumped on a trial basis in 2015, when a 300,000-tonne supertanker discharged at the newly opened deep-water port at Maday Island in Kyaukphyu. When the pipeline is fully functional, it will be capable of pumping 22 million tonnes of crude per annum—equivalent to about 4% of total Chinese demand in 2015.[25] The Sino-Myanmar pipelines join those from Kazakhstan and

Turkmenistan in delivering energy supplies overland, which Beijing deems vital for China's energy security.

For Beijing's strategists, the prize of gaining a western seaboard is the stuff of dreams. The oil and gas pipelines enable China to import energy supplies without requiring tankers from Africa and the Middle East to negotiate the narrow, pirate-infested waterway between Indonesia and Malaysia— the infamous Malacca Strait—which Beijing fears could be blockaded by the US Navy in a war. Three times as much oil passes through the Malacca Strait as through the Suez Canal, including roughly 80% of China's own oil imports. Although the current capacity of the Myanmar pipelines is small relative to China's vast energy needs, Beijing believes it goes some way to resolving the so-called "Malacca dilemma".

China's port at Maday Island is part of a broader plan to develop transport links to China from the Bay of Bengal. Efficient transport links from Kyaukphyu would enable China to import other raw materials directly, saving a journey of thousands of kilometres. In addition, establishing a trading hub there would allow firms from southwest China to export goods quickly and cheaply to India, Bangladesh and beyond. China calls this scheme the "Bangladesh–China–India–Myanmar Economic Corridor" (BCIM). It was conceived before the Belt and Road Initiative, but is almost certainly now viewed as part of this project. Above all, the economic corridor offers Beijing a big strategic prize: the chance to extend its sphere of influence into the Indian Ocean.[26]

The BCIM scheme would see new transport links from the southwestern province of Yunnan. Beginning in Kunming and ending in Kolkata, the proposed corridor loosely follows the path of the Ancient Tea Horse Road through Myanmar and Bangladesh, the old trading route once known as the Southern Silk Road. Beijing has a grand plan to build a parallel expressway and railway from Ruili to Kyaukphyu, with a separate road running through northern Myanmar, the Northeast States of India, and Bangladesh. The scheme's supporters say it will boost trade and investment in one of the most backward regions of Asia, long beset by tribal rebellion.

Since 2013, Kunming has hosted a China–South Asia Expo to promote trade along the corridor. When I visited in 2014, the jamboree heaved with shoppers haggling over Afghan carpets, Pakistani handicrafts, silks and textiles from India and Bangladesh, and Sri Lankan gemstones. It was held alongside the older Kunming Fair, a popular and colourful event that has run for two decades. The stalls in the exhibition halls were packed with local produce, selling everything from green Burmese jade and Pu'er tea to yak-bone jewellery and Tibetan leopard pelts. Lithe beauties from Yunnan's many minority groups pressed visitors to buy dry-aged ham and bags of mysterious edible fungus.

The upgrading of the old Kunming Fair is part of Beijing's blueprint for boosting development along China's frontiers. The "autonomous" regions of Xinjiang and Guangxi, which like Yunnan are home to large numbers of minorities with ethnic links over their borders, hold similar events directed at Central Asia and Southeast Asia respectively. Beijing believes greater cross-border cooperation will help nurture new markets and strengthen China's regional clout. In 2011,

China's State Council released a document calling for Yunnan to become a "bridgehead" to the countries of South and Southeast Asia, a plan known as "Opening up the Southwest". Its aim is to turn Kunming, a city of nearly 4 million people, into a regional gateway spearheading investment and trade flows over Yunnan's 4,000-km international border.[27]

In 2013, the four countries involved in the BCIM project met in Kunming and agreed to the broad thrust of the scheme, promising to identify realistic and achievable infrastructure projects. These could eventually include new railways, power transmission lines and telecoms networks, running over remote mountains and through thick jungle. But the initial focus is the construction of a 2,800-km highway from Kunming to Kolkata—winding through Ruili, Mandalay and Dhaka—which all four parties approved, in principle, in 2012. Opening 2014's China–South Asia Expo, Chinese vice-premier Wang Yang urged that work on the project be speeded up.

Planners in Kunming have talked about building regional trade routes since the 1990s, but the BCIM scheme only became a national priority in 2014, when Premier Li Keqiang mentioned it in his annual speech to the National People's Congress. It faces enormous obstacles—not least topographic—but progress is being made. China's Ministry of Transport has completed a plan for an expressway from Kunming to Kyaukphyu, which will split at Mandalay to follow the proposed BCIM route through Northeast India. The government in Dhaka is preparing to sign a memorandum of understanding with a Chinese construction company to build the Bangladesh leg of the highway, including an elevated expressway between the capital and the port city of Chittagong, where a Chinese firm runs a container port.

The scheme has not gone all China's way. In 2009 and 2011, China and Myanmar signed memoranda of understanding to develop a new special economic zone at Kyaukphyu under the management of CITIC Group, a Chinese state-owned conglomerate. This envisaged expanding the deep-sea port and developing an industrial zone and logistics terminus, linked by a US$20 billion railway line. But following strong local opposition, the government put the projects on hold. When the agreement expired in 2014, it said the railway would not go ahead. This was a blow to China, which had already built a new line from Kunming to Ruili. But the current frosty state of bilateral relations means that investing in a US$20 billion project remains a step too far.

Green shoots, however, are emerging. In December 2015, Myanmar's parliament finally granted contracts to CITIC Group to develop the deep-water seaport and industrial area, after years of languishing.[28] The US$14 billion project has brought renewed hope on the Chinese side that the expressway between Kyaukpyu and Ruili will finally be built. In 2014, the Myanmar government turned down a proposed US$2 billion Chinese loan to construct the proposed road, saying that it should be built as a joint venture with a local company on a build–operate–transfer basis. But a solution will probably be found: it is inconceivable that a country as impoverished as Myanmar can afford to block Chinese infrastructure investment for ever.

The multilateral nature of the BCIM project may help China to navigate the sensitive waters of popular politics. "The oil and gas pipeline did not receive nearly as much criticism in Myanmar as the Mytisone Dam and Letpadaung copper mine, as we cooperated with South Korea and other countries," notes Professor Lu Guangsheng, director of the Institute of Southeast Asian Studies at Yunnan University.[29] China's gas is delivered by a Daewoo-led consortium operating in the Shwe field, in which India is an additional investor—so it is not viewed as a purely Chinese project. That multilateral umbrella helped to shield China from the scale and depth of outrage experienced in Myitsone and Letpadaung.

If the BCIM highway goes ahead, the biggest winner may be the border town of Ruili, a remote jungle outpost that is fully 3,000 km from Beijing. A little over a decade ago, Ruili was China's very own Sin City, high on profits from the Burmese jade trade and rampant heroin smuggling. Chinese tourists crossed into Myanmar for a few hours to gamble in casinos and gawk at ladyboys performing tawdry sex shows. Junkie prostitutes shot up in the street and tested positive for HIV in the city's many venereal-disease clinics. "There wasn't even a fence or an official border crossing," a long-term resident told me. "People used to sell white powder by the roadside."[30]

That all changed in 2005, when the local government closed the border to tourists and cracked down on vice. Today Ruili has grown into semi-respectable middle age: the few tourists who still come are more likely to play golf than ogle pouting men with fake breasts. The city is less a den of iniquity than a giant wholesale market. Much of the economy is still fuelled by jade, the "green gold" dug from the mountains across the border; but it is also an export conduit for goods made in the manufacturing heartlands to the east. Nearly half of China's recorded trade with Myanmar crosses overland at Ruili, but the border is so porous that no one knows what it is really worth.

Already the entry point for the oil and gas pipelines, Ruili is gearing up to transform itself into Yunnan's gateway to South Asia and the Indian Ocean. Planners hope a new "experimental zone" with facilities for trade processing, logistics and storage will become an international trade hub on the road from Kunming to Kolkata. When I visited in 2014, the new zone had already received considerable investment, with more planned. Acres of new warehousing had sprung up, much of it still empty. Local officials want to build a cross-border city of 300,000 people—a "new growth pole" for southwest China. They plan to simplify customs controls and facilitate more cross-border trade, building on the success of the already tax-free enclave of Jiegao, a fingernail of land over the Shweli River from Ruili, right on the border with Myanmar.

Trucks arriving at Jiegao are greeted by a giant billboard of President Xi Jinping proclaiming, in English, "The Reforming does not pause and the Opening does not stop."[31] They drive there from all over China, offloading goods for export. I saw flat-packed motorbikes from Chongqing assembled on site and driven over the border into Myanmar. Jiegao's shops sell power tools, machinery, mobile phones, electronics—and Muslim headscarves. The biggest market, inevitably, is Gemstone City. Burmese traders are issued a small green "temporary residence permit" by the Yunnan government, but many are effectively permanent residents in China.

Parts of Jiegao felt thoroughly Burmese: dark-skinned men wearing *longyi* loaded brightly painted trucks with Chinese electronics; shopkeepers read newspapers in curly Brahmic script. The pavement was stained red with betel-nut juice and the working girls had white *thanaka*-pasted cheeks. Border crossings took seconds: more than 12 million official visits were made by foreign permit holders in Jiegao in 2014. Those without permits simply hopped through holes in the flimsy wire fence that separates the two countries. For a few crazy seconds, I stood with one leg in China and one in Myanmar. Local residents come and go as they please; border security is remarkably lax.

Chinese and Burmese residents in Ruili seem to rub along together fine, but there are tensions below the surface. "Those Burmese are not like we Chinese," a middle-aged Han woman told me. "They're wild, and fight in the streets; sometimes they even kill people. They don't have a good government like ours." She went on to tell a rambling story about a Han man who went into business with a village chief in Myanmar, investing his life savings in a coal mine. The business was very successful—until one day the Burmese partner decided he wanted it for himself. "He killed his Chinese partner, murdered his wife, and raped his daughter," she narrated, scurrilously. "The thing about the Burmese is that you never know what they're going to do next. Their tempers are as changeable as the weather."

亚洲梦

Ruili's massive investment requires an equally massive leap of faith in a productive future for China–Myanmar relations.

Much will depend on the new NLD government, effectively led by Aung San Suu Kyi in her capacity as "state counsellor". This position was specially created for her, as the Burmese constitution prohibits anyone with foreign family members from holding the office of predsident: Suu Kyi's late husband was British, as are her two children. Nevertheless, it is universally presumed that her new position will give her more power than the official president. In any case, as Myanmar's new foreign minister, Suu Kyi is officially responsible for shaping Myanmar's foreign policy—and there is no more important relationship than that with China.

It is a fascinating situation. Beijing stood behind Myanmar's military junta throughout Suu Kyi's long years in captivity; it had no interest in engaging with the pro-democracy forces nominally under her leadership. Yet Beijing knows it must work with Suu Kyi's new government, and Suu Kyi knows she must build a healthy relationship with Beijing. After all, one cannot choose one's neighbour. Six months before the NLD's landslide victory, in the summer of 2015, Beijing rolled out the red carpet. During that first visit to China, Suu Kyi met President Xi and was treated like a head of state. Human rights activists hoped she would raise the case of Liu Xiaobo, a fellow Nobel Laureate who is serving an eleven-year prison sentence for political crimes. Yet, despite her reputation as an ideologue, she was careful not to upset her hosts. In April 2016, China's foreign minister was the first foreign dignitary to visit the new government in Naypyidaw.

Since her release, Suu Kyi has fought hard to establish herself as a pragmatic politician, angering many idealistic supporters in the process. This has extended to Chinese investments, on which she has proven surprisingly accommodative. When the previous government asked her to chair the investigation committee set up to report on the controversy over the Letpadaung copper mine, Suu Kyi advised that the project be allowed to continue—for which she was roundly criticized. (Some analysts believe the former ruling party duped her into taking on this investigation, realizing she would look bad no matter what she advised.) In addition, she had little to say about China's controversial oil and gas pipelines, but has praised Xi Jinping's Belt and Road Initiative. So Beijing hopes Myanmar's new leader is someone with whom it can do business.

As foreign minister, Suu Kyi must decide whether two major Chinese investments should go ahead: the stalled Myitsone Dam and CITIC Group's special economic zone concession at Kyaukphyu. Beijing has consistently voiced its hope that work on the Myitsone Dam will restart, although China Power Investment itself has privately accepted that it must concentrate on smaller projects first. There is also popular support for scrutinizing the deal made with CITIC by the outgoing government in late 2015. With a lack of roads and power infrastructure inhibiting growth, Suu Kyi knows Myanmar cannot afford to push away Chinese investment. Her delicate task is to reassure China that responsible investment is welcome while simultaneously managing anti-Chinese sentiment on the street.

Suu Kyi must also work with China to help secure Myanmar's own fragile peace process. China observed peacekeeping talks with a dozen armed groups in 2011 and played a valuable role in coordinating talks between the government and the Kachin Independence Army the following year. Nevertheless, some observers (including the former Burmese government) believe it has aggravated the febrile situation in the border areas, supplying weapons to Wa and Kokang rebels.[32] If true, this is surely a further reason to bring China on board. The outgoing government agreed a ceasefire with seven armed ethnic groups in October 2015, but no concrete steps have been taken to make this lasting. Beijing has indicated it might be prepared to take on an official role in supporting dialogue between the government and the ceasefire signatories, especially with combatant groups on the China–Myanmar border.

If China and its companies behave responsibly, there is every chance that they will find the NLD government under Aung San Suu Kyi less troublesome than Thein Sein's awkward administration. Yet that does not change the fact that Beijing is in a far weaker position today than it could ever have foreseen in 2010. Then it hoped to turn Myanmar into its regional pawn; now it merely wants to restore normal diplomatic relations. With popular opinion unshackled, China and its firms will have to work hard to gain people's trust. If they can do so, bilateral trade will grow and further economic integration is inevitable: that is the natural consequence of living next to Asia's greatest economy. And if China invests well, it has huge potential to improve the lives of Burmese citizens. The people of Myanmar do have much to fear about a rising China—but they must find a way of growing with it.

CHAPTER 5

A STRING
OF PEARLS

FEAR AND LOATHING
IN THE INDIAN OCEAN

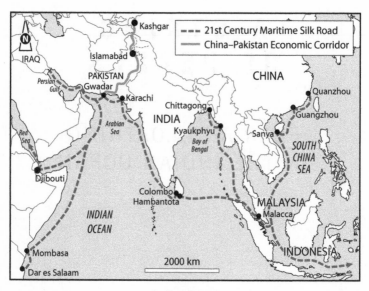

21st Century Maritime Silk Road
China–Pakistan Economic Corridor

Kashgar
Islamabad
IRAQ
Persian Gulf
PAKISTAN
Gwadar
Karachi
Chittagong
INDIA
Kyaukphyu
CHINA
Quanzhou
Guangzhou
Sanya
Red Sea
Arabian Sea
Bay of Bengal
SOUTH CHINA SEA
Djibouti
Colombo
Hambantota
MALAYSIA
Malacca
INDIAN OCEAN
Mombasa
Dar es Salaam
INDONESIA
2000 km

Indian Ocean

When a People's Liberation Army (PLA) Navy submarine docked at a Chinese-owned container port in Sri Lanka in September 2014, it seemed to confirm widespread fears in India about China's strategic ambitions. Hawkish military analysts in New Delhi believe that Beijing is systematically building naval facilities across the Indian Ocean, seeking to wrest strategic control of India's backyard. They have a colourful name for this dastardly plot to tighten a maritime noose around Mother India: the "string of pearls".[1]

The Chinese submarine was a *Song*-class diesel-electric vessel, flanked by a support ship. It docked at the Colombo International Container Terminal, a commercial port run by a Hong Kong-listed arm of the state-owned China Merchants Group. Several weeks later the vessels returned to Colombo, defying a warning from New Delhi that any presence of a Chinese submarine in Sri Lanka would be "unacceptable".[2] Responding to India's "security concerns", the Sri Lankan government said it was common practice for international naval vessels to dock in Colombo for refuelling and refreshments. Beijing added that the submarine was engaged in "anti-piracy escort missions" in the Gulf of Aden, where the Chinese Navy works closely with both its Indian and

US counterparts, and that the stopover was no more than a "routine port call".[3]

The explanations were reasonable, although it is unusual for submarines to be deployed in anti-piracy work and the PLA Navy's first stopover in Colombo can hardly be called routine. But the presence of a Chinese submarine in Sri Lanka caught the Indian Navy unawares, leading to questions in the Indian parliament and a stir in the media. When the Chinese Ministry of Defence later confirmed that it had also deployed a Type-093 *Shang*-class nuclear-powered attack submarine in the Indian Ocean, the news channel NDTV hysterically reported the beginning of "a great game" of submarine subterfuge, drawing on an old term for the strategic contest fought between the British and Russian empires for supremacy in central Asia. Quoting unnamed sources, NDTV reported that senior Indian Navy officers did not accept China's assertion that the submarine's deployment had been in aid of the anti-piracy mission off the coast of Somalia. Instead, they believed it was really part of "a carefully choreographed exercise to expand its military presence in the region".[4]

NDTV's report came just a few weeks after China had pledged to finance a staggering US$46 billion of investments in Pakistan, mainly to fund a 3,000-km "economic corridor" from the Arabian Sea to Xinjiang. The route will begin at Gwadar, a Chinese-run port on Pakistan's coast near the Iranian border, which Indian security experts fear will become a strategic base for the Chinese Navy in the Indian Ocean. Located near key shipping routes in and out of the Persian Gulf, the deep-water port is an important link in Xi Jinping's much-vaunted "21st Century Maritime Silk Road". Beijing says the initiative will improve connectivity between Asia and Europe, creating valuable new trade routes and boosting regional growth. But China's expansion into the Indian Ocean is causing jitters in both New Delhi and Washington.

These fears were articulated at an off-the-record media briefing given by a top US Navy officer in Delhi in March 2015. "There is no percentage in our momentum to improve relations with China," he said. "Ultimately China and the United States will not get along; the relationship is hollow. Where we can have the most effect is in our co-operation with India." He promised that the US would provide the Indian military with anything it needed, including fighter jets and technology to build aircraft carriers, to defend the Indian Ocean against the encroaching PLA Navy. Someone present at the briefing summed up his message as, "Let's work together to bugger the Chinese."[5]

INDIAN OCEAN

India's distrust of China dates back to its humiliating defeat in the Sino-Indian War of 1962, which erupted after a series of Himalayan border disputes beginning in the late 1950s. China launched simultaneous offensives into Indian-claimed territory in Aksai Chin, a mountainous desert sandwiched between Xinjiang, Tibet and Ladakh, and in what is now known as Arunachal Pradesh, a northeastern state bordering Tibet and Bhutan. The fighting was bitter, much of it fought at altitudes of over 4,000 metres, and the Indian Army was routed by China's far superior forces. More than 3,000 Indian soldiers were killed or missing in action; a further 4,000 were captured. "These losses were small by the standard of modern warfare," writes Ramachandra Guha in his magisterial history *India After Gandhi*, "yet the war represented a massive defeat in the Indian imagination."[6]

In the decade after Independence in 1947, India's prime minister Jawaharlal Nehru had talked of friendship between India and China as the basis for a "resurgent Asia". The burgeoning diplomatic ties between the two countries even had a jaunty Hindi catchphrase—*Hindi-Chini bhai-bhai*, meaning "Indians and Chinese are brothers". So China's invasion was greeted with shock as well as dismay: "Among the Indian public, the principal sentiment was that of betrayal, of being taken for a ride by an unscrupulous neighbour whom they had naively chosen to trust and support," Guha writes. Too late, Nehru realized that Chinese Communism was, above all else, a bellicose form of nationalism. More than fifty years on, the humiliation—and the betrayal—have not been forgotten.

The border dispute remains unresolved, a perennial thorn in Sino-Indian relations. India claims 38,000 square km of desolate mountain territory in southwestern Tibet, while China claims nearly 90,000 square km of Arunachal Pradesh, which Beijing refers to as "South Tibet". The situation is not helped by regular Chinese incursions over the Line of Actual Control, although there have been no military clashes since 1975. China's deepening cooperation with India's neighbours—Sri Lanka, Bangladesh, Nepal, Myanmar and the Maldives, but above all its arch-enemy Pakistan—is feeding further anxiety in New Delhi. It believes China is pursuing an old game of trying to box India into its subregion, preventing it from realizing its status as a great power. This began with the invasion of Tibet in 1950, a traditional buffer zone between China and India, and continues with Beijing's refusal to support New Delhi in its bid to become a permanent member of the UN Security Council.

The term "string of pearls" first appeared in a report on energy security prepared for the US Department of Defense by Booz Allen Hamilton (the contractor that once employed the infamous whistle-blower Edward Snowden). It described how China is, quite rationally, creating a network of ports to protect the sea lanes through which the bulk of its oil imports pass, especially in maritime choke points such as the Straits of Malacca and Hormuz.[7] Indian proponents of the theory have enthusiastically adopted the metaphor to describe how China is pursuing a policy of encirclement to choke India's defences. They point to a number of Chinese port facilities in the Indian Ocean that could be used by the PLA Navy. Going clockwise, these include a proposed deep-sea port at Sonadia near Chittagong in Bangladesh; the newly opened deep-sea port at Kyaukphyu in Myanmar, which serves China's oil pipeline to Yunnan; container ports at Hambantota and Colombo in Sri Lanka; and the ports of Karachi and Gwadar in Pakistan.

Indian faith in the "string of pearls" theory has only intensified since Xi Jinping announced his grand plan to build a Maritime Silk Road. In his speech to the Indonesian parliament in October 2013, Xi spoke of strengthening maritime cooperation and pursuing China's "shared destiny" with its neighbours. When Beijing released a policy document in

March 2015, it called for building new port infrastructure and links to inland transport networks; increasing the number of international sea routes; improving logistics, especially through enhanced use of information technology; dismantling trade and investment barriers; and deepening financial integration, partly by encouraging greater use of the renminbi.[8] Beijing says the Maritime Silk Road will bring mutual benefits; but security analysts in New Delhi believe China's growing presence in the Indian Ocean is really designed to project its naval power farther from home, and at India's expense.

One of the most vehement critics is Brahma Chellaney, a former adviser to India's National Security Council and professor of strategic studies at the New Delhi-based Centre for Policy Research, an independent think tank. Another Indian academic who studies the relationship between India and China described the former Harvard professor as a "demented lunatic", but Chellaney is worth listening to: he eloquently voices the negativity that many Indians feel towards China.[9]

I met Chellaney for dinner in the plush surroundings of Delhi's Taj Mahal Hotel.[10] "I have a deep-seated distrust of the authoritarian Chinese state," he declared before our food arrived, making little attempt at small talk. "China has a political system which relies on ultra-nationalism as its political credo. The Han state lays claims to lands which were never theirs." Xi Jinping's Belt and Road Initiative, he said, is the latest iteration of this line of thinking: China is using its economic muscle to project the power of the Han Chinese state over its borders. "In all the countries where they've made strategic gains they've used their engineering companies as the vanguard of international outreach," he explained.

> Commercial penetration is the forerunner to political penetration, and the integration of economic and military power. First they use engineering companies to create projects; then they bring in their own labour; then they acquire diplomatic influence. And finally they acquire strategic leverage.

Chellaney had no doubt about the underlying goal of China's investments in the Indian Ocean. "The Maritime Silk Road is just a cover for what China has been pursuing for a long time, which is the 'string of pearls'," he stated firmly. He is convinced that China's shift away from emphasizing its "peaceful rise", the principle that guided its diplomacy a decade ago, to its newly "proactive" foreign policy will end badly. "China is incrementally changing the status in Asia—it's called salami slicing," he said.

> But the system encourages aggression. If China keeps growing, in ten years' time other resurgent powers will emerge to check the exercise of Chinese power. China's behaviour has galvanized public opinion across Asia. In India, China's muscle flexing and cross-border incursions have changed the mood.

C Raja Mohan, author of *Samudra Manthan: Sino-Indian Rivalry in the Indo-Pacific* and director of the Carnegie Endowment's new India office, says it is only a matter of time before the "string of pearls" becomes a reality.[11] "If the Chinese military can use a civilian facility, then is that facility still civilian or military? Their ships will have to dock somewhere," he told me, referring to the stopover in Colombo.[12] His point is that China does not need to set up military bases overseas if its warships and submarines can rely on a friendly reception at commercial ports. The US Navy regularly docks in ports belonging to its allies—Singapore, for example, which hosts US vessels 150 times in an average year. The Chinese Navy has rarely taken advantage of its own more limited relationships, which partly explains why the docking in Colombo raised alarm bells in New Delhi.

Far from being an empty slogan, as its critics argue, Dr Mohan believes the Belt and Road Initiative heralds the beginning of a fundamental shift in Asian geopolitics. "The Chinese are coming: it's only a matter of when and how," he told me in his office at the National University of Singapore, where he spends two months of the year.

> As China goes global it's going to be in every goddamn place in the world. China has unparalleled scale and ambition. It is fulfilling a historic task of opening up Inner Asia. This is dramatic: it is spreading capitalism into central Asia. The only comparison is the British Raj. And China is doing it in a more sophisticated way than the US imperium. It's going to happen, so you need a strategy that builds on relations in the Indian Ocean.

Mohan believes that India should work with China when it is beneficial, such as on the "Bangladesh–China–India–Myanmar Economic Corridor" (BCIM). New Delhi has dragged its heels, mainly because the proposed highway will run close to the disputed border state of Arunachal Pradesh. It fears that the PLA could potentially march down the road into India, while open borders will make it harder to control the insurgencies it is fighting in its northeastern region. But it sees advantages in the BCIM scheme, too. India's impoverished Northeast States, which badly need new economic opportunities, have long pressed for better trade links with Yunnan. And cross-border trade could even prove a stabilizing force in Arunachal Pradesh. "We should collaborate with China on BCIM," said Mohan. "If we can sucker them into doing this for us, do it!"

Like the Maritime Silk Road, the BCIM scheme has geostrategic as well as commercial motives. But analysts who fear China's every move are exaggerating reality: Beijing is far more interested in securing alternative routes for its energy imports and in protecting commercial sea lanes than it is in building a new empire. China has understandable military interests in the Indian Ocean, but it knows that it cannot challenge the combined power of the US, Indian, Japanese and Australian navies, which are cooperating ever more closely. In any case, the Chinese enterprises creating the Maritime Silk Road are more concerned with making a profit than serving the strategic interests of the state. The truth is that President Xi's grand initiative is designed to advance China's interests primarily through economic development, not military might.

I found evidence of this during a visit to the Colombo South Container Terminal, where the Chinese submarine docked twice in 2014. Beijing's critics tend to assume that Chinese enterprises are stooges of the Chinese state, but most Chinese investments overseas are at least partly—and often wholly—commercial in nature. Colombo South Container Terminal is 85% owned by Hong Kong-listed conglomerate China Merchants Holdings International, which operates thirty-five terminals in thirteen countries, including eight in Europe. Its parent company is a state-owned conglomerate, so Beijing has some influence over its activities. But the listed arm is, above all, an experienced port operator that has entered Sri Lanka for one reason: to profit from growing trade volumes through the Indian Ocean.

China Merchants' US$550 million Colombo facility is just a short stroll from Galle Face, a grassy area near the city's business district where locals fly kites, stroll along the promenade, and snack at beachside kiosks. The terminal is world class: it can accommodate mega-ships carrying 19,000 containers, twice the capacity of Colombo's older terminals, and is one of only a few ports worldwide to operate 70-metre-high gantry cranes. It is a transhipment centre for Indian cargo bound for Europe, China and the US. Long-distance shipments are only cost-effective on mega-vessels, but India has few facilities for them. Loading and unloading in Colombo, 300 km south of India, saves shippers both time and money. "This is a purely commercial project, so we do not get support from the government," Lance Zuo, the assistant general manager, told me. "We are a global terminal operator," he explained, pointing to containers bearing the names of shipping companies from Denmark, Taiwan, South Korea and France, as well as China.

Managers expect the terminal to handle 2.4 million standard containers by 2018, cementing Colombo's position as the busiest container port in South Asia. It employs 7,500 locals, and full ownership will be transferred to the Sri Lanka Ports Authority after thirty-five years of operation. So even if this commercial port is a military base in disguise, it has no long-term strategic value. Far from being a shiny but threatening "pearl", the Colombo South Container Terminal is an excellent example of what Beijing claims the Maritime Silk Road is all about: building infrastructure, boosting transport efficiency, and creating new trade routes. "The idea of the Maritime Silk Road is very good if it means more logistics infrastructure," Sri Lanka's finance minister Ravi Karunanayake told me, despite criticizing many of China's other business dealings on the island.[13]

As China's commercial interests expand, it is perfectly natural for Beijing to seek to protect its assets overseas. There is nothing inherently threatening about Chinese naval vessels docking in friendly ports, as US ones have done for decades. "India should understand that China, while not an Indian Ocean state, has huge legitimate interests there," Mao Siwei, the former Chinese consul general in Kolkata and a leading thinker on Sino-Indian relations, argued in his blog after the submarine docking incident. "At the same time, China should not throw its weight around, just because it has money," he added, sternly: "India dominates in the region."[14]

PAKISTAN

India is reluctant to see Sri Lanka sucked into China's orbit, but it worries far more about China's "all-weather" friendship with Pakistan. In the Indian Ocean, these fears are directed 3,000 km northwest of Colombo at Gwadar. Back in 1958, when Oman ceded the western corner of the Makran coast to the new state of Pakistan, Gwadar was little more than a fishing village. In the 1960s, Pakistan's military rulers drew up plans to turn this desert outpost into an air and naval base that could serve as an alternative to Karachi, which is closer to the Indian border. Then, in the 1980s, Soviet strategists dreamed of transforming Gwadar into a conduit for exporting oil and gas out of central Asia. But the chaos after the withdrawal of Soviet troops from Afghanistan, followed by the dissolution of the Soviet Union itself, scuppered these plans.[15]

In 2000, when Pakistan's new leader General Pervez Musharraf asked China to fund a deep-water port at Gwadar, the dream became China's. Fantasizing about building pipelines to pump oil and gas into China from the Arabian Coast, Beijing agreed. It spent US$200 million on developing the first phase of a new deep-water port, which opened in January 2007. The Port of Singapore Authority (PSA) signed a forty-year contract to manage it. It was roughly at this point that Robert Kaplan, an American journalist and geopolitical analyst, visited Gwadar while researching his book *Monsoon*. "It evoked a nineteenth-century lithograph of Jaffa in Palestine or Tyre in Lebanon", he rhapsodized, describing "dhows emerging out of the white, watery miasma, laden with silvery fish thrown ashore by the fishermen, who were dressed in filthy turbans and *shalwar kameezes*, prayer beads dripping out of their pockets". He described his good fortune to see old Gwadar before it was swept away to build a new Dubai.[16]

Phase two of the development envisaged transforming Gwadar into a busy port and commercial hub, connected to the rest of the country by a new highway. Under PSA's management, Gwadar would gain four container berths, a bulk cargo terminal, two oil terminals, an oil refinery, a roll-on/roll-off terminal, and a grain terminal. The new highway would run to Quetta, the provincial capital of Balochistan, and connect to the existing network. But very little of phase two ever materialized: hardly any ships arrived, few new facilities were built, and Gwadar remained isolated. In 2012, 20,000 of the town's 80,000 residents left because of drought. Mired in a dispute with the Pakistani navy, which it claimed had refused to hand over land earmarked for port operations, PSA cut its losses. China Overseas Port Holdings Company, a subsidiary of China State Construction Engineering Corporation, took over the contract.

In 2013, when Gwadar effectively became a Chinese port, the dream of creating a viable conduit to the Arabian Sea looked a fantasy. But the Belt and Road Initiative, announced later that year, gave the project new impetus. In April 2015, during Xi Jinping's state visit to Pakistan, China agreed to finance US$46 billion of projects across Pakistan, including US$11 billion to upgrade Gwadar port and build new roads and a railway.[17] The "China–Pakistan Economic Corridor" will run from Gwadar, over the 4,700-metre-high Khunjerab Pass on the Chinese border, to Kashgar in the region of Xinjiang. A further US$34 billion was allocated to energy projects, presumably including the cost of building oil and gas pipelines alongside the expanded Karakoram Highway. Chinese surveyors quickly moved into Pakistan to determine how the infrastructure could be built across such difficult terrain.

The engineering challenge is enormous. More than a thousand construction workers died during the twenty years it took to build the original Karakoram Highway, which was completed in 1979 (though only opened to the public in 1986). The precariousness of this mountain road was highlighted in January 2010, when a huge landslide 150 km south of the Chinese border in the beautiful Hunza Valley created a lake that submerged the highway for 22 km. It took until September 2015 for the China Road and Bridge Corporation to complete five new tunnels and eighty bridges to reconnect the two sections of the highway.[18]

For China, the economic corridor has two aims: to open up an alternative route for oil imports from the Middle East, and to persuade Pakistan to do more to combat violent extremism seeping over its border. The vision is driven by strategic factors, not commercial logic. Even before the landslide in 2010, less than 10% of China's trade with Pakistan came over the land border with Xinjiang. Far from being economically sound, "this massive investment is actually a form of bribe", says one Beijing-based expert.[19] Government officials working on the Belt and Road project privately admit they expect to lose 80% of their investment in Pakistan. They have made similar strategic calculations elsewhere: in Myanmar they expect to lose 50%, in

Central Asia 30%.[20] The logic is that it is worth throwing away money if it helps China to expand its geopolitical influence.

In Pakistan, the biggest threat of all is poor security. Dozens of Chinese workers and engineers have been targeted by the Pakistani Taliban and other militant groups over the past fifteen years. Some militants see foreign nationals as a legitimate target in their fight against the Pakistan government; others want to stoke tension between Beijing and Islamabad. "Instead of being known as China's gateway to the Gulf, Pakistan has developed a reputation as the most dangerous country to be an overseas Chinese, with kidnappings and killings taking place with disturbing regularity," notes analyst Andrew Small in *The China–Pakistan Axis*.[21] Pakistan says it plans to establish a special security division of 12,000 guards to protect Chinese workers, and build a security fence around Gwadar. But attacks are inevitable.

They could occur at either end of the corridor, especially in Balochistan, where Gwadar is located. The province has experienced five separate rebellions since Pakistan was formed in 1947, as Baloch natives protest against in-migration by outsiders and government exploitation of their province's gas and mineral riches. (In this regard, Baloch grievances share much in common with those of Xinjiang's Uyghurs.) In 2004, the Baloch Liberation Army killed three Chinese engineers and injured nine when it blew up a bus carrying them to Gwadar; others survived rocket attacks on their hotel. "No matter how hard they try to turn Gwadar into Dubai, it won't work," Nisar Baluch, general secretary of the Baluch Welfare Society, told Kaplan. "There will be resistance. The future pipelines going to China will not be safe. The pipelines will have to cross our Baloch territory, and if our rights are violated, nothing will be secure."[22]

Nevertheless, Beijing clearly believes there is a strategic rationale for pumping billions of dollars into Pakistan, even if the money it actually commits is unlikely to match the astronomical headline figure. In terms of energy security, it justifies the expense with the same logic it applied in Myanmar: the threat of a blockade in the Malacca Strait means China needs to have alternative import routes. The cost of sending a barrel of oil from the Middle East to China via Gwadar would certainly be many times higher than shipping it by tanker to Shanghai, but it gives China a strategic backdoor if the front door is unavailable. In this regard, Gwadar plays a similar role to Kyaukphyu in the Bay of Bengal. Neither port solves the "Malacca dilemma", but they mitigate the danger of relying solely on ships transiting through the narrow throat that connects the Indian Ocean to the South China Sea.

Gwadar also provides something equally valuable: a permanent maritime base in the Indian Ocean, near the shipping lanes of the Persian Gulf and east Africa. Even if the "economic corridor" proves unviable—and there is a very high chance it will—Gwadar retains strategic value for the PLA Navy. China would dearly love to have naval access to Kyaukphyu, connected by land to Yunnan; but its fractious relationship with the Myanmar government means that is unlikely. China's close friendship with Pakistan makes Gwadar uniquely valuable. The port itself may never officially be a Chinese naval base, but naval *access* is what counts.

Analysts disagree over whether that makes Gwadar a threat to India. "Why would the Chinese put naval assets in Gwadar?" asks Kanti Bajpai, an expert on China–India relations at the Lee Kuan Yew School of Public Policy in Singapore. "They would be sitting ducks for the Indian Navy."[23] But China's options in the Arabian Sea are growing. In May 2015, shortly after President Xi's trip to Pakistan, a conventional *Yuan*-class submarine docked down the coast in Karachi, the first Chinese submarine to stop in the country. Shortly afterwards, Islamabad agreed to purchase eight diesel-electric attack submarines from China worth an estimated US$5 billion. Crucially, four will be built in Karachi—meaning not only that Pakistan will acquire the technology, but that China will gain a readymade maintenance facility for its own subs in the Indian Ocean.[24]

For India, this latest iteration of the China–Pakistan axis is wearingly familiar. Although China has no official allies, its friendship with Pakistan is actually closer than many formal alliances. Diplomats describe the bilateral relationship in comically sycophantic terms: it is "deeper than the deepest ocean", "higher than the highest mountain" and "sweeter than honey". In 1982, China proved its ardour by handing over enough enriched uranium for Pakistan's nuclear scientists to build two atomic bombs. But it was truly motivated less by love of Pakistan than by shared enmity of India: Beijing and Islamabad have long manipulated their mutual affections to keep New Delhi off-balance.

From New Delhi's perspective, therefore, its suspicion of China's maritime investments in Pakistan and across the

Indian Ocean is entirely reasonable. Whether those facilities form part of a coherent strategy to encircle India, however, is quite another matter. In truth, Indian paranoia about China's naval ambitions overstates reality: China does not yet control the South China Sea, let alone the Indian Ocean. Scare-mongering about a "string of pearls" is a useful ruse for the Indian Navy, which uses it to squeeze extra funding out of the national budget. Yet talk of a "China threat" could have unintended consequences. "The string of pearls doesn't really exist," says Bajpai, "but the Indian Navy really does believe in it. It's almost making the risk come true. If India deploys a naval strategy in that way, you can expect China to respond—making it into a reality."[25]

INDIA

The mutual distrust and rivalry between India and China has clear economic consequences. The relationship has improved enormously since its nadir in the 1960s and 1970s; both sides have cooperated in many multilateral settings over the past fifteen years, and bilateral trade rose from US$2 billion in 2000 to US$65 billion in 2014. But commercial relations nevertheless remain underdeveloped. Together, China and India have a population of 2.7 billion—approaching 40% of the global total—and a GDP exceeding US$13 trillion. They share a border nearly 4,000 km long. Yet China trades as much with Thailand as with its largest neighbour, and there are eight times as many flights between Beijing and Bangkok as there are between Beijing and Delhi. The weak ties between Asia's two giants are a gigantic missed opportunity for global trade and investment.[26]

Back in 2010, when Chinese premier Wen Jiabao visited India, both sides tried to shift the tense relationship onto a friendlier footing. They agreed an ambitious target to increase bilateral trade to US$100 billion by 2015 while simultaneously reducing India's trade deficit with China. Indian critics of the relationship complain that China exports vast quantities of consumer and capital goods to India, while India merely exports a few shiploads of iron ore in return. India would like to export more pharmaceuticals and IT services to China, but claims tariff walls keep them out. After Premier Wen's visit, Indian exports to China actually fell by one-fifth over the following four years, even as Chinese imports grew by 40%. The trade deficit doubled to around US$40 billion.

When Narendra Modi became Indian prime minister in May 2014, there was renewed optimism that the relationship would improve. As chief minister of Gujarat, his home state, Modi had visited China four times to court investment. With his technocratic, no-nonsense approach, Beijing saw someone with whom it could do business. Later that year, President Xi Jinping led a large trade delegation to India, visiting Gujarat and pledging to help plug India's legendary infrastructure deficit. "With rich experience in infrastructure building and manufacturing, China is ready to contribute to India's development in these areas," Xi told Modi.[27] At the end of talks in New Delhi, they agreed that China would help modernize India's ageing railway system, cooperate on building environmentally friendly "smart cities", and establish special economic zones in Gujarat and Maharashtra, both on India's west coast. Xi promised to give more market access to Indian exports, including pharmaceuticals and agricultural produce.

Unfortunately, Xi's trip was undermined by a border standoff in the mountainous region of Ladakh, where New Delhi accused Chinese soldiers of building a road in Indian territory. Calling for an early settlement on the disputed common border, Modi said the "true potential of our relations" would not be realized until there was "peace in our relations and in the borders".[28] Indian diplomats were shocked and puzzled that Beijing would deliberately seek to mar the talks, embarrassing both sides. But the truth is that the incursion was neither planned nor coordinated by Beijing. Insiders say that when the Indian Army put up a new observation post, the PLA crossed into Indian territory to knock it down. They did so as a matter of course, neither informing Beijing nor considering the diplomatic fallout.[29] Xi left India having promised US$20 billion of investment—far below the US$100 billion figure that had been widely touted.

Ahead of Narendra Modi's first visit to China as prime minister in May 2015, I sat down to lunch with Gurcharan Das, a businessman and author who advises the Modi government. Before retiring to become a full-time writer, Das was chief executive of Procter & Gamble in India and Southeast Asia, and then headed its global strategic planning unit. We met at Wasabi, an eye-wateringly expensive Japanese restaurant in Delhi's Taj Mahal Hotel. "China helps me to understand India," Das began, munching on a US$15 piece of sashimi flown in that morning from Tokyo's Tsukiji fish market. "China has always been a strong state with a weak society. India is the opposite: it has always been a weak state with a strong society. The fact is you need both: a strong state to get things done, and a strong society to hold it accountable. China needs to fix its politics, and India its governance."[30]

It would be to both countries' advantage to work more closely together, he said, moving on to the theme of Modi's plan to transform India into a manufacturing powerhouse. "India needs to expand and be part of China's trading network. India hasn't offered a level playing field for Chinese imports. We need to be more confident and open up," he said, sipping a cup of chilled sake. "It would be best if China invested in manufacturing here, so we can make the goods India needs in India. This is Modi's dream. Chinese investment has been held back by red tape and defence fears. We also need to be more self-confident about that," he continued, addressing the border issue.

> The benefits of free trade outweigh protectionism, but security fears have overshadowed investment so far. We desperately need to settle the border question and make it an economic relationship. We want to put the dispute over Arunachal Pradesh behind us.

In the event, Modi's visit to China brought plenty of smiling photo shoots but precious little substance. Xi's decision to invite Modi to his own home province of Shaanxi indicated that both sides wanted to put past rancour behind them: it is unusual for Chinese leaders to meet their counterparts outside

Beijing. But there is still little evidence that India is ready to let China build the infrastructure needed to underpin Modi's signature "Make in India" policy, which aims to replicate part of the East Asian development model. Some progress has been made: India has warily given the green light to the BCIM scheme of building a new highway linking China with Kolkata, and China Railway Corp is undertaking a feasibility study to build a 2,200-km high-speed railway from Delhi to Chennai, on India's southeast coast. Whether these projects ever go ahead, however, is far from certain. The economic potential in strengthening ties between China and India will remain unfulfilled so long as security concerns continue to overshadow the relationship.

Those concerns are partly behind India's push to bolster relations with the countries on China's periphery. In 2015, Modi made the first visit by an Indian prime minister to Sri Lanka in twenty-seven years, and he has expanded India's engagement with Japan, the US, Australia, Vietnam, Mongolia and South Korea. The relationship with Japan is particularly noteworthy: Modi has an obvious rapport with Japanese prime minister Shinzo Abe, which has delivered a contract for a new US$15 billion bullet-train railway line from Mumbai to Ahmedabad—an area of economic diplomacy in which China and Japan compete fiercely. Modi responded positively to Abe's attempt to construct a coalition opposed to Beijing's expansionism in maritime Asia, saying that Asian powers needed to push back against China's "expansionist mind-set".[31]

For China, there are also worrying signs of a budding strategic alliance between India and the US. President

Obama told the Indian parliament as early as 2010 that the relationship between the world's two most populous democracies would "be one of the defining partnerships of the 21st century".[32] The rise of China is pushing both sides closer together: the US needs India to maintain its primacy in Asia, while India needs US support to shore up its position as a great regional power. Washington believes that bringing India into its security network is critical, because its sheer size makes it a natural bulwark against Chinese expansionism. Its location near the Persian Gulf and the African seaboard also gives it strategic access to sea lanes carrying China's oil and gas imports. With India on board, the US believes it can strengthen its grip across the whole of Asia, extending in an arc from the Western Pacific, across Southeast Asia, and into the Indian Ocean region. In 2015, India signed a "Joint Strategic Vision" with the US, pledging cooperation on maritime security and freedom of navigation across the Indian Ocean and western Pacific—an agreement pointedly aimed at China.

New Delhi will be careful not to move too decisively towards Washington, as Modi is serious about seeking closer economic cooperation with China. Yet, sadly, there is little hope of a genuine breakthrough in India–China relations. Despite whispers within India's diplomatic community that China could be ready to come to a deal on the border, that remains unlikely. As Brahma Chellaney put it to me, "China just leads India around the mulberry bush, again and again." Beijing is happy with the status quo, which keeps India preoccupied on its eastern flank even as it nervously eyes Pakistan to the west. And Modi, who came to power on a ticket of Hindu nationalism, cannot compromise on such a visceral matter of national pride.

SRI LANKA

Narendra Modi's two-day state visit to Sri Lanka in March 2015 was a breakthrough for relations between India and its southern neighbour, long scarred by India's failed intervention in Sri Lanka's civil war in the late 1980s. When I arrived in Colombo the day before the Indian leader, the road from the airport was lined with fluttering Indian tricolours and khaki-clad soldiers with rifles. Posters of Modi declared, "Welcome to Sri Lanka!"

Modi's visit was the first by an Indian prime minister since Rajiv Gandhi signed the Indo-Sri Lanka Peace Accord in Colombo in 1987. Under a temporary truce, Sri Lankan troops withdrew from the north of the island and an Indian peacekeeping force arrived to disarm militant groups there, including the Liberation Tigers of Tamil Eelam (LTTE). But the peacekeepers rapidly became embroiled in a war with the "Tamil Tigers", as they were better known in the West. In one particularly gruesome incident, Indian soldiers were accused of massacring up to seventy civilians in a teaching hospital in Jaffna. When nationalist resentment to the Indian presence grew, the Sri Lankan government demanded the peacekeepers' withdrawal. By that time, over 1,000 Indian soldiers had been killed. A year later, in 1991, Rajiv Gandhi was assassinated by a suicide bomber from the LTTE. Bilateral relations stalled, leaving room for China to become the leading foreign presence in Sri Lanka.

Sri Lanka's new coalition government, elected in January 2015, had invited Modi to become the first Indian prime minister to address the national parliament. Playing up their shared heritage, Modi declared the two countries to be "the closest neighbours in every sense", and said he brought "the greetings of 1.25 billion friends, and millions of fans of Sri Lankan cricket". With their common cultures, he said, India and Sri Lanka should naturally be one another's closest economic partner. "My vision of an ideal neighbourhood is one in which trade, investments, technology, ideas and people flow easily across borders," he declared. "Connecting this vast region by land and sea, our two countries can become engines of regional prosperity." Finally, he emphasized security across the Indian Ocean: "The security of our two countries is indivisible. Equally, our shared responsibility for our maritime neighbourhood is clear."[33]

Lurking behind these fine words, though never mentioned, was the shadow of China. As neighbours, India and Sri Lanka are indeed natural economic partners—but the reality is that China's economic influence in Sri Lanka is many times greater than India's. For Modi, this would have been obvious from the moment he arrived. From the airport, his limousine enjoyed a smooth drive into Colombo down a perfectly flat expressway punctuated with electronic toll booths—superior to any road in India.[34] And from his hotel suite overlooking the Indian Ocean, he would have viewed the giant cranes of the deepwater Colombo South Container Terminal lifting boxes onto one of the world's largest container ships. Both the airport expressway and the container terminal were built and financed by Chinese enterprises.

These are precisely the kind of projects envisaged by China's leaders when they wax lyrical about "going global" and "win–win diplomacy". Just a week before Modi's visit to Colombo, in his report to the National People's Congress, Premier Li Keqiang laid out the government's plans to encourage more Chinese companies to participate in infrastructure investment projects overseas. He said the government would work to increase China's international market share of machinery and equipment, especially in the power, communications and transport industries. And he promised to broaden the channels for utilizing China's foreign exchange reserves, both to support China's own firms and to help foreign countries build up their production capacities.[35]

At its best, Chinese economic diplomacy has the capacity to deliver the mutual benefits it promises. Yet Sri Lanka's experience also shows the ugly side of Chinese business overseas. In 2009–14, China financed projects worth nearly US$5 billion on the island.[36] In addition to roads and ports, its enterprises built bridges, railways, a coal-fired power station and an international airport. These projects were arranged under the previous government led by the thuggish president Mahinda Rajapaksa, who was ousted from power in the January 2015 election. One of the reasons for his downfall was his allegedly corrupt relationship with China. During the election campaign, the opposition's manifesto made a thinly veiled reference to China's neo-colonial designs on the island:

"The land that the White Man took over by means of military strength is now being obtained by foreigners by paying ransom to a handful of persons."[37]

Rajapaksa's close relationship with China had political origins. Beijing supplied the majority of the weapons used by his government to end the island's twenty-six-year civil war in 2009, which culminated in the slaughter of up to 40,000 Tamil civilians. Despite accusations of genocide, China prevented the issue from coming up at the UN Security Council and being brought before the Human Rights Commission. "The Rajapaksa government projected China as the ultimate friend and saviour of Sri Lanka," Paikiasothy Saravanamuttu, head of the Centre for Policy Alternatives think tank, told me over coffee in Colombo. "Internationally China was our insurance policy against allegations of war crimes. China stood as the champion and protector of the Global South against the goliath of Western powers and India."[38]

I asked Karu Jayasuriya, minister of public administration and democratic governance in the new coalition government, how China's business dealings had worked under Rajapaksa. We met at Jayasuriya's elegant home in south Colombo, designed by Geoffrey Bawa, one of the most influential Asian architects of the 20th century. Dressed in flowing white robes and with a scholarly manner, he explained how Sri Lanka's trading links with China went back to a "rubber for rice" agreement more than six decades ago. As a businessman, Jayasuriya had himself worked closely with the Chinese. In the late 1970s, as China began to open up to the world, he started a soap factory to export to China. Then, in the 1980s, he shipped a million rubber seeds to Hainan Island free of charge, after Malaysia, Thailand and Sri Lanka had declined to do so. "The Chinese were very grateful," he said.[39]

Relations between the two countries had stayed friendly. "After the civil war finished, we couldn't get adequate financing from other countries, so we had to go to China," he explained. Chinese firms solicited projects to the government, which did not bother to open them to competitive bidding. Rajapaksa's administration, he said, had commissioned wasteful vanity projects funded by Chinese banks and built by Chinese enterprises. The banks charged high interest rates, allowing the firms to pay fat kickbacks to Rajapaksa's cronies. According to one estimate, nearly 70% of Sri Lanka's infrastructure projects during that period were funded and built by China, helping to push the island's foreign debt up from 36% of GDP in 2010 to more than 90% by 2015.[40] A huge chunk of government expenditure had gone on servicing Chinese debts.

The economic fallout from Rajapaksa's sweetheart deals with Chinese contractors is a litany of white elephants. A new airport in Rajapaksa's small home town of Hambantota shut its doors for want of passengers, while the second phase of the town's unneeded container port was suspended. Hambantota's new cricket stadium and conference centre are barely used, like so many vanity projects across China. "Rajapaksa named them all after himself, even while he was still alive!" Jayasuriya exclaimed, shaking his head. Even the island's much-needed expressway and power station were built at considerably more expense than they should have been. Costs were routinely ramped up to 40–60% above the original contract price, he explained, with the cut siphoned off to grasping politicians: "The Chinese companies went along with this to get the business."

Chinese banks benefited from issuing loans far above usual commercial rates. In Africa and other developing regions, China has a reputation for handing out soft loans at an artificially low cost. One of Washington's original objections to China's proposal to set up the Asian Infrastructure Investment Bank was its fear that any Chinese bank would undercut other lenders with cheap loans and no strings attached. Yet, in Sri Lanka, Rajapaksa's administration allowed Chinese lenders to milk the island as a cash cow.

These high interest rates are one of the biggest bones of contention between the new government and Beijing. "The Chinese are not providing gifts," Ravi Karunanayake, Sri Lanka's fast-talking, barrel-chested finance minister told me in his Colombo home, a large villa with stucco pillars, barricaded behind a high metal gate. "They've lent us US$5 billion on very, very commercial terms. Most of the loans are at about 6%, but the highest is 8.8%."[41] By comparison, multilateral lenders typically charge well under 2%. "The high costs come from nothing other than corruption, but we do not want taxpayers to pay for the past decisions of a corrupt regime," he continued, sitting at his desk in front of a photograph in which he was shaking hands with a grinning Bill Clinton.

Following the election of the new government, the chief symbol of the struggle to extricate Sri Lanka from China's clutches was a US$1.5 billion luxury real estate project known as Colombo Port City. The developer, China Communications

Construction Company, planned to build on 233 hectares of reclaimed land in Colombo bay. Under the deal, the state-owned but Hong Kong-listed developer would lease 88 hectares for ninety-nine years and own 20 hectares of Sri Lankan territory outright. President Xi inaugurated the project in person in September 2014. After jointly cutting a red ribbon with a smiling Rajapaksa, the two presidents watched a dredger pump an arc of sand into the water to initiate the reclamation process.[42]

When Sri Lanka's new government swept into power in January 2015, it vowed to scrutinize Chinese-sponsored projects. In March that year, work on Colombo Port City was suspended. In addition to legal concerns about the ownership of the land, there were doubts about the project's financial viability and environmental impact. Although up to 300,000 people could eventually live in the development, no one had bothered to assess its impact on water, sewerage or transport. When I visited that month, the large artificial sandbank that had emerged out of the harbour was littered with stationary diggers. Signs tied to the perimeter fence announced that the project would not restart till it had obtained "approval from relevant government institutions".

The Colombo Port City deal was made with support at the highest level, without due process. This is typical of the Chinese approach to striking investment and construction deals overseas. Chinese businessmen, diplomats and financiers know how to wine, dine and flatter foreign elites, especially the members of politically dubious regimes shunned by Western investors and multilateral financiers. China's policy of non-interference in the internal affairs of other countries brings many commercial opportunities, but it also means Chinese enterprises become associated with the corrupt regimes with which they do business. That makes them particularly vulnerable to shifts in public opinion and the changing political fortunes of their foreign partners.

The environment for Chinese enterprises in Sri Lanka changed dramatically when the new government came to power. "We mean business when we say we want clean, transparent, good governance," Karunanayake told me, forcefully. "Perhaps Chinese companies had to be corrupt in the past, but if they do that now they will be disqualified." He said Colombo would renegotiate a number of hefty loan repayments due to Chinese banks. "What we're saying to the Chinese is this: 'We're in a tough spot. Please help us by taking a haircut on our debt.'" In early 2015, a Sri Lankan minister told reporters that a Chinese lender, presumably China Exim Bank, had agreed to issue a large loan at a 2% interest rate to enable Sri Lanka to pay off previous loans taken out at 6.9%.[43] Beijing clearly realized that it was not in its best interests to alienate Sri Lanka's new government, especially when the island holds so much strategic importance.

But Sri Lanka's optimistic new government has also learned how hard it is to extricate itself from China's clutches. By late 2015, facing falling foreign exchange reserves and a balance of payments crunch, it sought an emergency loan from the IMF. It also turned, once again, to Beijing. Having announced that work on Colombo Port City would restart, it began to discuss a plan for Chinese investors to build a special economic zone in Hambantota, alongside the Chinese-built seaport and airport. China is considering a plan to build ships there, which would certainly fuel Indian concern, especially since a Sri Lankan defence official said the suspension of Chinese naval ships docking in Sri Lanka might also be reconsidered. "The stance on China has completely changed," cabinet spokesman Rajitha Senaratne told Reuters. "Who else is going to bring us money, given tight conditions in the West?"[44]

Money talks, and China has much more of it than anyone else—even after haemorrhaging foreign exchange in 2015–16 to support its own falling currency. Sri Lanka's new government is carefully treading a line between demanding that Chinese enterprises play by the rules and not alienating a vital source of investment. When new Sri Lankan president Maithripala Sirisena visited Beijing in 2015, he was careful to emphasize that the problems facing Chinese firms "[do] not lie with the Chinese side", instead blaming Rajapaksa's regime.[45] "What we want from the Chinese is investment that can be converted into trade," Finance Minister Karunanayake explained to me. "So far there are almost no Chinese investments—only loans. It's all financing for construction projects. We would like the Chinese to invest in infrastructure, logistics and industrial production for export."[46]

This is precisely the kind of investment that China's Belt and Road Initiative promises. But China will need to be smarter about how it operates in democracies like Sri Lanka: its chastening experience there, however brief, demonstrates how vulnerable its foreign investments are to shifting political winds. China remains influential in Sri Lanka, but it is unlikely to regain the seemingly unassailable position it once occupied—just as it will struggle to rule the roost again in Myanmar. Sri Lanka may be open to Chinese investment, but it is actively seeking more cooperation with companies in India, Japan, the US and Europe.

For China, Sri Lanka offers a test case of how nimbly its leaders and enterprises can react to the vicissitudes of foreign politics. "The Chinese do not quite understand how to deal with countries that are democracies, where you have political transitions as we have seen here," said Saravanamuttu at the Centre for Policy Alternatives, sucking hard on a Dunhill ciga-rette. "They would rather deal with a corrupt dictatorship and not worry about it."[47] But this is far from the first time that China's foreign business dealings have turned sour in a polit-ically unstable country. And at some point, Beijing may find it is time to reconsider its policy of working with corrupt elites.

For China to realize its Asian dream, it has to live up to its promises of delivering mutually beneficial development. For as long as the suspicion remains that Beijing's much-vaunted "win–win" diplomacy really represents a double victory for China—and that its friendly words about shared commercial gain are really a smokescreen for more self-interested objec-tives—it will fail to win the trust of its neighbours.

CHAPTER 6

FIERY WATERS

MAPPING THE
SOUTH CHINA SEA

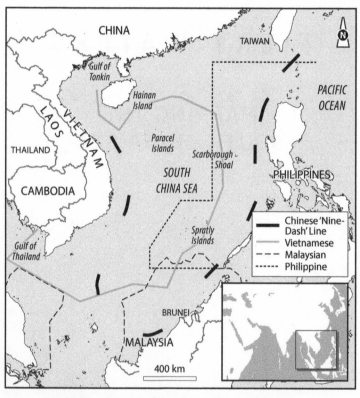

Major territorial claims in the South China Sea

Early on the morning of 23 May 2014, Le Thi Tuyet Mai took a taxi to the front gate of Reunification Palace in Ho Chi Minh City. On the site where the Vietnam War ended on 30 April 1975, she doused herself in fuel and set herself alight. Palace guards put the fire out within a few minutes, but the sixty-seven-year-old was already dead. Beside her burnt corpse, police found banners with hand-written slogans denouncing China's actions in the South China Sea: "Demand unity to smash the Chinese invasion plot", one said.[1]

Le Thi Tuyet Mai's suicide came a week after anti-Chinese protests and deadly riots spread across Vietnam. Factories with Chinese characters on their signboards were attacked, looted, vandalized and torched, including many owned by Taiwanese firms. Hundreds of Chinese and Taiwanese fled the country, fearing for their lives.[2] The protests were ignited by the decision of China National Offshore Oil Corporation (CNOOC) to park an oil rig 120 nautical miles off the Vietnamese coast in waters claimed by both China and Vietnam. CNOOC established an exclusion zone around its US$1 billion rig, *Haiyang Shiyou* ("Ocean Oil") *981*, and began drilling on 2 May. When Vietnam sent ships and boats to disrupt operations, they were rammed by Chinese vessels. It was the most serious incident in the long-standing territorial dispute between China and Vietnam since the Johnson South Reef Skirmish in 1988, when seventy Vietnamese soldiers were killed. On the streets of Vietnam, it proved a trigger for simmering anti-Chinese feelings to come to the boil.

The Chinese rig was positioned 17 nautical miles off the southwestern edge of the Paracels, a group of 130 coral islands, reefs and sandbanks roughly equidistant from the coastlines of China and Vietnam. Distributed over a maritime area the size of Northern Ireland or Connecticut, the Paracels are claimed by China, Taiwan and Vietnam, but have been controlled by China since it defeated South Vietnamese forces in a maritime battle in 1974. Since the 1980s, Beijing has poured money into bolstering its position in the islands, which are located about 350 km southeast of Hainan Island, home to China's major submarine base. On Woody Island, the largest, it has built a sizeable artificial dock and a runway capable of handling fighter aircraft and small passenger planes. Since July 2012, the island has officially served as the administrative centre of Sansha, a prefecture-level "city" of Hainan province that administers China's territorial claims across the South China Sea. Its thousand or so residents are served by shops, offices, hostels, canteens, a post office, a bank, a school and a hospital. Beijing is doing everything it can to turn a once uninhabited island into an indisputable piece of its territory.[3]

No fair observer denies that China has a decent claim over the Paracels—though it is certainly no better than Vietnam's. But several hundred kilometres to the south, China's assertion of sovereignty over the Spratly Islands is dubious in the extreme. The Spratlys are an archipelago of more than 750 islands, islets, reefs and atolls lying off the coasts of southern Vietnam, Malaysia and the Philippines. Some or all of these land features are claimed by six states. The example of the James Shoal, which Beijing attests is the "southernmost point of Chinese territory", shows how farcical its claims have become. Far from being a genuine land formation, the James Shoal is actually a sandbank whose highest point lies a full 22 metres under the sea. It is also located more than 1,500 km from Hainan Island, the most southerly part of Chinese territory uncontested by other countries. The coast of Malaysia, by contrast, is just 80 km away. Yet Beijing says its historical claims trump geography.

China has constructed more than 3,000 acres of artificial islands in the South China Sea since 2014, according to the US Department of Defense.[4] It has focused its most intensive land reclamation efforts in the Spratly Islands, building seven new islets there in 2014–15 alone. Vietnam, Malaysia, the Philippines and Taiwan all began reclaiming land earlier, but China has done so on a much larger scale. Satellite photos released by the Center for Strategic and International Studies in Washington in 2015 showed Chinese dredgers sucking sediment off the seabed and dumping it onto previously submerged sandbanks.[5] At Fiery Cross, China's most strategically significant island in the Spratlys, it has built port facilities, radar installations and an airstrip long enough to land large transport aircraft. Although Beijing claims most of the construction is for civilian purposes, it is clearly intent on boosting its naval and air capabilities. It has even admitted that it needs a stronger defensive presence in the Spratly Islands precisely because they are so far from the Chinese mainland.[6]

To its Southeast Asian neighbours, China's behaviour in the South China Sea amounts to a clear policy of expansionism. Here, Xi Jinping's much-vaunted "Chinese Dream" looks much more like a nightmare. In February 2016, the Pentagon confirmed that China had deployed advanced surface-to-air missiles on Woody Island, and few observers would be surprised if it placed missiles on the Spratly Islands, too.[7] Fearing the growing militarization of the South China Sea, Washington has sided with the other claimants in the dispute. It has frequently warned Beijing over its "aggressive" actions, and sailed warships near disputed islands. The former Philippines president Benigno Aquino repeatedly compared China's regional expansion to that of Nazi Germany in the 1930s.[8] "Just as German soil constituted the military front line of the Cold War," warns Robert Kaplan, an author and security analyst who has advised the Pentagon, "the waters of the South China Sea may constitute the military front line of the coming decades."[9]

亚洲梦

In 1975, Deng Xiaoping told his Vietnamese counterpart Le Duan that the islands of the South China Sea had "belonged to China since ancient times". Since then, these words have appeared in innumerable official documents to support China's claim to waters that stretch far into the natural territory of Southeast Asian nations.[10] Beijing buttresses its claim with a map that shows a U-shaped line made up of nine or ten dashes, sometimes likened to a "cow's tongue", running down the coast of Vietnam, along the coasts of mainland Malaysia and Borneo, and looping back up past the islands of the Philippines to Taiwan. Beijing says the map shows its historical ownership of almost the entire South China Sea, but has never properly explained its historical basis. The truth is that China's claims of ancient sovereignty in the South China Sea are mostly historical nonsense.

For nearly 2,000 years, the South China Sea and the littoral communities of Southeast Asia were a polyglot place of trade and exchange. Land borders were unfixed and maritime boundaries did not exist. There is no archaeological evidence that Chinese ships made trading voyages across the South China Sea until the 10th century, when traders from the kingdom of Minnan set off from the port of Quanzhou in modern-day Fujian province. Chinese trading fleets only began to outnumber those of Southeast Asian traders in the late 16th century—but in no sense did the islands they sailed past "belong" to China. The Ming court sent naval expeditions through the South China Sea under the great eunuch admiral Zheng He in the early 15th century, but this outward-looking period lasted just thirty years. When the Ming Empire turned inwards, Zheng's maps were burned and his ships left to rot. "China didn't possess another naval ship capable of reaching the islands of the South China Seas until it was given one by the United States 500 years later," writes Bill Hayton in his excellent history of the region.[11]

In the 18th century, as Chinese merchants and labourers began to seek their fortunes across Southeast Asia, an "informal empire" began to develop around the rim of the South China Sea. Thousands of Chinese migrants set up plantations or worked in mines, forming communities across the region. But neither these migrants nor the Qing authorities paid much attention to the vast expanse of blue beyond the coast. Chinese merchants generally sailed close to land, fearing that a mythical archipelago off the coast of Indochina blocked access to the seas beyond. This was finally disproved by a hydrographer with the British East India Company in 1821, who published the first chart of the South China Sea containing reasonably accurate maps of the Paracel and Spratly archipelagos. Yet the Chinese state remained geographically in the dark: "There are big rocks, but we do not know anything about them," the writer Wang Wentai wrote of the Spratlys in 1843.[12]

The basis for the current boundaries of the South China Sea were set by the European powers that colonized much of Southeast Asia in the 19th century, creating fixed states and demarking borders along Westphalian lines. Yet this was to the polities in the region an entirely alien concept. The authority of traditional rulers typically radiated from the centre of their kingdoms, diminishing with distance. National boundaries had always been vague, and maritime boundaries vaguer still. Modern political borders were only established as Western nations divvied up territory between them, extending these boundaries into the sea. In China, modern notions of sovereignty took many years to catch on: the first map produced by China's new republican government after the overthrow of the Qing Empire showed no borders at all.

In 1914, a Chinese cartographer published a map purporting to show the extent of China's historic territory when the Qianlong Emperor ascended to the throne in 1735. It showed a line drawn across the South China Sea that went no farther south than 15 degrees north, midway down the Vietnamese coast. The only islands within the line were the Pratas, southwest of Taiwan, and the Paracels. But when, in 1933, the French government announced that it had annexed the Spratly Islands some 1,000 km to the south, the Chinese government reacted. "All our professional geographers say that Triton Island [in the Paracels] is the southernmost island of our territory," its Military Council noted in a secret report. "But we could, maybe, find some evidence that the nine islands [in the Spratlys] were part of our territory in the past."[13] That year it established the Review Committee for Land and Water Maps. In 1935, the committee published a list of islands rightfully belonging to China—including ninety-six in the Spratlys.

A year later, one of the founders of the China Geographical Society went a step further. Bai Meichu was a fervent nationalist who had previously published a map of "Chinese national humiliation" showing the extent of territory lost by China at the hands of European and Japanese imperialists. Demarcating China's "rightful" territory, his *New China Construction Atlas* included a U-shaped line looping around almost the entire South China Sea, as far south as the James Shoal. A similar map, showing a U-shaped line formed by 11 dashes, was published by China's Nationalist government in 1947.[14] After the establishment of the People's Republic of

China in 1949, the new Communist government adopted the map, which was redrawn with nine dashes.

That map has since become the basis of China's claim to "sovereign rights" over approximately 85% of the South China Sea. In May 2009, when China submitted a map to the United Nations Commission on the Limits of the Continental Shelf, it included a "nine-dash line" marking China's "indisputable sovereignty over the islands in the South China Sea and the adjacent waters".[15] This was the first time the "nine-dash line" had been used in an international context, yet it is now clearly marked on every official map of China.

Quite understandably, China's Southeast Asian neighbours reacted with fury. The publication of the map triggered a rapid deterioration in regional relations, which had improved enormously over the previous twenty years. Despite his statement about the islands of the South China Sea belonging to China since "ancient times", Deng Xiaoping had been careful not to press China's territorial claims in the farther reaches of the South China Sea, preferring to stress the potential for economic cooperation. Indeed, Deng used to say that the foreign policy breakthrough he was most proud of was *not* the full normalization of China's relations with the United States—it was the transformation of China's relationship with the countries of Southeast Asia. Once a deadly enemy, China had become their potential partner.[16]

But in 2009 these years of shrewd diplomacy started to unravel. After presenting its map to the UN, China began to press its territorial claims in the South China Sea with more force. It warned Exxon Mobil and BP to stop explorations in waters off Vietnam and began to harass fishing vessels from other countries. For the first time, it started to talk of the 3.5 million square km sea as a "core interest", on a par with Tibet and Taiwan. This persuaded Washington to join the fray. Secretary of State Hillary Clinton asserted that freedom of navigation in the South China Sea, through which more than half of the world's merchant tonnage passes, was a US "national interest". This provoked a furious response from China's then foreign minister Yang Jiechi at an annual meeting of the Association of Southeast Asian Nations (ASEAN) in Hanoi in July 2010. "China is a big country and other countries are small countries, and that's just a fact," he fulminated.[17]

China's aim was to set the framework in the South China Sea, pushing its smaller neighbours to conform. Indonesia, the biggest power in the organization, reacted by pressing for greater cohesion within ASEAN. China's nationalist *Global Times* newspaper warned that ASEAN nations would hear the "sound of cannons" if they did not back down.[18] But Beijing's belligerent stance backfired: after it pressurized Myanmar and Cambodia to do its bidding within ASEAN, Bangkok and Singapore closed ranks with Jakarta and Hanoi, in a rare example of collective resolve. Worse, it persuaded Southeast Asian nations to move closer again to the US—just what had infuriated Beijing in the first place. In 2012, as part of its "pivot to Asia", the US announced plans to revamp its naval deployment across the world's oceans, with 60% to be concentrated in the Pacific by 2020.[19] China's relations with ASEAN duly deteriorated further, as it used naval vessels to enforce a fishing ban in waters off the Scarborough Shoal near the Philippines, which responded in January 2013 by making an arbitration appeal to a UN tribunal.[20]

亚洲梦

This was the incendiary situation inherited by President Xi Jinping and Premier Li Keqiang when they took over as China's leaders in March 2013. At the outset, they appeared intent on returning relations to a more positive footing. Sweeping through Southeast Asia in a blizzard of trade and investment deals, Premier Li proposed a new "political consensus" based on expanding mutual benefit, and inked a treaty on "good neighbourliness".[21] President Xi followed by signing comprehensive strategic partnerships with Indonesia and Malaysia to increase security cooperation and improve economic ties. The new diplomacy culminated in Xi's call, first made in Jakarta in October 2013, to build a 21st Century Maritime Silk Road.

But the friendly smiles rapidly melted away as Beijing's new "proactive" diplomacy bared its teeth. The first sign of a more aggressive approach came that November, when China set up an Air Defence Identification Zone (ADIZ) over the East China Sea. This covered the contested Senkaku Islands, known as the Diaoyu Islands in China, which Beijing maintains Japan stole from it in 1895. Any aircraft flying over the East China Sea must report its flight path and respond to inquiries from the Chinese military. China's argument with Japan is underpinned by a simmering sense of historical wrongdoing that does not apply in Southeast Asia; yet many military analysts nevertheless await a Chinese decision to declare a second ADIZ in the South China Sea.

In early 2014, China turned its attention south. It reasserted its right to regulate fishing across all the waters contained within the "nine-dash line", and it massively ramped up its programme of land reclamation. Then, for all the talk of mutual development and cooperation, it sent *Haiyang Shiyou 981* to drill for oil off Vietnam's coast, setting off the violent anti-Chinese protests that ended with Le Thi Tuyet Mai's self-immolation. After its short-lived charm offensive, China's foreign policy in maritime Southeast Asia had swung to outright provocation, sowing anxiety and bewilderment across the region.

Since 2014, China's policy in the South China Sea has become openly expansionist. Despite repeatedly promising not to militarize the region, it has done precisely that. If placing advanced surface-to-air missiles on reclaimed islands is not militarization, as China claims, it is hard to know what is.[22] Ostensibly, China's bull-headed stance looks like a grand strategic error: why undo years of positive diplomacy for so little obvious gain?

It is surely not, primarily, about securing new hydrocarbons. Experts believe the South China Sea contains relatively little oil and gas, and what little there is would be hard to extract: the geology is troublesome and the region suffers from powerful summer typhoons. In a report published in February 2013, the US Energy Information Administration estimated the South China Sea contains commercially viable reserves of 11 billion barrels of oil—certainly worth exploiting, but not enough to excite the oil majors.[23] By comparison, Venezuela has proven oil reserves of nearly 300 billion barrels. More to the point, most of the South China Sea oil is to be found within individual countries' exclusive economic zones near the coasts; only a fraction lies within the disputed territory of the U-shaped line. China imported 336 million tonnes of crude oil in 2015, equivalent to about 2.5 billion barrels.[24] So even if it secured all of the oil lying under the South China Sea, it would only be enough to satisfy its oil needs for a few years. The South China Sea is far more important as a shipping route for oil than for the oil that lies beneath it.

China's true motivation in the South China Sea is to gain strategic control of its shipping lanes. The South China Sea carries a third of global maritime traffic, including most Chinese exports, and more than 80% of China's oil imports. Beijing, quite rationally, is building a military presence to protect its energy supply lines—a job that is currently done by the US, a geopolitical rival. It is also determined, understand-ably, to ensure security in its own backyard. Some analysts argue that China is merely repeating what the US did in the 19th century, when it ousted European nations from the Caribbean Sea.[25] "From a Chinese point of view, I believe it makes eminently good sense to turn the South China Sea into a giant Chinese lake," says John Mearsheimer, a celebrated political scientist. "The Chinese should want to call all the shots in the South China Sea, just the way the United States calls all the shots in the Caribbean."[26] It is only logical, in his view, for China "to want to dominate Asia the way the United

States dominates the western hemisphere"—starting with an adjacent sea crowded with smaller and much weaker powers.

This is straightforward realpolitik. Yet Beijing tries to buttress its position by selectively invoking legal principles to justify its actions. It is a signatory to the United Nations Convention on the Law of the Sea (UNCLOS), which seeks to provide a modern legal basis for maritime claims. Under the convention, habitable islands are entitled to an exclusive economic zone (EEZ) of 200 nautical miles out to sea. The Paracel Islands lie within Vietnam and China's overlapping EEZs, but China has no valid legal claim to the most southerly and easterly rock formations of the South China Sea, many of which are not naturally habitable in any case. Nevertheless, China's official map clearly marks the Spratly Islands and Scarborough Shoal, a triangle-shaped chain of reefs and rocks located 120 nautical miles off the coast of the Philippines, as its territory. It justifies this claim by appealing to historical precedent.

Beijing refuses to accept UN arbitration over its maritime disputes. It has exempted itself from UNCLOS's compulsory settlement procedure for several categories of disputes, including those relating to maritime delimitation. Following the Philippines' arbitration appeal to an international tribunal hosted at the Permanent Court of Arbitration in The Hague, it refused to participate in the proceedings. Instead, it launched a propaganda campaign denouncing the "law-abusing tribunal" as illegitimate.[27] Nevertheless, the tribunal determined that it had jurisdiction to consider seven of Manila's fifteen submissions. Its unanimous verdict, announced in July 2016, went further than anyone expected. It found there was no legal basis for China to claim historic rights within the "nine-dash line", ruled that Scarborough Shoal is a rock entitled only to a 12 nautical mile territorial sea, and found that none of the land features in the Spratlys are islands entitled to an EEZ. It did not delimit any boundaries or rule on the sovereignty of the islets themselves, but it did invalidate China's claims outside the territorial seas that surround them. It could therefore declare that certain sea areas claimed by China are actually within the existing EEZ of the Philippines, and that China's occupation of Scarborough Shoal had violated Manila's sovereign rights.[28] Beijing declared the verdict "null and void", but as a signatory of UNCLOS, it is legally bound by it.

Beijing attests the tribunal had no jurisdiction under UNCLOS to make its verdict. It is important for Beijing to pay lip service to the Convention, because it is happy to invoke it when it suits its own ends. In a statement sent to the UN in June 2014, for example, China's foreign ministry contended that Vietnam's attempt to disrupt the *Haiyang Shiyou 981* drilling rig constituted "serious infringements upon China's sovereignty" and "gross violations of the relevant international laws, including ... UNCLOS". It claimed that China's effective administration of the nearby Paracels invalidated any territorial dispute: "Since it is closer to Chinese territory, the rig is in Chinese waters."[29] Yet that is precisely the basis of the Philippines' claim over the Scarborough Shoal, which is located closer to its coastline than to any Chinese territory. China also uses its effective control of the Paracels to deny that any legitimate dispute with Vietnam exists—precisely Japan's approach

212

to the Senkaku Islands, which have been administered by Tokyo for 130 years. Beijing, unsurprisingly, wants Tokyo to admit that the Senkakus are indeed disputed. All that can be said of Beijing's arguments is that they are consistently inconsistent.

China's refusal to abide by the rules weakens its political position. In 2002, China and ASEAN member states signed the "Declaration of the Conduct of Parties in the South China Sea", agreeing not to escalate maritime tensions, to resolve territorial disputes by peaceful means, and to abide by the principles of international law, including UNCLOS.[30] It also made agreements both with Vietnam in 2011 to resolve sea-related disputes "through friendly negotiations and consultations" and with the Philippines in 2012 to withdraw its ships from Scarborough Shoal. Far from honouring these agreements, China simply took whatever unilateral action it judged would strengthen its territorial position. The refusal to accept the verdict of the tribunal in The Hague is simply a more egregious example of an oft-repeated pattern. When it comes to matters of security and sovereignty, China will happily thumb its nose at rules set in the West. International law means little if no one is willing to enforce it.

In sum, Beijing picks and chooses arguments to help support its claims, but refuses to be bound by them. It invokes high-sounding principles, but brazenly pursues any policy it believes will strengthen its hand. It insists on resolving disputes bilaterally, but will reach out to the UN or act independently as it sees fit. It talks responsibly about solving disputes through peaceful means, but its actions are aggressively unilateralist—a strategy that the Vietnamese call "talk and take".[31] Wang Yi, China's foreign minister, expressed the contradictory impulses shaping China's foreign policy at a press conference during the annual meeting of the National People's Congress in 2014. "We are willing to listen to voices from our neighbouring countries and respond to their doubts about China's neighbourhood policy," he said, quite reasonably. "But", he continued, injecting some steel, "we will defend every inch of territory that belongs to us."[32]

亚洲梦

China's piece-by-piece expansionism in the South China Sea has been likened to slicing salami. It is careful to ensure that each new piece of territory it slices off is too small to provoke a war in itself, but the accumulated loss will, in time, radically alter the balance of power.[33] So far, this policy has been reasonably successful: China's position in the South China Sea is far stronger than it was a decade ago. But its behaviour is jeopardizing a long-standing principle of its diplomacy—that foreign policy should support domestic ends. The Ministry of Foreign Affairs affirmed this view in a 2011 white paper: "The central goal of China's diplomacy is to create a peaceful and stable international environment for its development."[34] Xi Jinping himself has stated that China's proactive foreign policy must strive "to safeguard peace and stability" in its neighbourhood.[35] Yet the South China Sea has rarely felt less stable.

China's unremitting salami slicing may backfire. As it continues to upset its neighbours, China is pushing them ever more firmly into the arms of its only genuine strategic competitor—the US. In February 2016, President Obama hosted a special summit with ASEAN leaders at the Sunnylands estate in California. According to the official joint statement, "it marked a watershed year for both ASEAN and for the increasingly close US–ASEAN strategic partnership". The participants reaffirmed mutual respect for "the sovereignty, territorial integrity, equality and political independence of all nations" and the shared commitment to "maintain peace, security and stability in the region", including "ensuring maritime security and safety".[36] Washington then announced a US$250 million initiative to bolster naval and coast guard capabilities in the South China Sea, and the US Congress authorized it to assist Brunei, Indonesia, Malaysia, the Philippines, Singapore, Taiwan and Vietnam in strengthening their maritime security.

All this is clear evidence, Beijing believes, that the US is building an anti-China alliance with ASEAN, along with Japan, Australia and India. US leaders have repeatedly called for a halt to "reclamation, construction and militarization" in the South China Sea, and have backed up these demands with occasional shows of military force. In May 2015, a US Navy surveillance aircraft ignored a Chinese command to leave the Spratly Islands. This brought a belligerent response from Beijing's nationalistic *Global Times* newspaper, which declared that a "US–China war is inevitable in the South China Sea" unless Washington backed down.[37] In October 2015, the US sailed a destroyer near reclaimed Chinese islands in the Spratlys, receiving public praise from Australia, Japan and the Philippines. And in February 2016, it sent another destroyer to patrol within 12 nautical miles of Triton Island in the Paracels, after it was reported that China had deployed advanced surface-to-air missiles on Woody Island.

Why is the US so worried about China's expansion in the South China Sea? One issue that cannot be ignored is Taiwan. Among the many reasons for China to strengthen its position in the South China Sea is to put military pressure on its "renegade province", or even to facilitate a future blockade or invasion. From a US strategic perspective, Taiwan is at least as important as the Philippines. And from a political perspective, it is much more important: the "Taiwan caucus" in Congress consisted of 205 members in 2016, making it the largest country caucus on Capitol Hill.[38] It is also one of the most active special-interest groups in the legislature. Defending Taiwan is embedded deep in America's China strategy: immediately after President Jimmy Carter normalized relations with the PRC in 1978, Congress passed the Taiwan Relations Act as a counterbalance. The Act requires the US to intervene militarily if China attacks or invades Taiwan. The ultra-realists in the US foreign policy establishment, starting with Henry Kissinger in the 1970s, would happily sacrifice Taiwan to reach a satisfactory accommodation with Beijing. But such a solution is politically impossible so long as Taiwan retains support in Congress.[39]

Yet there is a still greater fear: that China's expansionism in the South China Sea is part of Beijing's grand strategy to replace the US as the dominant power in Asia. The US has enjoyed seventy years as the unrivalled master of the Asia-Pacific, where its powerful military presence has helped to bring both peace and stability—a point emphasized by Singaporean prime minister Lee Hsien Loong in his opening speech at the Shangri-La Dialogue, an annual Asian security summit, in 2015.[40] The US is hardly going to hand over leadership of Asia willingly. Purely in economic terms, so much US trade moves through the South China Sea that it has a genuine national interest in policing it. It is partly for this reason that Washington has carefully built up an alliance structure to defend its interests, and is so determined to defend the "rules-based order" that underpins its power. At 2016's Shangri-La Dialogue, US Secretary of Defense Ashton Carter demanded that "everyone [must play] by the same rules". Hammering home his point, he warned China that it "could end up erecting a Great Wall of self-isolation" if it did not.[41]

For its part, China sees "the rules-based order" as a rigged system designed both to contain its legitimate rise and to prop up the US *imperium*. In the US's "pivot to Asia", Beijing sees proof of Washington's efforts to stymie its attempts to build a regional sphere of influence. Further proof was the Obama administration's sponsorship of the Trans-Pacific Partnership trade agreement, which Beijing initially saw as a strategic ploy to strengthen US influence in the Asia-Pacific at China's expense. Although China did not meet the agreed criteria for members, that obstacle did not prevent Vietnam from joining. Defense Secretary Carter seemed to confirm the accuracy of this interpretation in April 2015, when he said that "passing TPP is as important to me as another aircraft carrier".[42] President Obama followed up that November, declaring that "if we don't pass this agreement—if America doesn't write those rules—then countries like China will".[43]

Where does this leave us? China's white paper on military strategy released in July 2015 made it clear that the Chinese military would fight back if attacked.[44] So any US military action in the region risks being perceived by Beijing as an act of war. When nationalist emotions run high, it is foolish to dismiss the chance of war outright—yet a conflagration in the South China Sea remains unlikely. China requires regional stability to deliver domestic growth and prosperity: a conflict with the US would be a huge strategic error, because it would undermine its economic rise. The US has 365,000 active servicemen in the Asia-Pacific, a powerful regional security alliance, and by far the world's most powerful military. Beijing believes its long-term goals in Asia are best served by keeping the uneasy peace and patiently establishing "facts in the water". So China will continue to test Washington's resolve, but it has no interest in provoking the US into military action. Beijing is careful, for example, to ensure that its reclamation efforts do not threaten international shipping.

That is why fears that the South China Sea is a cauldron on the verge of bubbling over are probably wide of the mark. China is determined to regain its historical position as the central power in eastern Asia, but it is not in its interest to force the US's hand. This is especially true now that China's greatest regional competitor—Japan—is gearing up to play a larger security role. President Shinzo Abe came to power in 2012 on the back of a promise to repeal some of the restrictions imposed on Japan's military in its pacifist post-War constitution. As a staunch US ally, Japan would certainly act in concert with the US in the event of a conflict. The current machinations in the

South China Sea therefore amount to shadow boxing: China is not militarily strong enough to take the area by force, and it has no choice but to play the long game.

The overriding question now is how Donald Trump's government responds to China's provocations. Beijing viewed the Obama administration as lily-livered and its policies in Southeast Asia as irritating but largely ineffectual. President Obama's Asia team was criticized by many in Washington as the weakest since World War II, with little interest in developing a coherent China strategy. More hawkish observers argue that Washington should formulate a coherent policy to contain China and ramp up the US military presence in the South China Sea. But a concerted effort to prevent China's rise would risk escalating tensions to genuinely dangerous levels. In the end, the US will surely have to accept China's desire to play a bigger role in its backyard, and find a way to shape a new regional order that serves everyone's interests.

VIETNAM[45]

Vietnam's National Museum of History, located in the heart of Hanoi's French Quarter, once went under the exotic moniker of the École Française d'Extrême Orient.[46] Built in 1925–32 by the French architect Ernest Hebrard, it features an octagonal tower with mustard-yellow walls and a terracotta-tiled roof—an audacious, and largely successful, attempt to blend traditional Vietnamese and French architecture. Visitors to the museum's ornamental garden, which is decorated with Buddhist statues and ancient stone steles, can find respite from

Hanoi's savage sun in the shade of a giant tree dripping with tropical creepers.

The museum holds an array of Neolithic tools, pots and jewellery, glazed ceramics, bronze drums and funerary objects. Among its most splendid treasures are a series of voluptuous statues dating back to the Kingdom of Champa, a Hindu civilization that flourished a thousand years ago on the coast of central Vietnam. But the National Museum of History is really a celebration of one thing: Vietnam's 2,000-year struggle for independence against invading Chinese armies. From 40 AD to 938 AD—from the Han Dynasty to the Tang Dynasty—the glass displays contain description upon description of Vietnamese heroes rebelling against oppressive occupiers. "During the period when the Han Empire dominated Nam Viet," one display contends, "the population resisted all attempts at cultural assimilation by the Chinese over a period of one thousand years." Once the Chinese yoke had finally been thrown off, other displays explain, Vietnam spent a further thousand years repelling invasion after invasion from the north.

One famous victory, during the Song invasion of 1076–77, saw General Ly Thuong Kiet smash a reputed Chinese force of 1 million foot soldiers, 100,000 horses and 2 million labourers. According to the official history, the Chinese retreated with just 23,400 men and 3,174 horses. "The Song wasted 5,190,000 ounces of gold for this war," a caption reads, next to an exhibit of ancient swords and daggers used to spill invading Chinese blood. National identity, it hammers home, was forged by fighting Chinese invaders. Yet the four lines of rhyming verse attributed to General Ly Thuong Kiet celebrating the victory

were written in classical Chinese—for this was a highly Sini-
cized society, with close cultural links to the very people its
own people so despised. The steles erected to commemorate
Vietnamese victories, engraved with Chinese characters, were
identical to similar stone memorials found all over China.

The largest stele in the museum, four metres high by nearly
two metres wide, celebrates the Lam Son Uprising against the
occupying Ming army in the early 15th century. Under the
leadership of the nobleman Le Loi, the Vietnamese forces
spent a decade grinding down the Chinese troops, emerging
victorious. In 1428, Le Loi founded the Le Dynasty, and
today every city in Vietnam has a street named after him. Yet
the object chosen to commemorate his famous victory was
entirely Chinese in inspiration and design. Inscribed with classical Chinese and decorated with swirling Chinese dragons,
the giant stone stands atop a huge, smiling turtle—a mystical
symbol of longevity and fortune in Chinese culture. For all
Vietnam's long, bloody and proud history of resistance against
the northern invader, Chinese culture permeated every aspect
of local life—from the language and cuisine, to the arts and acts
of worship. To this day Vietnamese is larded with Chinese loan
words, and the cultural influence from the north is obvious.

The National Museum is a paean, in concrete form, to the
Vietnamese struggle for independence. The history it projects
defines Vietnamese nationhood in opposition to China; but
the truth is rather more complex. Most of this nationalist
narrative, journalist and historian Bill Hayton writes, is "anach-
ronistic myth": the heroic struggles against the "Chinese"
were often really disputes between regional rulers who spoke

similar languages.[47] "The truth is that, however much we hate the Chinese, we are basically the same as them," one unusually frank speaker told me over coffee in Ho Chi Minh City. "Historically the Viet people come from the lands south of the Yangtze River in southern China, and then moved further south into modern Vietnam."[48] In the Vietnamese tradition, ninety-nine Yue (or Viet) clans were incorporated and acculturated into China; only one, the Nan Yue—the southern Viets—kept their identity. The first time the two countries known today as China and Vietnam fought a war was in 1979, when Vietnam battled off an incursion by tens of thousands of People's Liberation Army troops.

The salient point for modern relations between China and Vietnam is that most Vietnamese still regard China as the eternal enemy. Whereas US Army veterans returning to Vietnam are invariably greeted with friendliness—despite fighting against the winning Communist forces in the Vietnam War—Chinese businessmen and tourists are treated warily. Since the oil rig debacle, public opinion has turned even more hostile. According to the 2015 Pew Research Survey on global attitudes, Vietnamese hold an overwhelmingly negative view of China. Seventy-four percent of those surveyed said they viewed China "unfavourably", more than in any country other than Japan.[49] It is common to hear people talk of being "born with anti-Chinese feeling in our blood": the hatred many ordinary Vietnamese feel for their northern neighbours is visceral.

In the political sphere, these feelings are complicated by the debt owed by the Communist Party of Vietnam (CPV) to its big brother in Beijing, which supplied the Communist North with rice and rockets during its bitter struggle with the South, in what the Vietnamese call the Resistance War Against America. Relations deteriorated in the late 1970s, when the Vietnamese Politburo concluded that the Khmer Rouge regime in neighbouring Cambodia, which had been attacking Vietnamese border villages, was a proxy of China. Tensions were exacerbated by Vietnam's close relationship with the Soviet Union, China's arch enemy. After Vietnam invaded and occupied Cambodia in 1978, China and Vietnam fought a brief border war in 1979. This was followed by a naval skirmish over the Johnson South Reef in the Spratly Islands in 1988.

As the Soviet Union began to dissolve, however, China began to reassert its grip over its little Communist brother. After both sets of Communist Party leaders met for secret talks in Chengdu in 1990, bilateral ties were officially normalized. The CCP's political influence in Hanoi grew rapidly in the 1990s, and is retained to this day. Ordinary Vietnamese believe the political and military establishments to be riddled with Chinese spies. Much patriotic anti-Chinese sentiment contains within it implicit criticism of the Vietnamese Communist Party, which is still considered too close to Beijing.

One of the most virulent critics of China's political influence is Tuong Lai, a former head of the Academy of Social Sciences of Vietnam and an adviser to two former Vietnamese prime ministers. A frequent contributor to the op-ed pages of the *New York Times*, Tuong Lai advocates further economic reform and a closer relationship with the US.[50] In this he is representative of a band of Vietnamese dissidents pushing for political reform. In 2013, he helped pen an open letter to the

Party's general secretary, Nguyen Phu Trong, urging consti-
tutional changes to "ensure that real power belongs to the
people".[51] Other critics would not get away with voicing such
forthright views, but Tuong Lai is too well-connected (and
probably too old) to be sent to jail.

On a hot May morning in Ho Chi Minh City, I jumped on
the back of my translator's scooter and joined the rush-hour
madness for the thirty-minute ride to Tuong Lai's home in the
south of the city. Millions of motorbikes buzzed like a giant
swarm of angry bees as we flew past mangrove swamps and
the rusting warehouses of the old port on the Saigon River.
Silver haired and casually dressed in a striped polo shirt, Tuong
Lai greeted us in a modern, airy flat decorated with framed
posters of classical Vietnamese poetry written in traditional
Chinese characters. Over green tea served in bamboo cups,
he launched into a long history of Vietnam's troubled relations
with the Chinese. "The struggle against an expansionist China
is the struggle against the evil inside Vietnamese leadership—
the ones who follow Chinese ideology," he began. "China is
becoming increasingly aggressive in the South China Sea.
This is a tremendous threat to Vietnam's sovereignty." The
failure of General Secretary Trong to complain about China's
provocative maritime actions during his visit to Beijing in
2015 was "an act of treason", he declared, waggling his index
finger passionately.[52]

Rising to his theme, Dr Tuong explained how China was
deliberately challenging the US for leadership in Asia. "The
current expansionist policy of Beijing in the South China Sea
is a consistent policy," he continued.

The policy of "keeping a low profile" was just a tactical move by Deng Xiaoping, waiting for a right time to project Chinese power overseas. The security environment in the 21st century is very complicated for Washington, which is facing many difficulties around the world, especially in the Middle East and with Russia. China's leaders have realized this is the right time to change their approach.

China's ambition, he concluded, is to finish what it has been trying to do for 2,000 years: "China wants to turn Vietnam into a vassal state. The South China Sea is the focal point in China's grand strategy to become a superpower."

In Hanoi, the official line is less provocative. It goes something like this: "China is our big neighbour, whether we like it or not. This is the tyranny of geography. So we should do our best to work with China and not deliberately irritate it."[53] Yet that stance is increasingly being questioned, even among the pro-Beijing faction within the CPV. Institutional ties still exist between the two Communist parties, but they are fraying. Under a foreign policy framework approved by Vietnam's Politburo in 2013, Vietnam treats China as a partner on economic and ideological matters, and as an adversary in the South China Sea. But following the oil rig incident in 2014, which underlined Chinese contempt for both Vietnam's sovereignty and international law, the pro-Beijing faction seemed to be in retreat. "Vietnam has always wanted peace and friendship with China," Prime Minister Nguyen Tan Dung said that year. "But we cannot trade our sacred independence and sovereignty for some elusive peace or any type of dependence."[54]

Xi Jinping's visit to Vietnam in November 2015, the first by a Chinese president in a decade, was billed by Western media as Beijing's attempt to claw back its lost influence. His trip was carefully timed ahead of the CPV's 12th National Congress in January 2016, a meeting of Communist leaders that would determine who would rule Vietnam for the next five years. Xi's visit was greeted by street protests in Hanoi and Ho Chi Minh City, and anti-Chinese protests on social media. But Xi also received a twenty-one-gun salute in Hanoi, where he was granted a rare invitation to address the National Assembly. In his twenty-minute speech, Xi laid it on thick: "China and Vietnam enjoy comradely and brotherly friendship," he said, "drinking water from the same river." He spoke of the "traditional friendship" and "mutual trust" between the two neighbours.[55] Xinhua, the official Chinese press agency, reported that Xi's speech was greeted "warmly"; but his friendly exhortations were actually received in stony silence. "The atmosphere was very tense," an anonymous Vietnamese official told the *Washington Post*.[56]

President Xi used the latter half of his speech to press for further economic cooperation. "Both sides should join efforts to create a regional order and environment that bring more benefits to Asia and the world at large," he said. For Beijing, such "win–win cooperation" is really about boosting regional prosperity under a Chinese-led regional order—precisely what patriotic Vietnamese want to avoid. Beijing is only too aware how economically reliant Vietnam is on China. A full 20% of Vietnam's trade is with its northern neighbour, which is the source of nearly 30% of its imports.[57] The bilateral trade deficit, which hovers around the US$25 billion mark, vexes Hanoi. It knows that its export industries, on which so much of its future growth depends, rely on imports of raw materials and inputs from China.

Economically, Beijing has most of the leverage. Consider the following facts. Vietnam's GDP of US$194 billion in 2015 was smaller than the economies of its provincial Chinese neighbours, Guangxi (US$270 billion) and Yunnan (US$220 billion), even though they are ranked among China's poorest provinces. Vietnam would like to resemble Guangdong, China's export powerhouse, but Guangdong's economy is six times larger. Guangdong's exports were worth US$746 billion in 2014, compared with Vietnam's US$150 billion.[58] Much of northern Vietnam is mountainous and poor, and reliant on China for electricity. After the oil rig incident in 2014, a debate raged across Vietnam about the economic costs of "escaping from China". Hanoi's economists calculated that GDP would shrink by 10–15% if China placed sanctions on it.[59] If Vietnam is to develop, it literally cannot afford to alienate Beijing.

For its part, China sees huge potential to invest more in Vietnam. For all Beijing's high-flown rhetoric about being the engine of Asian development, China's investment record there is unimpressive. Chinese bauxite mines and processing facilities in the scenic Central Highlands are popularly regarded as exploitative. The owners have been accused of harming the local environment and shipping in their own workers, inciting protests. A canal clearance project undertaken by a Chinese firm in Ho Chi Minh City is regarded as a disaster. And protestors blocked a national highway for five days in

April 2015 demanding an end to pollution from a Chinese-built power station. China's accumulated investment of US$8 billion in Vietnam ranks ninth, far behind bigger investors like South Korea, Japan and Taiwan, and now also eclipsed by the US.[60]

In his speech to the National Assembly, President Xi specifically mentioned improving transport infrastructure between the two countries under the Belt and Road Initiative.[61] Here China's ambitions tie in with existing projects with multilateral backing. In 2009 the Asian Development Bank identified twenty-one "flagship" infrastructure projects—twelve transport projects and nine energy projects—crucial for regional growth. Among them was a new expressway to connect the region of Guangxi in southern China with Hanoi in north Vietnam, via the border province of Lang Son. Here and in other parts of the Greater Mekong Subregion, the ADB believes that a more efficient transport artery will boost trade and investment, and give impoverished farmers better access to markets.[62]

Vietnamese and Chinese officials have been promising great things for Lang Son for a decade. In 2008 a "border gate economic zone" was formally established to create an economic corridor running from Guangxi to Hanoi and the port city of Haiphong. In 2013, following Premier Li Keqiang's visit, Vietnam and China agreed to set up a new economic zone there, along with three others on the border. They talked of building bonded warehouses and an industrial park to welcome export processors from China. The Hanoi–Lang Son Expressway, they promised, would be completed by 2015.[63]

When I visited Lang Son that summer, however, construction on the expressway had yet to begin. The bus from Hanoi wound through glorious countryside along an old highway that showed little evidence of trade, commerce or industry. Farmers in conical hats walked water buffalo through the fields; villagers sipped iced tea at the roadside. Lang Son City, which is located just 15 km from the Chinese border, could have been anywhere. No one I spoke to understood Chinese, even in the large central market. Even stranger was the absence of trucks shipping Chinese goods over the border. Unlike the market towns of northern Laos or northeastern Myanmar, where markets bustle with Chinese traders, China felt a long way away. A busy cross-border economic corridor this most certainly was not.

Anti-Chinese feelings run especially deep in Lang Son, for centuries the first port of call for Chinese marauders. In the 1979 border war, the city was captured and partly destroyed by the invading Chinese army, which conducted fierce house-to-house fighting in the streets. With memories of the war still fresh, it is no surprise that locals remain wary of China. In principle, Beijing's financing and infrastructure push has much to recommend it: China's own experience shows how vast investment can successfully stimulate economic development. Yet China cannot simply push its development model over its borders without first overcoming the weight of history and popular fear.

China's ambitions in Vietnam are also hampered by its constructions firms' reputation for shoddy building practices. Take China Railway Group (CRG), which is building part of Hanoi's new urban rail system, financed with US$419 million of Chinese development aid loans. When I visited one of its new stations in May 2015, I found a construction site filled with rubble, twisted rebar and pools of fetid water. The railway was running three years behind schedule and way over budget. The previous December, a scaffolding collapse had rained steel and concrete onto a taxi carrying three passengers. Barely a month before that, a motorcyclist was killed after reels of steel fell from the same construction site. CRG has built thousands of kilometres of railway track across China, yet Hanoi residents fear that the metro will collapse. CRG's corporate logo is conspicuous by its absence in the city: it is in no one's interest to advertise Chinese involvement.[64]

In Ho Chi Minh City, where two Japanese companies are building that city's first metro system, the scene was altogether different. In the central square opposite the ornate French-built opera house, a billboard showed a red Japanese sun next to a yellow Vietnamese star; it informed passers-by that the project was an example of "Vietnam–Japan Friendship and Cooperation". Shimizu and Maeda, the two Japanese contractors, receive funding from their government's aid agency—part of Tokyo's effort to ramp up Japanese aid and investment in the face of Chinese competition. While Chinese investment is resented, Japanese investment is embraced.

亚洲梦

I watched the progress on the metro from my window in the Hotel Continental Saigon, supposedly the oldest in the city. Built in the 1880s, the hotel's white Doric columns and cream façade evoke the lost colonial age of French Indochine. By the 1930s, Saigon was regarded as one of the great colonial metropolises of the East. Today, though colonial offices and villas are felled one after another to make way for high-rise buildings, tourists still throng to the twin spires of the Roman Catholic cathedral and the magnificent edifice of the General Post Office. In truth, Saigon at that time was home to around only 125,000 people, including barely more than 12,000 French. Compared to Shanghai, whose population approached 3 million—including more than 100,000 foreigners—it was little more than a trading outpost. By the 1950s, as the French colonial project was coming to an end, Graham Greene took up residence in the Hotel Continental and penned his classic tale of its disintegration, *The Quiet American.*

More than half a century later, Saigon is beginning to fulfil its promise. Renamed Ho Chi Minh City after falling to Communist troops in May 1975, its population has swollen to 10 million, making it easily the second largest city in mainland Southeast Asia, behind only Bangkok.[65] The streets thrum and roar with the noise of 6 million scooters, and there is an excellent choice of international cuisine. If economic reforms can push development beyond its commercial capital, Vietnam may thrive while maintaining its economic independence. The prospect of closer ASEAN economic integration, combined with growing domestic consumption and low labour costs, have already turned it into a hub for foreign manufacturers. It has plenty of economic suitors: after China, Vietnam attracted more greenfield FDI than any other country in Asia in 2014 (though it was overtaken in 2015 by India and Indonesia).[66]

One reason for optimism had been Vietnam's inclusion in the US-led Trans-Pacific Partnership, a multilateral trade pact designed to encompass 40% of the global economy. Vietnam was expected to be the biggest winner among the twelve members of the TPP, before Donald Trump's election radically reduced the chances of it ever being ratified. According to one assessment, its economy would gain 11% and exports jump 28% within a decade, reducing its trade reliance on China.[67] If Vietnam were to let state-owned enterprises die and keep steering support to the private sector, in accordance with the TPP's original anti-competition provisions, a reformed pact could yet benefit the economy. Given that the TPP was expected to provide the impetus for market-opening reforms, some Vietnamese viewed it as merely the latest episode in the country's 2,000-year struggle for independence from China.

The significance of the TPP, says Professor Tuong Lai, went far beyond economics. Vietnam's membership "would realign geopolitical relations in the region and help stave off China's expansionism in the South China Sea", he argued in an April 2015 piece for the *New York Times*.[68] Hanoi began negotiations on the TPP back in 2008, but Vietnamese analysts say the US had to cajole it through the process. Hanoi's uncertainty probably reflected residual distrust of the US within the Vietnamese Communist Party. But the visit by Communist Party leader Trong to Washington in July 2015, where he was received by President Obama in the Oval Office, capped a year of frenzied diplomacy between the two countries. Vietnam's decision to sign up to the TPP in February 2016 marked an important step in its counterbalance against China.

The burgeoning relationship between the US and Vietnam was on full show in May 2016, when President Obama's visit brought excited crowds onto the streets of Hanoi—in marked contrast to Xi's strained visit six months earlier. More than four decades after the Vietnam War ended, Vietnam is one of the most US-friendly nations in Asia: 78% of Vietnamese citizens had a favourable view of the US in 2015, according to the Pew global attitudes survey.[69] The corresponding figure for China was just 19%.[70] Announcing the lifting of a decades-long ban on the sale of military equipment to Vietnam, Obama insisted that the move was "not based on China".[71] But his comments were clearly aimed at Beijing: "Vietnam will have greater access to the equipment you need to improve your security. Nations are sovereign and no matter how large or small a nation may be, its territory should be respected," he said. "Big nations should not bully smaller ones. Disputes should be resolved peacefully."[72]

"China's behaviour is pushing Vietnam closer to the US," Dr Truong-Minh Vu, director of the Centre for International Studies think tank in Ho Chi Minh City, told me over lunch.

> After the South China Sea issue blew up in 2009, the government began to discuss how to deal with Chinese assertiveness. It began to pursue a policy of balancing and hedging—economically, diplomatically and militarily. Vietnam has moved closer to the US, Japan, Russia and India.[73]

In addition to a proposed free trade agreement with the EU, Vietnam has signed similar agreements with South Korea and the Russia-led Eurasian Economic Union. It is rapidly modernizing its navy and has begun conducting joint operations with elements of the US Pacific Fleet—though it will be careful not to get too close to the US. "Vietnam does not want to be seen to be choosing sides and allying itself against China," Vu explained.

The geographical reality is that Vietnam cannot escape entirely from China's orbit, yet nor is it condemned to be controlled by its giant neighbour. Since no one doubts Beijing's intention to secure effective control of the South China Sea, Hanoi must formulate a tough-minded response that does not cripple the country economically. "The focus of the debate is not about whether Vietnam should submit to or distance itself from China," Murray Hiebert of the Center for Strategic and International Studies testified to US Congress in May 2015, "but rather how and to what extent it can use its growing partnerships with countries such as the United States, Japan and India to keep Chinese assertiveness in check."[74]

For Beijing, Vietnam is an acid test of its Asian diplomacy. In June 2015, ahead of General Secretary Trong's visit to Washington, CNOOC once again moved its oil rig close to Vietnam's coast. Trong, who unexpectedly won the power struggle to remain Party leader in January 2016, is generally seen as a member of the pro-China faction. But his successful meetings with President Obama signalled Hanoi's drift away from Beijing in order to protect its strategic autonomy. It was further evidence that Beijing's uncompromising stance in the South China Sea, for all its apparent rapprochement with new Philippines president Rodrigo Duterte in October 2016, risks pushing its neighbours into the US's welcoming arms.[75]

"China's goal of forging 'common prosperity' cannot work in Vietnam so long as there are conflicts of sovereignty in the South China Sea," said Dr Vu. "They need to understand that they can buy neither our sovereignty nor our good will with money."[76]

CONCLUSION

CONCLUSION

Do countries march towards great power status by design, or slip into it by necessity? History shows it is usually a bit of each. As Xi Jinping pursues his vision of "great power diplomacy", he has tossed the old doctrine of self-restraint in foreign matters aside. The pursuit of national rejuvenation—the "Chinese Dream"—is a deliberate attempt to restore China's traditional leadership in Asia, not just as a great power but as a force of regional development. China is carefully using economic diplomacy to win its neighbours over to its vision, backed by the implicit threat of commercial sanctions and military action.

The truth is that China has little choice but to start acting like a great power. Given its enormous population and the tremendous economic growth of the past three decades, it is simply too big to pretend otherwise. US and EU officials have long called for China to play an active role in global affairs—to become a "responsible stakeholder", in the words of the former US deputy secretary of state Robert Zoellick.[1] Now that its leaders are beginning to accept this status, pursuing a more vigorous foreign policy and building international institutions of their own, the US and some of its Asian allies have responded with disquiet. Yet the growing weight of China's economic and strategic interests means that it cannot afford *not* to play a more active global role. Simply put, in order to protect its interests abroad China must interfere in other countries' affairs. That is what great powers do.

What are these interests it needs to protect? China's national security law, enacted in July 2015, helped clarify what it means by its "core interests".[2] With regard to foreign policy, it boils down to the principle of sovereignty and defending territorial integrity. In addition to Taiwan, Tibet and Xinjiang, foreign policy officials have made it clear that Beijing now regards the South China Sea and the Japanese-held Senkaku Islands as core interests. Arunachal Pradesh in India, which state media have taken to calling "South Tibet", may also fall within this category. In Chinese eyes, it is not expansionary to claim territory that it regards as rightfully its own.

President Xi's newly "proactive" foreign policy in Asia offers a straightforward deal: China will deliver trade, investment and other economic goodies to all partners that accommodate—or, at the very least, do not challenge—its core interests. China relies on economic diplomacy because it lacks political leverage. Unlike the US, whose power in Asia comes from its regional alliance structure, it needs economic partners to further its geopolitical ends. The strategic goal of the Belt and Road Initiative is to promote China as an engine of development, weaving a web of interdependence across Asia and beyond. Beijing hopes the incentive of massive infrastructure investment will persuade Asian countries to put their economic interests above security concerns.

China's long-term aim is to tie its neighbours' prosperity to its own advancement, in what it calls a "community of common destiny". Will it succeed? In the first place, Beijing will struggle to gain trust, especially in political systems which rely on popular support. This is obviously true in countries that have territorial disputes with China or harbour historical resentment against it, such as Vietnam and India. But across Asia, China's concept of "win–win" diplomacy is often dismissed as code for "double win to China". No one seriously believes that China is motivated by spreading development over its borders, especially as its firms hardly have an impressive record of pursuing enlightened self-interest.

Even some of China's own foreign policy advisers warn that its expanding economic reach will provoke a backlash, as it has already done in Myanmar and Sri Lanka. Chinese firms, many of them state owned, have a reputation for operating with little care for local sensitivities—whether that means shipping in Chinese labourers or harming the environment. They are happy working with local elites and unelected officials, but much less adept at dealing with civil society. That can be effective while favoured partners remain in power, but authoritarian regimes have a tiresome habit of collapsing. Shifting political winds have already scuppered large investments abroad, and will continue to do so.

China will struggle to convince much of the Asian public that it has good intentions. It is viewed quite favourably in Pakistan, Malaysia and Indonesia, according to the Pew Research Survey on global attitudes; but views are far more mixed in the Philippines and India, and overwhelmingly negative in Vietnam and Japan.[3] Anecdotal evidence in Mongolia, Kazakhstan, Kyrgyzstan and the Russian Far East suggests that the fear of Chinese "invasion", fed by historical memory and years of anti-Chinese Soviet propaganda, retains popular currency. Although these countries will happily accept Chinese investment, this fear will also breed resentment.

The reality is that China will become a much more visible presence across Asia in the coming decades. As Chinese firms expand into new markets and millions of Chinese people move overseas to find work, Beijing will find itself inexorably pulled into the messy reality of foreign politics. This first became apparent in the spring of 2011—not in Asia, but in northern Africa. As turmoil engulfed Libya, China evacuated more than 35,000 Chinese workers by plane, ship, bus and truck. It voted in the UN Security Council to sanction Muammar Gaddafi for mistreatment of his people, and agreed to a second resolution that eventually led to NATO-sponsored regime change.[4]

Beijing's uncharacteristic intervention in a foreign state reflected a hard-nosed reality: seventy-five Chinese companies had invested an estimated US$18.8 billion in Libya, and it had to protect both its citizens and its assets. Overthrowing another country's authoritarian leader is not something that China's own authoritarian leaders take lightly, for obvious reasons; but the events in Libya gave them no choice. It is not hard to envisage a crisis in Asia requiring a similar intervention. China's greater assertiveness is not just an ideological shift as it looks to restore national glory: it is a necessary consequence of its expanding commercial and strategic reach.

China already has an estimated 5 million nationals living overseas, but the demands on the Chinese state will only grow as the Belt and Road Initiative progresses. Pakistan, where

China has pledged to fund enormous investments, is the biggest security risk. "Chinese citizens are being killed, and more will be killed," warns David Sedney, a former US deputy assistant secretary of defence for Afghanistan, Pakistan and Central Asia, who advises the Chinese government on its strategy in that region.[5] Islamabad is training a special security division with thousands of guards to protect Chinese nationals working on the "China–Pakistan Economic Corridor", one of the biggest projects connected to the Silk Road Economic Belt. But Beijing fears insecurity will spill over the border into its own restive region of Xinjiang. In Pakistan, as in neighbouring Afghanistan, China has found it impossible to separate economic and security issues.

President Xi Jinping has promised to use the power of the Chinese state, including military force, to keep Chinese citizens safe. At the 18th Party Congress in 2012, Xi's first as Communist Party chief, "protecting nationals abroad" was finally made a political priority.[6] A defence white paper published in 2013 stated for the first time that the People's Liberation Army must provide security for Chinese interests abroad. Even before it was national policy, Chinese forces led a hunt in 2011 for the killers of thirteen Chinese sailors in the Golden Triangle—the meeting point of Myanmar, Laos and Thailand—even though the murders were committed outside China. The investigation resulted in the extradition, prosecution and execution of a Burmese gang leader in Yunnan, and in Chinese patrols down the Mekong River.[7]

China's economic diplomacy is premised on the promise of mutual benefit—yet this policy will come under strain wherever state power breaks down and Chinese interests are threatened. If a massacre of Chinese workers occurred in Pakistan or elsewhere, Beijing would feel enormous domestic pressure to intervene directly. In the past, the Ministry of Foreign Affairs has even received calcium tablets in the post sent by nationalist critics lamenting its failure to show more backbone.[8] President Xi's shift to a proactive foreign policy is designed to project China as a great power, but it is also a reaction to the reality of what being a great power entails.

History shows that "trade follows the flag", but also that "the flag follows trade": British India was a trading colony under the auspices of the East India Company until the violent uprising of 1857 persuaded the Crown to impose direct rule.[9] No one is predicting a Chinese Raj, but Beijing's resolve to defend both its core national interests and the rights of its citizens means that non-interference in foreign affairs is no longer an option. As economic realities push China towards great-power status, China will have to project more political and military muscle across Asia—whether it wants to or not.

亚洲梦

In 1890, Kaiser Wilhelm II of Germany launched a bellicose "New Course" in foreign affairs that culminated in the carnage of World War I. An Italian cartoon in 1915 depicted the gluttonous emperor, moustachioed and eagle-helmeted, attempting to eat the world.[10] How long before Xi Jinping's face appears on similar cartoons? China has not fought a war since 1979, but it has become fashionable to draw comparisons between its rise and that of imperial Germany.[11] These comparisons are unfair:

China's militarism has barely extended beyond building a base or two in the South China Sea. Yet the spectre of a more interventionist China, willing to throw around its economic and military weight, terrifies its neighbours.

China, its leaders never tire of declaring, is a peaceful country. But their attempt to look and talk tough does nothing to dispel anxiety about the "China threat". Take the goose-stepping display of military power that brought Beijing to a standstill on 3 September 2015. "We Chinese love peace," President Xi Jinping told hundreds of millions of people viewing across the world. "No matter how much stronger it may become, China will never seek hegemony or expansion."[12] Yet the 12,000 troops and deadly arsenal of intercontinental ballistic missiles, advanced bomber tanks and assault helicopters told another story. This was not the only occasion on which China has projected mixed messages about its military intentions. Speaking in Paris in 2014, President Xi quoted Napoleon's old adage about China being a sleeping lion which, when it wakes, "will shake the world". "The lion has already awakened," Xi roared. "But it is a peaceful, amiable and civilized lion."[13]

Soviet-style military displays and Napoleonic invocations about waking lions hardly inspire faith in China's intrinsically peaceful nature. But the truth is that China views itself as the threatened party, not as the threat. This is not as ridiculous as it sounds: Asia's security system is dominated and sponsored by the US, which maintains several regional defence agreements and formal alliances with Japan, South Korea, the Philippines, Thailand and Australia. These are supplemented by a security partnership with Singapore and by evolving relationships with Vietnam, Malaysia, Indonesia and India. So China's sense of insecurity is not paranoia: it really *is* ringed by US allies.

Quite rationally, China is determined to dilute the US's grip on security in its neighbourhood. At an international security conference in Shanghai in 2014, President Xi unveiled a new "Asian security concept", essentially calling for Asian security to be left to Asians.[14] Everyone knew what he really meant: the role of the US must diminish. The problem for China is that few Asian countries want the US to leave the region, as they view its presence as vital for maintaining the balance of power. In fact, their biggest complaint about the Obama administration was its reluctance to make good on the "pivot to Asia" (subsequently re-branded a "rebalance"). "We want a strong US to take the lead," one Asian ambassador told me in an interview in Washington, DC.[15]

This was not a hawkish call for a more assertive US policy to contain a rising China—quite the opposite. Asian diplomats are frustrated by the US reluctance to address the strategic implications of China's rise: they lament Washington's refusal to acknowledge China as a great power that must be accommodated within the regional security structure. They support the vital role played by the US in maintaining regional peace and stability, but are keenly aware of geopolitical reality—that China lies at the heart of Asia, which it regards as its sphere of influence. "Currently there can be no happy outcome," said the ambassador. "Keeping the status quo is not an option as China's growing power means relative strengths in the region have changed."

The US affirms that its China policy is about engagement, not containment. But it continues to regard China as a strategic rival to be kept in its place. After announcing the "pivot to Asia", the Obama administration bolstered military relationships with its regional allies, favoured Southeast Asian countries in maritime disputes with China, and lobbied its friends against joining Chinese initiatives such as the Asian Infrastructure Investment Bank. Sceptical observers in Beijing viewed the Trans-Pacific Partnership trade and investment deal, which included twelve Pacific Rim countries but not China, as just another attempt by the US to undercut its legitimate ambitions as a great power—even if the official line on both sides was that China would be free to join at a later date. This is not a situation that can continue indefinitely.

Biannual summits between China and the US have made moderate progress on small issues, but have studiously avoided one of the great strategic questions of our time: how can China grow within a security system dominated and sponsored by Washington? The US ignores the issue because it does not accept China as an equal power. China has no desire to negotiate, because it believes it is making slow but steady progress towards supplanting the US. It will keep flexing its economic muscles and stick to its policy of incrementally gaining control over the South China Sea. Yet future leaders must address this issue before friction turns into conflict.

Among Washington hawks, there is a clamour for a new grand strategy to contain Beijing. One view is that that the US must do all it can to prevent China from replacing it as the dominant power in Asia, which means the US military must intensify its naval and air presence in the South China

Sea.[16] This approach would only bring the threat of war closer. Saner voices within the foreign policy community believe the US needs to reach a tacit accommodation with Beijing. That means finding a way to acknowledge China's global ambition and yielding to it greater freedom of action in its own region, while keeping the US's own strategic presence intact.

The latter strategy is in tune with the prevalent view across much of Asia. China's economic pull is real, but not potent enough to convince its neighbours that they are better off without a US security presence. Most Asian countries are united in their support of the US as a counterbalance to Chinese power. Yet they will oppose any US policy that could anger their giant neighbour, placing them in a precarious position: no one wants to be the meat in a US–China sandwich. They acknowledge that China, an economic superpower with an increasingly powerful military, is unwilling to play second fiddle to anyone in its own backyard, and it is foolhardy to seek to contain it.

It is hardly my place to prescribe how the US and China should avoid war. I do believe, however, that the US and its regional allies must accept China's determination to carve out its own sphere of influence across Asia. And having accepted the inevitability of China's rise, the safest course of action is to accommodate it within a remodelled regional security structure. Whether China would accept such an accommodation is another question, and much will depend on the relative strengths of both sides in the decades to come. But as China pursues its vision of national rejuvenation, something has to give. If it does not, the "Chinese Dream" could tragically morph into an Asian nightmare.

NOTES

I travelled to a dozen countries in the course of my research, spending weeks interviewing, talking, listening and looking. All the on-the-ground reporting was carried out in 2014–15, except for a visit to Myanmar in early 2013. I spoke to government ministers, officials, diplomats, consultants, businesspeople, journalists, academics, researchers, NGO workers, traders and, yes, taxi drivers. Most of these conversations were on the record, but some people asked not to be named. As a journalist at heart, I have quoted people where appropriate, but I have not attempted to credit all my sources.

The notes that follow are not designed to be exhaustive. I read thousands of books, reports and articles in the course of my research, both in English and in Chinese, and I do not believe readers would find it useful if I listed all of them. Instead I have drawn attention to the most important sources, especially books and significant articles, and given credit where it is due. I have also done my best to source all policy speeches and data.

Much of the raw material for the book can be found in articles published for the clients of Gavekal Research and Gavekal Dragonomics in 2013–16. I have directed readers' attention to the original articles when it seemed useful to do so.

Introduction

1   A version of this introduction originally appeared in Miller, "The Chinese dream: the empire strikes back" in *China Economic Quarterly*, Gavekal Dragonomics, November 2015.

2   I have taken this potted history from many sources. One particularly useful account for the earlier history is Odd Arne Westad's *Restless Empire: China and the World Since 1750*, Bodley Head, London (2012).

3 Alexander V Avakov, *Two Thousand Years of Economic Statistics, Years 1-2012: Population, GDP at PPP, and GDP Per Capita*, Algora, New York (2015).

4 Angus Maddison, *Monitoring the World Economy*, OECD Development Centre, Paris (1995), http://www.ggdc.net/maddison/Monitoring.shtml.

5 See, eg, "Backgrounder: China's WWII contributions in figures", Xinhua, 3 September 2015, http://news.xinhuanet.com/english/2015-09/03/c_134582291.htm.

6 For an excellent account of how historical memory has helped construct national identity, see Zheng Wang, *Never Forget National Humiliation: Historical Memory in Chinese Politics and Foreign Relations*, Columbia, New York (2012).

7 http://www.chinatoday.com/general/china-flag-emblem-anthem.htm.

8 Xi Jinping made his first public comments on the "Chinese Dream", also translated as "China Dream", when he visited "The Road Toward Renewal" exhibition at the National Museum of China on 29 November 2012 almost immediately after coming to power. See "Xi pledges 'great renewal of Chinese nation'", http://news.xinhuanet.com/english/china/2012-11/29/c_132008231.htm. For a similar report in Chinese, see "Xi Jinping: chengqian qihou jiwang kailai jixu chaozhe zhonghua minzu weida fuxing mubiao fenyong qianjin", *People's Daily*, 29 November 2012, http://politics.people.com.cn/n/2012/1129/c1024-19744072.html.

9 The chief source for the following paragraphs is Orville Schell and John Delury, *Wealth and Power: China's Long March to the Twenty-First Century*, Little, Brown, London (2013).

10 Xi made this speech while inspecting a military base in Guangzhou. The "Chinese Dream" of national rejuvenation, he said, was also a "dream of a strong country and a strong military". See "Bixu jianchi fuguo he qiangjun xiang tongyi nuli jianshe gonggu guofang he qiangda jundui", *China Youth Daily*, 13 December 2012, http://zqb.cyol.com/html/2012-12/13/nw.D110000zgqnb_20121213_1-01.htm.

11 See Miller, "Goose stepping into isolation", Gavekal Research, 3 September 2015.

12 Off-the-record author interview in Beijing, 29 June 2015.
13 February 2012. The concept of *xinxing daguo guanxi* was elaborated in a July 2012 essay by Cui Tiankai, then vice foreign minister, and Pang Hanzhao: "Xinshiqi zhongguo waijiao quanjuzhong de zhong-mei guanxi" in *China International Strategy Review 2012*, Beijing University Institute of International Relations.
14 See Xi Jinping's speech "Rang mingyun gongtongti yishi zai zhoubian guojia luodi shenggen ("Let the sense of community of common destiny take deep root in neighbouring countries") at a Party work conference on regional diplomacy on 25 October 2013: http://news.xinhuanet.com/politics/2013-10/25/c_117878944.htm. *Zhoubian waijiao* is officially translated as "peripheral diplomacy", but I prefer "neighbourhood diplomacy" or "regional diplomacy".
15 See David Shambaugh, "The illusion of Chinese power" in http://nationalinterest.org/feature/the-illusion-chinese-power-10739, and *China Goes Global: The Partial Power*, Oxford University Press, New York (2013).
16 "Central Conference on work relating to foreign affairs was held in Beijing", 29 November 2014, http://www.fmprc.gov.cn/mfa_eng/zxxx_662805/t1215680.shtml.
17 The CCP has long celebrated its role in ending a "century of humiliation" (*bainian guochi*) to help legitimize its rule.
18 The Chinese characters spell *yazhou meng*, which means "Asia(n) Dream". I have used the simplified characters introduced by the PRC government in the 1950s. The *meng* character on the front cover uses the traditional, unsimplified character for "dream".
19 http://databank.worldbank.org/data/download/GDP.pdf.
20 I believe I was one of the first to suggest this. See "A Chinese Bretton Woods", Gavekal Research, 12 June 2014. I have since moderated my opinion: see "A boring infrastructure bank", Gavekal Research, 30 June 2016.
21 The term "China's California" is used by Thant Myint-U in "Asia's new great game", *Foreign Policy*, 12 September 2011, http://foreignpolicy.com/2011/09/12/asias-new-great-game/. For a fuller account, see his *Where China Meets India: Burma and the New Crossroads of Asia*, Faber & Faber, London (2011).

22 For a useful roundup of Xi's speeches on the "Chinese Dream" in which he talks about China becoming "wealthy and strong" (*fuqiang*), see "Xi Jinping zongshuji 15 pian jianghua xitong chanshu 'zhongguo meng'", *People's Daily Online*, 19 June 2013, http://theory.people.com.cn/n/2013/0619/c40531-21891787.html.

23 See "Full text: Xi's speech at commemoration of 70th anniversary of war victory", *China Daily*, 3 September 2015, http://www.chinadaily.com.cn/world/2015victoryanniv/2015-09/03/content_21783362.htm.

24 *The China Dream: Great Power Thinking and Strategic Posture in the Post-America Era*, CN Times Books (2015), p 100. The book was published in Chinese in 2010.

25 In the world of international relations, "realists" believe that geopolitics is a Darwinian survival of the fittest: great power politics entails competition, conflict and war. John J Mearsheimer, one of the world's leading "realist" thinkers, says that "survival is the primary goal of great powers". See JJ Mearsheimer, *The Tragedy of Great Power Politics*, Norton, New York (2001).

1 "One Belt, One Road"

1 I was told this by my neighbours in a small village in Beijing's rural Huairou County, where I rent a cottage in the shadow of the Great Wall. Ignoring the edict not to burn any naked flames, I fired up the barbeque in any case.

2 "Chinese president proposes Asia-Pacific dream", http://www.2014apecceosummit.com/apec/news1/1721.jhtml.

3 "Jianchi zhengque yi li guan jiji fahui zeren daguo zuoyong", *People's Daily*, 10 September 2013, http://opinion.people.com.cn/n/2013/0910/c1003-22862978.html.

4 "Deng Xiaoping's '24-Character Strategy'", http://www.globalsecurity.org/military/world/china/24-character.htm.

5 See, eg, "Hurt the feelings of the Chinese people", *China Digital Times*, http://chinadigitaltimes.net/space/Hurt_the_feelings_of_the_Chinese_people.

6   I am indebted to Christopher Johnson for his excellent summary of China's evolving foreign policy in "President Xi Jinping's 'Belt and Road' Initiative: A practical assessment of the Chinese Communist Party's roadmap for China's global resurgence", CSIS, March 2016.

7   http://news.xinhuanet.com/english2010/china/2011-09/06/c_131102329.htm.

8   http://www.fmprc.gov.cn/mfa_eng/wjb_663304/wjbz_663308/activities_663312/t1093870.shtml.

9   "Foreign Minister Wang Yi meets the press", 8 March 2014, http://www.fmprc.gov.cn/mfa_eng/wjb_663304/wjbz_663308/2461_663310/t1135385.shtml.

10 http://www.fmprc.gov.cn/mfa_eng/zxxx_662805/t1215680.shtml.

11 "China's Xi demands accelerated FTA strategy", Xinhua, 6 December 2014, http://news.xinhuanet.com/english/china/2014-12/06/c_133837015.htm.

12 "Vision and actions on jointly building Silk Road Economic Belt and 21st-Century Maritime Silk Road", 28 March 2015, http://www.fmprc.gov.cn/mfa_eng/zxxx_662805/t1249618.shtml.

13 "President Xi Jinping delivers important speech and proposes to build a Silk Road Economic Belt with Central Asian countries", 7 September 2013, http://www.fmprc.gov.cn/mfa_eng/topics_665678/xjpfwzysiesgjtfhshzzfh_665686/t1076334.shtml.

14 2 October 2013, http://www.asean-china-center.org/english/2013-10/03/c_133062675.htm.

15 "Vision and actions on jointly building Silk Road Economic Belt and 21st-Century Maritime Silk Road", op cit.

16 Ibid.

17 Ibid.

18 "Jointly build the 21st Century Maritime Silk Road by deepening mutual trust and enhancing connectivity", 29 March 2015, http://www.fmprc.gov.cn/mfa_eng/zxxx_662805/t1249761.shtml.

19 Author interview with Christopher Johnson, Washington, DC, 30 September 2015.

20 Ibid.

21 The full list of members can be found on the AIIB website: http://euweb.aiib.org/html/aboutus/introduction/Membership/?show=0.

22 This is how ADB officials referred to it on the sidelines of their annual meeting in May 2014, held in Astana, which I attended.

23 See Miller, "A Chinese Bretton Woods", op cit.

24 "ADB head will be 'very happy' to work with China's Asia infrastructure bank", Reuters, 2 May 2014, http://www.reuters.com/article/kazakhstan-adb-banking-idUSL6N0NO1ZG20140502.

25 Here is the salient passage: "The Chinese government will integrate its domestic resources to provide stronger policy support for the Initiative. It will facilitate the establishment of the Asian Infrastructure Investment Bank." See "Vision and actions on jointly building Silk Road Economic Belt and 21st-Century Maritime Silk Road", op cit.

26 See Miller, "A petty and short-sighted hissy fit", Gavekal Research, 17 March 2015.

27 Ahead of the ceremony, *China Daily* printed a version of the speech Lou later gave at the ceremony: "Inclusive AIIB can make a difference", 25 June 2015, http://usa.chinadaily.com.cn/epaper/2015-06/25/content_21101260.htm.

28 The "Agreement on the New Development Bank" is available at http://brics.itamaraty.gov.br/images/pdf/BRICSNDB.doc.

29 "China-led Development Bank AIIB Will be Lean, Clean and Green, Says its President", *Wall Street Journal*, 22 January 2016, http://www.wsj.com/articles/china-led-development-bank-will-be-lean-clean-and-green-says-head-1453479933.

30 "What is the Asian Infrastructure Investment Bank?", http://euweb.aiib.org/html/aboutus/AIIB/?show=0.

31 "AIIB's First Annual Meeting of its Board of Governors held in Beijing: Governors note progress during the Bank's first 6 months of operation", http://www.aiib.org/html/2016/NEWS_0625/123.html.

32 See Miller, "A boring infrastructure bank", op cit.

33 The analysis of the lending capabilities of AIIB and China's policy banks over the next three pages relies heavily on the work of my colleague Arthur Kroeber. See "Financing China's global dreams", *China Economic Quarterly*, Gavekal Dragonomics, November 2015.

34 See Henry Sanderson and Michael Forsythe, *China's Superbank:*

Debt, Oil and Influence—How China Development Bank is Rewriting the Rules of Finance, Wiley, Singapore (2013).

35 *The Global Competitiveness Report 2015-16*, "Competiveness rankings", World Economic Forum, http://reports.weforum.org/global-competitiveness-report-2015-2016/competitiveness-rankings/.

36 *Infrastructure for a Seamless Asia*, Asian Development Bank Institute, Tokyo (2009), http://adb.org/sites/default/files/pub/2009/2009.08.31.book.infrastructure.seamless.asia.pdf.

37 Some of this section originally appeared in Miller, "Asia's infrastructure arms race", Gavekal Dragonomics, 30 June 2015.

38 See Naohiro Kitano and Yukinori Harada, *Estimating China's Foreign Aid 2001–2003*, JICA Research Institute, June 2014, https://jica-ri.jica.go.jp/publication/assets/JICA-RI_WP_No.78_2014.pdf. Further information can be found in the *China's Foreign Aid (2014)* white paper, http://news.xinhuanet.com/english/china/2014-07/10/c_133474011.htm. See also Miller, "Asia's infrastructure arms race", op cit.

39 "Cabinet decision on the Development Cooperation Charter", 10 February 2015, http://www.mofa.go.jp/files/000067701.pdf.

40 "Stronger ties with ASEAN vital to Japan's security: ODA paper", *Kyodo*, 13 March 2015, http://www.japantimes.co.jp/news/2015/03/13/national/stronger-ties-asean-vital-japans-security-oda-paper/#.VYEsdPmqpBd.

41 "Japan unveils $110 billion plan to fund Asia infrastructure, eye on AIIB", Reuters, 21 May 2015, http://www.reuters.com/article/2015/05/21/us-japan-asia-investment-idUSKBN0O617G20150521.

42 See "Strategy and Action Plan for the Greater Mekong Subregion Southern Economic Corridor", ADB (2010), http://www.adb.org/sites/default/files/publication/28006/gms-action-plan-south.pdf.

43 "Don't penalize us for using AIIB, says Cambodian minister", *Nikkei Asian Review*, 21 May 2015, http://asia.nikkei.com/Features/The-Future-of-Asia-2015/Don-t-penalize-us-for-using-AIIB-says-Cambodian-minister.

44 Author interview in Phnom Penh, 22 May 2015.

45 See Andrew Batson, "Can the New Silk Road revive China's exports?", Gavekal Dragonomics, 17 February 2015.

46 See Tom Miller, "Investing along the New Silk Road", Gavekal Dragonomics, 4 March 2015.

47 "Tongchou xietiao you xu tuijin 'yidai yilu' jianshe de difang gang'an xianjie gongzuo chengxiao chu", http://www.sdpc.gov.cn/gzdt/201511/t20151120_759153.html.

48 Neither the "port alliance" not the investment in Malacca is listed by NDRC. The "port alliance" is between the Chinese ports of Dalian, Taicang, Shanghai, Ningbo, Fuzhou, Xiamen, Guangzhou, Shenzhen, Haikou and Qinzhou and the Malaysian ports of Bintulu, Johor, Kuantan, Malacca, Penang and Port Klang. See "China, Malaysia tout new 'port alliance' to reduce customs bottlenecks and boost trade", *South China Morning Post*, 9 April 2016, http://www.scmp.com/news/asia/southeast-asia/article/1934839/china-malaysia-tout-new-port-alliance-reduce-customs.

49 "2015 nian yu 'yidai yilu' xiangguan guojia jingmao hezuo qingkuang", 21 January 2016, http://www.mofcom.gov.cn/article/tongjiziliao/dgzz/201601/20160101239881.shtml.

50 Author interview in Beijing, 29 May 2015.

51 Author interview, 19 May 2015.

2 Marching West

1 The Khan Shatyr Entertainment Centre, which translates as "the tent of the khan", was designed by London-based Foster + Partners. See http://www.fosterandpartners.com/projects/khan-shatyr-entertainment-centre/.

2 The murky nature of "ownership", together with changing annual production outputs, makes it impossible to come up with a definitive figure. But I heard "one-quarter" from several well-informed sources in 2014–15, and it is my own best estimate.

3 "President Xi Jinping delivers important speech and proposes to build a Silk Road Economic Belt with Central Asian countries", 7 September 2013, http://www.fmprc.gov.cn/mfa_eng/topics_665678/xjpfwzysiesgjtfhshzzfh_665686/t1076334.shtml.

4   Two useful sources on the history of the region are Westad's *Restless Empire*, op cit, and Michael Clarke, "The 'centrality' of Central Asia in world history, 1700–2008: From pivot to periphery and back again?" in Mackerras and Clarke (eds), *China, Xinjiang and Central Asia: History, Transition and Crossborder Interaction into the 21st Century*, Routledge, London and New York (2009).

5   China regularly refers to the "three evils", though this expression is not actually used in the charter itself. See http://www.soi.org.br/upload/34b4f65564132e7702726ee2521839c790b895453b-6de5509cf1f997e9e50405.pdf.

6   See "Chinese Premier Wen Jiabao's speech at opening session of second China–Eurasia Expo", Xinhua, 3 September 2012, http://en.people.cn/90883/7933186.html.

7   "Wang Jisi: 'xijin', zhongguo diyuan zhanlue de zai pingheng", *Global Times*, 17 October 2012, http://opinion.huanqiu.com/opinion_world/2012-10/3193760.html.

8   This argument has been forcefully made by Rafaello Pantucci and Alexandros Peterson in a number of articles, notably in "China's Inadvertent Empire", *The National Interest*, November–December 2012, http://nationalinterest.org/print/article/chinas-inadvertent-empire-7615. Pantucci and Peterson also co-founded an excellent blog: www.chinaincentralasia.com. Tragically, Peterson was killed in January 2014 in an attack on a restaurant in Kabul, where he was working at the American University.

9   See, eg, "Hundreds face trial over deadly Xinjiang riots", *The Guardian*, 24 August 2009, https://www.theguardian.com/world/2009/aug/24/china-trials-xinjiang-riots.

10 A version of the next few paragraphs originally appeared as a book review I wrote for *The Spectator*. See "China's repressive policy towards its Islamic fringe has badly backfired", 1 August 2015, http://www.spectator.co.uk/2015/08/chinas-repressive-policy-towards-its-islamic-fringe-has-badly-backfired/. Much of the information in this section comes from Nick Holdstock, *China's Forgotten People: Xinjiang, Terror and the Chinese State*, IB Tauris, London (2015). The body count is my own, taken from adding up the reported deaths that year.

11 The report can be seen here: https://na-production.s3.amazonaws.com/documents/ISIS-Files.pdf.

12 See http://english.alarabiya.net/en/perspective/analysis/2016/03/02/China-s-proxy-war-in-Syria-Revealing-the-role-of-Uighur-fighters-.html.

13 See, eg, "Chinese embassy in Kyrgyzstan hit by suicide bomb attack", *Financial Times*, 30 August 2016, https://www.ft.com/content/23243e7e-6e82-11e6-9ac1-1055824ca907#axzz4JMS4K4O7.

14 "Beijing Vows to Strike Back After Kyrgyzstan Attack", *China Digital Times*, 7 September 2016, http://chinadigitaltimes.net/2016/09/beijing-vows-strike-back-kyrgyzstan-embassy-attack/.

15 Khorgos has several different names and pronunciations, depending on who you are talking to and your preferred language. In Kazakh and Uyghur, it is pronounced and written *Qorgas*; in Russian, *Khorgos*; in Chinese, *huo'erguosi*. *Horgos* is also heard.

16 See, eg, "The Silk Railroad of China–Europe Trade", Bloomberg, 21 December 2012, http://www.bloomberg.com/news/articles/2012-12-20/the-silk-railroad-of-china-europe-trade, and "China's bold gambit to cement trade with Europe—along the ancient Silk Road", *Los Angeles Times*, 1 May 2016, http://www.latimes.com/world/asia/la-fg-china-silk-road-20160501-story.html.

17 "DHL opens China–Turkey intermodal corridor", *Lloyd's Loading List*, 18 December 2015, http://www.lloydsloadinglist.com/freight-directory/news/DHL-opens-China-Turkey-intermodal-corridor/65139.htm#.WAYnwuArJN0.

18 See "Carec 2020: A strategic framework for the Central Asia Regional Economic Cooperation 2011-2020", Asian Development Bank (2012), http://www.carecprogram.org/uploads/docs/CAREC-Publications/2012/CAREC-2020-Strategic-Framework.pdf.

19 See http://www.carecprogram.org/index.php?page=ci-knowledge-sharing.

20 Off-the-record author interview in Beijing, 21 April 2015.

21 Author interview, 2 September 2014.

22 All interviews in and around Kashgar took place on 23–24 August 2014.

23 Isaac Stone Fish, "China's hottest cities and Kashgar", *Newsweek*, 25 September 2010, http://europe.newsweek.com/chinas-hottest-cities-and-kashgar-72333?rm=eu.

24 Much of this section originally appeared as "Blood and bazaars on the New Silk Road", Gavekal Dragonomics, 22 October 2014.

25 "Zhe shi shangtian cigei dangdai zhongguoren zui fenghou de liwu." On their website (http://www.chinaincentralasia.com), Pantucci and Peterson translate General Liu's comments as "Central Asia is the thickest piece of cake given to the modern Chinese by the heavens". This is a colourful but, in my opinion, inaccurate translation.

26 My chief source for the section on energy in Central Asia is Marlene Laruelle and Sebastien Peyrouse, *The Chinese Question in Central Asia: Domestic Order, Social Change, and the Chinese Factor*, Columbia, New York (2012). I also used their book extensively as background for the chapter. Another useful account is Alexander Cooley, *Great Games, Local Rules: The New Great Power Contest in Central Asia*, Oxford University Press, New York (2012).

27 My driver's mixed loyalties, both to his Kyrgyz ethnicity and to the Chinese Party-state, illustrated the complex nature of personal and national identity in this part of China.

28 It's a cliché, but the quality and reach of China's hard infrastructure really is extraordinary. I had no problem chatting to friends in Beijing from the mountainous border of Xinjiang, but I still struggle to get a mobile signal in central Oxford.

29 Drug smuggling is rife across China's western borders, both in Xinjiang and Yunnan. The biggest source of opiates in China is the "Golden Crescent" region: Afghanistan, Pakistan and Iran. Heroin is trafficked into Xinjiang via Pakistan, Tajikistan, Kazakhstan and Kyrgyzstan, including over the Irkeshtam Pass. I do not imagine, however, that many drugs are trafficked in the opposite direction by notebook-toting Englishmen. See Murray Scot Tanner, "China confronts Afghan drugs: Law enforcement views of 'The Golden Crescent'", CNA, March 2011, https://wikileaks.org/gifiles/attach/134/134547_China%20Heroin.pdf.

30 All interviews in Osh took place on 26 August 2014.

31 Quoted in Roman Muzalevsky, "China–Kyrgyzstan–Uzbekistan railway scheme: Fears, hopes and prospects", *Eurasia Daily Monitor*, Jamestown Foundation, 30 May 2012.

32 Author interview in Almaty, 6 May 2014.

33 Interview with Deirdre Tynan, Central Asia Project Director at International Crisis Group, in Bishkek, 28 August 2014.

34 See Chris Rickleton, "Kyrgyzstan: Racketeers taking aim at Chinese entrepreneurs", 10 January 2014, http://www.eurasianet.org/node/67928. EurasiaNet, financed by George Soros and his Open Society Institute, is an invaluable English-language source on Central Asia.

35 I was thinking here of the interviews with Chinese immigrants in Howard W French, *China's Second Continent: How a Million Migrants are Building a New Empire in Africa*, Knopf, New York (2014).

36 All author interviews in Bishkek took place on 28–29 August 2014.

37 Author interview in Beijing, 20 August 2014.

38 Much of this section originally appeared as "Travels along the New Silk Road: The economics of power", Gavekal Dragonomics, 24 October 2014.

39 Hillary Clinton has talked of Putin's efforts to "re-Sovietize" Eurasia. See "Clinton calls Eurasian integration an effort to 'Re-So-vietize'", Radio Free Europe Radio Liberty, 28 July 2016, http://www.rferl.org/content/clinton-calls-eurasian-integration-ef-fort-to-resovietize/24791921.html.

40 Quoted in Michael Clarke, "Understanding China's Eurasian Pivot", *The Diplomat*, 10 September 2015, http://thediplomat.com/2015/09/understanding-chinas-eurasian-pivot/. I found *The Diplomat* magazine an invaluable source of information for under-standing China's foreign policy across Asia.

41 Author interview in Almaty, 7 May 2014.

42 Author interview, 6 May 2014.

43 "Links to Prosperity: Connectivity, Trade, and Growth in Devel-oping Asia" ADB panel meeting, 4 May 2014.

44 Author interview, 29 August 2014.

45 See http://en.kremlin.ru/events/president/transcripts/49433.

46 "China to build 400km/h train for Russia's high-speed railway",

Russia Today, 6 June 2016, https://www.rt.com/business/345535-china-train-russia-kazan/.

47 See *China's Central Asia Problem*, 27 February 2013. The executive summary is available here: https://www.crisisgroup.org/asia/north-east-asia/china/china-s-central-asia-problem.

48 Quoted in Mira Milosevich, "Russia and China", FAES, 17 September 2014, http://www.fundacionfaes.org/en/analysis/127/rusia_y_china.

3 In the Heat of the Sun

1 The chapter title is inspired by Jiang Wen's classic Beijing film of 1994, set during the Cultural Revolution. See https://en.wikipedia.org/wiki/In_the_Heat_of_the_Sun.

2 Sarongs are called *longyi* in Myanmar.

3 For more on the "Go West" policy, see Miller, *China's Urban Billion: The Story Behind the Biggest Migration in Human History*, Zed, London (2012).

4 "Zhongguo shida jichang", http://baike.baidu.com/view/2144319.htm, and "List of busiest airports by passenger traffic", Wikipedia, https://en.wikipedia.org/wiki/List_of_busiest_airports_by_passenger_traffic#2015_statistics.

5 "Guowuyuan guanyu zhichi yunnan sheng jiakuai jianshe mianxiang xinan kaifang zhongyao qiaotoubao de yijian", 3 November 2011, http://www.gov.cn/zwgk/2011-11/03/content_1985444.htm.

6 Much of this section originally appeared as "No bridgehead too far in China's expanding empire", Gavekal Dragonomics, 7 April 2014, and "In Laos, all roads lead to China", Gavekal Dragonomics, 8 April 2014.

7 My writing on Southeast Asia, including Laos, was informed by Peter Church (ed), *A Short History of South-East Asia*, Wiley, Singapore (2009).

8 See "China ranks largest investor in Laos", Thai PBS, 20 September 2014, http://englishnews.thaipbs.or.th/china-ranks-largest-investor-laos/. Thailand was a slightly bigger trade partner in 2015, according to the CIA's World Factbook, https://www.cia.gov/library/publications/the-world-factbook/fields/2050.html#la.

9 "China plans $31b investment for border zone with Laos", *China Daily*, 20 October 2015, http://europe.chinadaily.com.cn/business/2015-10/20/content_22229728.htm.

10 For more information, see http://www.adb.org/publications/greater-mekong-subregion-economic-cooperation-program-overview.

11 I remember a torturous bus journey from northern Laos to Luang Prabang in August 2011, when we got stuck in the mud. It was long enough for me to get through a good chunk of *Anna Karenina*.

12 All author interviews in Udomxai were conducted on 4–5 March 2014.

13 I personally discovered this in July 2012, when a good friend of mine tragically died in the city.

14 "New Thai, Lao PDR bridge completes 'missing link' in key regional corridor", 11 December 2013, http://www.adb.org/news/new-thai-lao-pdr-bridge-completes-missing-link-key-regional-corridor.

15 7 March 2014.

16 I crosschecked this information with a number of media and government sources. See, eg, "China, Laos sign a railway deal", *China Daily*, 14 November 2015, http://www.chinadaily.com.cn/business/2015-11/14/content_22456633.htm. After so many holdups, however, only time will tell if the railway is actually built.

17 "China, Thailand sign rail, rice, and rubber deals", *The Diplomat*, 4 December 2015, http://thediplomat.com/2015/12/china-thailand-sign-rail-rice-and-rubber-deals/.

18 "Changing Asia: China's high-speed railway diplomacy", *The Strategist*, 2 December 2013, http://www.aspistrategist.org.au/changing-asia-chinas-high-speed-railway-diplomacy/.

19 1 *mu* is less than one-fifth of an acre or 0.06 hectares.

20 TV presenter Simon Reeve visited the resort during its construction for his *Tropic of Cancer* travel documentary, which was aired on BBC in April 2010. A clip can be viewed at https://www.youtube.com/watch?v=28hDqzDGVn0 . A promotional video for the resort is available, in Chinese, at https://www.youtube.com/watch?v=k7OdftN2ksQ.

21 See, eg, "Laos's Chinese gamble", *The Diplomat*, 24 December 2010, http://thediplomat.com/2010/12/laoss-chinese-gamble/.

22 "Dok Ngiew Kham Group pays US$6.3m in taxes", Vietstock, 4 February 2015, http://en.vietstock.com.vn/2015/02/dok-ngiew-kham-group-pays-us63m-intaxes-71-195753.htm.

23 Author interviews at the Golden Triangle Special Economic Zone took place on 6 March 2014.

24 "China to spur investment in Laos", *Vientiane Times*, 10 May 2016, http://www.nationmultimedia.com/aec/China-to-spur-investment-in-Laos-30285603.html.

25 "Leadership changes and upcoming Obama visit give us new opportunities in Laos", CSIS, 4 February 2016, https://www.csis.org/analysis/leadership-changes-and-upcoming-obama-visit-give-us-new-opportunities-laos.

26 I am indebted to John Ciorciari for sharing his insights on China–Cambodian relations. I recommend his paper "A Chinese model for patron–client relations? The Sino-Cambodian partnership", *International Relations of the Asia-Pacific*, 25 November 2014, http://irap.oxfordjournals.org/content/15/2/245.short.

27 See "Asian leaders at regional meeting fail to resolve disputes over South China Sea", *New York Times*, 12 July 2012, http://www.nytimes.com/2012/07/13/world/asia/asian-leaders-fail-to-resolve-disputes-on-south-china-sea-during-asean-summit.html?_r=0.

28 "Cambodia's Hun Sen proves a feisty ASEAN Chair", *Wall Street Journal*, 4 April 2012, http://blogs.wsj.com/indonesiarealtime/2012/04/04/cambodias-hun-sen-proves-a-feisty-asean-chair/.

29 Reliable foreign investment data in Cambodia are hard to come by, but this is my best estimate of the current situation after cross-checking numerous sources. See, eg, "Chinese Investment to 'Bear Fruit Soon', *Khmer Times*, 21 December 2015, http://www.khmertimeskh.com/news/18940/chinese-investment-to----bear-fruit-soon---/.

30 "China's Exim Bank to fund US$1.7b refinery in Cambodia", *Shanghai Daily*, 17 October 2013, http://www.shanghaidaily.com/Business/finance/Chinas-Exim-Bank-to-fund-US/shdaily.shtml.

31 "China to invest $9.6b in Cambodia", *Phnom Penh Post*, 1 January 2013, http://www.phnompenhpost.com/business/china-invest-96b-cambodia.

32 All author interviews in Phnom Penh took place on 21–22 May 2015.

33 IMF, World Economic Outlook Database, http://www.imf.org/ external/pubs/ft/weo/2016/01/weodata/index.aspx.

34 Council for the Development of Cambodia, http://www.cdc-crdb. gov.kh/cdc/aid-management-cambodia.html. Also see Miller, "Asia's infrastructure arms race", op cit.

35 "When it comes to Chinese aid Cambodia should be cautious", AEC News, 18 July 2006, http://aecnewstoday.com/2016/when- it-comes-to-chinese-aid-cambodia-should-be-cautious/#axzz 4FLu6Oy4b.

36 David Roberts, *Political Transition in Cambodia 1991–1999: Power, Elitism and Democracy*, London, Routledge (2001).

37 http://www.transparency.org/cpi2015.

38 "Cambodia's top ten tycoons", Wikileaks Cable Viewer, https:// wikileaks.org/plusd/cables/07PHNOMPENH1034_a.html.

39 "Royal repays $421m loan early", *Phnom Penh Post*, 31 January 2011, http://www.phnompenhpost.com/business/royal-repays- 421m-loan-early.

40 "Cambodian mobile firm CamGSM gets $591 mln funding", *Reuters*, 4 November 2010, http://uk.reuters.com/article/cambodia- camgsm-idUKSGE6A30G020101104.

41 See Simon Denyer, "The push and pull of China's orbit", *Washington Post*, 5 September 2015, http://www.washingtonpost.com/ sf/world/2015/09/05/the-push-and-pull-of-chinas-orbit/. I thoroughly recommend Denyer's "China's Back Yard" series, to which this article belongs.

42 Quoted in John D Ciorciari, "China and Cambodia: Patron and client?", IPC Working Paper Series Number 121, 14 June 2013, p 17.

43 Denyer, "The push and pull of China's orbit", op cit.

44 The fact that he used the Chinese names for the Paracel Islands (*Xisha*) and Spratly Islands (*Nansha*) is telling.

45 Quoted in "As Cambodia approaches China over the US, it should remember Machiavelli's lessons", *The Diplomat*, 11 August 2015, http://thediplomat.com/2015/08/as-cambodia-approaches- china-over-the-us-it-should-remember-machiavellis-lessons/.

46 See, eg, "ASEAN talks fail over South China Sea dispute", Al Jazeera, 13 July 2012, http://www.aljazeera.com/news/asia-pacific/2012/07/201271381350228798.html.

47 Quoted in Ciorciari, "China and Cambodia: Patron and client?", op cit.

48 "Face Off", *Focus ASEAN*, 2 September 2013, http://sea-globe.com/cpp-cnrp-cheam-yeap-son-chhay/.

49 "Half a million Cambodians affected by land grabs: Rights group", Radio Free Asia, 1 April 2014, http://www.rfa.org/english/news/cambodia/land-04012014170055.html.

50 See "Developer, soldiers 'destroyed homes', 28 January 2014, Open Development Cambodia, https://opendevelopmentcambodia.net/news/developer-soldiers-destroyed-29-homes/.

51 Ciorciari, "A Chinese model for patron–client relations? The Sino-Cambodian partnership", op cit.

52 "China, Cambodia boost cooperation during Hun Sen's visit", *The Diplomat*, 21 October 2015, http://thediplomat.com/2015/10/china-cambodia-boost-cooperation-during-hun-sens-visit/.

4 California Dreamin'

1 Burma was officially renamed Myanmar, an old usage, in 1989 by the then-ruling military junta. The UN accepted the change and everyone I met on my trip called it "Myanmar". That is what I use here, though I occasionally use "Burmese" as an adjective.

2 Author interview in Yangon with Dr Wong Yit Fan, then country head of Jardine Matheson. All author interviews in this chapter took place in Yangon and Mandalay in January 2013, unless otherwise stated.

3 According to David Steinberg in *Burma/Myanmar: What Everyone Needs to Know*, Oxford University Press, New York (2010), *paukpaw* is variously translated as "cousins, brotherhood, or a relation based on kinship". The term is only used to describe the relationship between the people of China and Myanmar. For a non-specialist, Steinberg's book is an indispensable guide to the history and politics of Myanmar, and is an important background source for this chapter.

4   See, eg, Sun Yun, "Has China lost Myanmar?", *Foreign Policy*, 15 January 2013, http://foreignpolicy.com/2013/01/15/has-china-lost-myanmar/. I also recommend Sun's articles "China's strategic misjudgement on Myanmar", *Journal of Current Southeast Asian Affairs*, 31, 1 (2012), 73–96 and "Chinese investment in Myanmar: What lies ahead?", Stimson, September 2013.

5   The US "pivot to Asia" was later renamed a "rebalance". Introduced by the Obama administration in 2012, it is a strategic initiative to strengthen the US's security alliances and presence in east Asia. It is widely interpreted in China as part of a "China containment" policy.

6   See Thant Myint-U in "Asia's new great game", op cit.

7   The military junta moved the capital from Yangon (Rangoon) to Naypyidaw, in the centre of Myanmar, in 2006.

8   "Power shift won't hurt Sino-Myanmese ties", 10 November 2014, http://www.globaltimes.cn/content/951736.shtml.

9   "Myanmar to continue friendly policy toward China: Aung San Suu Kyi", Xinhua, 17 November 2015, http://news.xinhuanet.com/english/2015-11/17/c_134826571.htm.

10   Much of this chapter was originally published in Miller as "The Myanmar dilemma", GK Dragonomics, 29 April 2013, and as "Myanmar: Going solo" and "Chinese immigration: On the Road to Mandalay", *China Economic Quarterly*, June 2013.

11   The Myanmar government recognizes 135 distinct ethnic groups. Ethnic Burmans (officially called Bamar) comprise roughly two-thirds of the population. "Burmese" refers to the whole nation, not to any particular ethnic group.

12   For one of the best organized campaigns, see https://www.internationalrivers.org/campaigns/irrawaddy-myitsone-dam-0.

13   Author interview with Sun Yun in Washington DC, 2 October 2015.

14   Since its merger with State Nuclear Power Technology, CPI has been known as State Power Investment Corporation (SPIC). See http://eng.spic.com.cn/.

15   Off-the-record interview in Yangon, 21 January 2013.

16   Author interview in Beijing, 8 January 2013.

17   See, eg, "SPIC donates electrical equipment to Myanmar flood-hit areas", http://eng.spic.com.cn/NewsCenter/CorporateNews/201605/t20160503_262376.htm.

18   "China's intervention in the Myanmar–Kachin peace talks", East–West Center, *Asia Pacific Bulletin*, No 200 (2013).

19   "Myanmar Bombings in Yunnan Killed 4 Chinese", *The Diplomat*, 14 March 2015, http://thediplomat.com/2015/03/its-official-myanmar-bombings-in-yunnan-killed-4-chinese-citizens/.

20   Burmese *longyi* are similar to the lungi worn by men in Bangladesh and many parts of India.

21   "China remains top investor of Myanmar", MITV News, 19 March 2016, http://www.myanmaritv.com/news/foreign-investment-china-remains-top-investor-myanmar.

22   https://www.youtube.com/watch?v=Whd63L0q8Uw.

23   http://www.mofcom.gov.cn/article/i/jyjl/j/201602/20160201258595.shtml.

24   Global Witness, *Jade: Myanmar's 'Big State Secret'*, October 2015, https://www.globalwitness.org/en/campaigns/oil-gas-and-mining/myanmarjade/.

25   "Myanmar section of the Myanmar–China oil pipeline starts trial operation", 4 February 2015, http://www.cnpc.com.cn/en/nr2015/201502/2cea6be48e4e43e7a4bcfa77080d8314.shtml.

26   Much of the section on the BCIM scheme was originally published in Miller as "Beijing eyes the Bay of Bengal", Gavekal Dragonomics, 14 August 2014.

27   See "Guowuyuan guanyu zhichi yunnan sheng jiakuai jianshe mianxiang xinan kaifang zhongyao qiaotoubao de yijain", 3 November 2011, http://www.gov.cn/zwgk/2011-11/03/content_1985444.htm.

28   "China's CITIC wins projects to develop Myanmar economic zone", Reuters, 31 December 2015, http://www.reuters.com/article/myanmar-citic-project-idUSL3N14K1D720151231.

29   Author interview in Kunming, 5 June 2014.

30   Author interview, 4 June 2014.

31   The same slogan was also printed in Chinese and Burmese.

32   See, eg, "Myanmar Kokang rebels deny receiving Chinese weapons", Radio Free Asia, 13 February 2015, http://www.rfa.org/english/news/myanmar/kokang-02132015185129.html.

5 String of Pearls

1   Some of this chapter was originally published in Miller as "Maritime Silk Road or 'String of Pearls'?", Gavekal Dragonomics, 23 April 2015.

2   See, eg, "Chinese submarine docking in Lanka 'inimical' to India's interests: Govt", TNN, 3 November 2014, http://timesofindia.indiatimes.com/india/Chinese-submarine-docking-in-Lanka-inimical-to-Indias-interests-Govt/articleshow/45025487.cms.

3   "China: Submarine docking in Sri Lanka was routine", ECNS, 26 September 2014, http://www.chinadaily.com.cn/china/2014-09/26/content_18668407.htm.

4   http://www.ndtv.com/india-news/navy-alert-to-chinese-nuclear-submarine-threat-in-indian-ocean-767781.

5   My source prefers to remain unnamed.

6   See *India After Gandhi: The History of the World's Largest Democracy*, Pan, London (2007), p 336. I have relied on Guha's history for much of the historical account of Sino-Indian relations.

7   *Energy Futures in Asia*, Booz-Allen & Hamilton (2004), https://books.google.no/books/about/Energy_Futures_in_Asia.html?id=5En2PgAACAAJ&hl=en.

8   "Vision and actions on jointly building Silk Road Economic Belt and 21st-Century Maritime Silk Road", op cit.

9   See, eg, "A silk glove for China's iron fist", Project Syndicate, 4 March 2015, https://www.project-syndicate.org/commentary/china-silk-road-dominance-by-brahma-chellaney-2015-03?barrier=true.

10   Author interview, 27 March 2015.

11   *Samudra Manthan: Sino-Indian Rivalry in the Indo-Pacific*, Carnegie Endowment, New York (2012).

12   Author interview in Singapore, 11 March 2015.

13   Author interview in Colombo, 13 March 2015.

14 "Strive for a win–win outcome on the Indian Ocean", Thinker Blog, 20 March 2015, http://maosiwei.blog.21ccom.net/%3Fp%3D127/. Translation by China Policy (http://policycn.com/).

15 For a history of Gwadar and background on the China–Pakistan relationship, I have drawn on Andrew Small's *The China–Pakistan Axis: Asia's New Geopolitics*, Hurst, London (2015).

16 Robert Kaplan, *Monsoon: The Indian Ocean and the Future of American Power*, Random House, New York (2011), p 71.

17 See, eg, "China readies $46 billion for Pakistan trade route", *Wall Street Journal*, 16 April 2015, http://www.wsj.com/articles/china-to-unveil-billions-of-dollars-in-pakistan-investment-1429214705?mg=id-wsj.

18 See "KKH Re-Alignment: 94% work on the project completed so far, remaining to be completed by Sep 25 this year", *Pamir Times*, 27 June 2015, http://pamirtimes.net/2015/06/27/kkh-re-alignment-94-work-on-the-project-completed-so-far-remaining-to-be-completed-by-sep-25-this-year/.

19 Author interview in Beijing, 19 June 2015.

20 Author interview with Sun Yun in Washington, DC, 2 October 2015.

21 Small, *The China–Pakistan Axis*, op cit, pp 98–99.

22 Quoted in Kaplan, *Monsoon*, op cit, p 78.

23 Author interview, 11 March 2015.

24 "Pakistan, China finalize 8-sub construction plan", *Defense News*, 11 October 2015, http://www.defensenews.com/story/defense/naval/submarines/2015/10/11/pakistan-china-finalize-8-sub-construction-plan/73634218/.

25 Author interview, 11 March 2015.

26 Parts of this section were originally published in Miller as "A Sino-Indian powerhouse?", Gavekal Dragonomics, 8 May 2015.

27 See Xi Jinping's speech, "Towards an Asian century of prosperity", published by *The Hindu*, 17 September 2014, http://www.thehindu.com/opinion/op-ed/towards-an-asian-century-of-prosperity/article6416553.ece.

28 "India's Modi: Border peace needed to realise China ties", Reuters, 18 September 2014, http://www.reuters.com/article/india-china-border-idUSD8N0RB01A20140918.

29 Author interview with Douglas Paal, vice president for studies at the Carnegie Endowment for International Peace, in Washington, DC, 1 October 2015. Paal was informed by sources in Beijing.

30 Author interview, 25 March 2015.

31 See "India and Japan link up to counter China's 'expansionist' mind-set", *Wall Street Journal*, 2 September 2014, http://blogs. wsj.com/chinarealtime/2014/09/02/india-and-japan-link-up-to-counter-chinas-expansionist-mind-set/.

32 https://www.whitehouse.gov/the-press-office/2010/11/08/ remarks-president-joint-session-indian-parliament-new-delhi-india.

33 See "Text of PM's address to the Sri Lankan Parliament", 13 March 2015, http://www.pmindia.gov.in/en/news_updates/text-of-pms-address-to-the-sri-lankan-parliament/.

34 Certainly according to my experience of travelling around India. My opinion was backed up by the South Asia correspondent for a major international newspaper.

35 See "Full text: Report on the work of the government (2015)", 16 March 2015, http://english.gov.cn/archive/publications/ 2015/03/05/content_281475066179954.htm.

36 This is the figure I was given by Sri Lankan investment officials during interviews in March 2015.

37 See "China's Indian Ocean influence at risk in Sri Lanka election", Bloomberg, 6 January 2015, http://www.bloomberg.com/news/ articles/2015-01-06/china-push-for-indian-ocean-influence-at-risk-as-sri-lanka-votes.

38 Author interview, 13 March 2015.

39 Author interview, 13 March 2015.

40 For this high estimate of Sri Lanka's foreign-debt ratio, see http:// time.com/4077757/sri-lanka-china-financial-crisis-ravi-karun-anayake-interview/. But I found a confusing number of different estimates. A prominent Chinese academic gave me a figure of 88%, while a former central banker puts the figure nearer 60% (see http://www.sundaytimes.lk/160221/business-times/foreign-debt-commitments-trigger-macro-financial-risks-183602.html). Using Central Bank of Sri Lanka data, I calculated a *public* external debt-to-GDP ratio of 34% at the end of 2015.

41   Author interview, 13 March 2015.

42   The launch of Colombo Port City can be viewed at https://www.
youtube.com/watch?v=RO79WgJMz_w.

43   See Kalinga Seneviratne, "Sri Lanka turning anew into a geopolitical
battle ground—Analysis", *Eurasia Review*, 30 January 2016, http://
www.eurasiareview.com/30012016-sri-lanka-turning-anew-into-
a-geopolitical-battle-ground-analysis/. A smaller loan was granted
by Exim Bank later that year: see "Cabinet approves fresh loan from
China EXIM Bank", 9 June 2016, http://www.ft.lk/article/546991/
Cabinet-approves-fresh-loan-from-China-EXIM-Bank.

44   "Short of options, Sri Lanka turns back to Beijing's embrace", 10
February 2016, http://www.reuters.com/article/us-sri-lanka-china-
idUSKCN0VJ2RX.

45   "China's Sri Lanka project back on track", *China Daily*, 26 March
2015, http://usa.chinadaily.com.cn/world/2015-03/26/content_
19917566.htm.

46   Author interview, 13 March 2015.

47   Author interview, 14 March 2015.

6 Fiery Waters

1   See "Vietnamese woman dies in self-immolation protest against
China", Associated Press, 23 May 2014, https://www.theguardian.
com/world/2014/may/23/vietnamese-woman-dies-self-immola-
tion-protest-china, and "Vietnamese woman burns self to protest
China: Official", *Thanh Nien News*, 24 May 2014, http://www.
thanhniennews.com/society/vietnamese-woman-burns-self-to-
protest-china-official-26601.html.

2   See, eg, "At least 21 dead in Vietnam anti-China protests over oil
rig", *The Guardian*, 15 May 2014, https://www.theguardian.com/
world/2014/may/15/vietnam-anti-china-protests-oil-rig-dead-
injured.

3   See, eg, "China's secret weapon on disputed island: Beer and
badminton", Tea Leaf Nation, 8 Match 2016, http://foreignpolicy.
com/2016/03/08/china-woody-island-sansha-paracels-south-
china-sea-dispute-secret-weapon-beer-badminton/.

4   "Pacom chief: China's land reclamation has broad consequences", *DoD News*, 24 July 2015, http://www.defense.gov/News-Article-View/Article/612689.

5   An ocean of ink has been spilled on the South China Sea in recent years, but by far the most informative single source is CSIS's Asia Maritime Transparency Initiative. Its website (https://amti.csis.org/) features the latest news, in-depth articles, satellite photos, diagrams and an "island tracker".

6   See Fu Ying's comments about the "need for defence capacities", in "US militarizing South China Sea: Spokesperson", Xinhua, 4 March 2016, http://news.xinhuanet.com/english/2016-03/04/c_135155264.htm.

7   "US expects 'very serious' talks with China after missile reports", Reuters, 17 February 2016, http://uk.reuters.com/article/uk-south-chinasea-china-missiles-idUKKCN0VP2V6.

8   See, eg, "Philippine's Aquino revives comparison between China and Nazi Germany", Reuters, 3 June 2015, http://www.reuters.com/article/us-japan-philippines-idUSKBN0OJ0OY20150603.

9   Robert Kaplan, *Asia's Cauldron: The South China Sea and the End of a Stable Pacific*, Random House, New York (2014), p 15.

10 See, eg, this foreign ministry statement: "Set aside dispute and pursue joint development", http://www.fmprc.gov.cn/mfa_eng/ziliao_665539/3602_665543/3604_665547/t18023.shtml.

11 See Bill Hayton, *South China Sea: The Struggle for Power in Asia*, Yale, London (2014), p 26. I have relied on Hayton's account for much of the historical background to China's claims in the South China Sea.

12 Quoted in ibid.

13 Quoted in ibid.

14 The 1947 map is reproduced in a US Department of State paper called "China: Maritime claims in the South China Sea", part of its *Limits in the Seas* series. See http://www.state.gov/documents/organization/234936.pdf.

15 The letter which accompanies the map was addressed to Ban Ki-Moon, secretary-general of the UN. Both can be seen here: http://www.un.org/depts/los/clcs_new/submissions_files/vnm37_09/chn_2009re_vnm.pdf.

16 See OA Westad, "Saying boo to bullyboy", *China Economic Quarterly*, June 2013.

17 "US takes a tougher tone with China", *Washington Post*, 30 July 2010, http://www.washingtonpost.com/wp-dyn/content/article/2010/07/29/AR2010072906416.html.

18 "China paper warns of 'sound of cannons' in sea dispute", Reuters, http://www.reuters.com/article/us-china-seas-id USTRE79O1MV20111025.

19 "Leon Panetta: US to deploy 60% of navy fleet to Pacific", BBC News, 2 June 2012, http://www.bbc.co.uk/news/world-us-canada-18305750.

20 The case was made under Annex VII to the United Nations Convention on the Law of the Sea (UNCLOS) and registered with the Permanent Court of Arbitration in The Hague. The case can be viewed here: https://pcacases.com/web/view/7.

21 See "Full text: Premier Li Keqiang gives joint written interview to media in ASEAN countries", Xinhua, 8 October 2013, http://news.xinhuanet.com/english/china/2013-10/08/c_125496903.htm.

22 See, eg, "Fu Ying: Defence ability is not equivalent to militarization", Xinhua, 4 March 2016, http://news.xinhuanet.com/english/video/2016-03/04/c_135156002.htm.

23 "Contested areas of South China Sea likely have few conventional oil and gas resources", http://www.eia.gov/todayinenergy/detail.cfm?id=10651.

24 "Amid global price rout, China crude oil imports hit record", Reuters, 13 January 2016, http://www.reuters.com/article/us-china-economy-trade-crude-idUSKCN0UR0DU20160113.

25 See, eg, Kaplan, *Asia's Cauldron*, op cit. The US's efforts to dominate the Greater Caribbean in the early 19th century was a key element of the "Monroe Doctrine", as President Monroe sought to prevent European nations from further colonizing the Americas. Kaplan points out that Monroe did not seek to keep European navies out of the Caribbean altogether—just as no serious analyst believes China would ever attempt to block the sea lanes of the South China Sea.

26 Mearsheimer, the doyenne of "offensive realism", believes that China is structurally determined to challenge the hegemonic US, and that war is inevitable. This quotation comes from an interview

in Bill Callahan's short film *Mearsheimer vs Nye on the Rise of China*, https://vimeo.com/131276478.

27 See, eg, "Spotlight: Law-abusing tribunal issues ill-founded award on South China Sea arbitration, draws worldwide criticism", Xinhua, 12 July 2016, http://news.xinhuanet.com/english/2016-07/13/c_135508301.htm.

28 The press release of the tribunal decision is available here: https://pcacases.com/web/sendAttach/1801.

29 "The Operation of the HYSY 981 Drilling Rig: Vietnam's Provocation and China's Position", Ministry of Foreign Affairs, 8 June 2014, http://www.fmprc.gov.cn/mfa_eng/zxxx_662805/t1163264.shtml.

30 The statement can be viewed here: https://cil.nus.edu.sg/rp/pdf/2002%20Declaration%20on%20the%20Conduct%20of%20Parties%20in%20the%20South%20China%20Sea-pdf.pdf.

31 Thanks to David Brown for pointing this out.

32 "Wang Yi outlines China's foreign policy vision", *The Diplomat*, 11 March 2014, http://thediplomat.com/2014/03/wang-yi-outlines-chinas-foreign-policy-vision/.

33 See, eg, "Salami slicing in the South China Sea", *Foreign Policy*, 3 August 2012, http://foreignpolicy.com/2012/08/03/salami-slicing-in-the-south-china-sea/.

34 "Full text: China's peaceful development", 6 September 2011, http://news.xinhuanet.com/english2010/china/2011-09/06/c_131102329_2.htm.

35 See Xi's work conference speech on regional diplomacy, "Let the sense of community of common destiny take deep root in neighbouring countries", 25 October 2013, http://www.fmprc.gov.cn/mfa_eng/wjb_663304/wjbz_663308/activities_663312/t1093870.shtml.

36 16 February 2016, https://www.whitehouse.gov/the-press-office/2016/02/16/joint-statement-us-asean-special-leaders-summit-sunnylands-declaration.

37 "China state paper warns of war over South China Sea unless US backs down", Reuters, 25 May 2015, http://in.reuters.com/article/southchinasea-china-usa-idINKBN0OA07N20150525.

38 "US Congress marks Taiwan Relations Act anniversary", *Taipei Times*, 14 April 2016, http://www.taipeitimes.com/News/taiwan/archives/2016/04/14/2003643940.

39 Thanks to my colleague Arthur Kroeber for reminding me of the enduring importance of the Taiwan question in US politics.

40 https://www.iiss.org/en/events/shangri%20la%20dialogue/archive/shangri-la-dialogue-2015-862b/opening-remarks-and-keynote-address-6729/keynote-address-a51f.

41 https://www.iiss.org/en/events/shangri%20la%20dialogue/archive/shangri-la-dialogue-2016-4a4b/plenary1-ab09/carter-1610.

42 Speech at Arizona State University: "Remarks on the next phase of the US rebalance to the Asia-Pacific", 6 April 2015, http://www.defense.gov/News/Speeches/Speech-View/Article/606660/remarks-on-the-next-phase-of-the-us-rebalance-to-the-asia-pacific-mccain-instit.

43 "The battle over President Obama's trade deal has officially arrived", *Washington Post*, 5 November 2015, https://www.washingtonpost.com/politics/obama-administration-prepares-to-launch-long-fight-over-trade-pact/2015/11/05/8299ad32-8326-11e5-8ba6-cec48b-74b2a7_story.html.

44 The full paper can be seen here: http://www.chinadaily.com.cn/china/2015-05/26/content_20820628.htm.

45 Part of this chapter was originally published in Miller as "For Beijing, it's goodnight Vietnam", Gavekal Dragonomics, 17 July 2015.

46 The museum website is here: http://baotanglichsu.vn/subportal/en/Home/mid/29453A92/.

47 Hayton, *South China Sea: The Struggle for Power in Asia*, op cit.

48 Author interview, 25 May 2015. I was speaking to a highly connected businessman, who preferred not to be named.

49 See "Global ratings for China", http://www.pewglobal.org/2015/06/23/2-views-of-china-and-the-global-balance-of-power/.

50 See, eg, "What Vietnam must do now", *New York Times*, 6 April 2015, http://www.nytimes.com/2015/04/07/opinion/what-vietnam-must-now-do.html?_r=1, and "Vietnam's angry feet", 6 June 2013, http://www.nytimes.com/2013/06/07/opinion/vietnams-angry-feet.html.

51 Quoted in Thomas Fuller, "In hard times, open dissent and repression rise in Vietnam", *New York Times*, 23 April 2013, http://www.nytimes.com/2013/04/24/world/asia/vietnam-clings-to-single-party-rule-as-dissent-rises-sharply.html.

52 Author interview, 26 May 2015.

53 Author interview with Dr Truong-Minh Vu, director of the Center for International Studies at the University of Social Sciences and Humanities in Ho Chi Minh City, 25 May 2016.

54 Quoted in Tuong Lai, "Vietnam's overdue alliance with America", *New York Times*, 11 July 2014, http://www.nytimes.com/2014/07/13/opinion/sunday/vietnams-overdue-alliance-with-america.html.

55 "Xi Jinping delivers important speech at National Assembly of Viet Nam, stressing to bear big picture in mind and join efforts to open up new situation of China-Viet Nam comprehensive strategic partnership of cooperation", 6 November 2015, http://www.fmprc.gov.cn/mfa_eng/topics_665678/xjpdynxjpjxgsfw/t1313676.shtml.

56 "China's assertiveness pushes Vietnam toward an old foe, the United States", *Washington Post*, 28 December 2015, https://www.washingtonpost.com/world/asia_pacific/chinas-assertiveness-pushes-vietnam-toward-an-old-foe-the-united-states/2015/12/28/15392522-97aa-11e5-b499-76cbec161973_story.html.

57 See World Bank's WITS database, http://wits.worldbank.org/CountrySnapshot/en/VNM.

58 See World Bank, "Vietnam: Country at a glance", http://www.worldbank.org/en/country/vietnam, and provincial data from China's National Bureau of Statistics, http://data.stats.gov.cn/english/easyquery.htm?cn=E0103.

59 I was given the 10–15% figure by a reporter at the Tuoi Tre newspaper in Ho Chi Minh City, but I am unable to locate the relevant report.

60 Vietnam Ministry of Finance, Statistics, http://www.mof.gov.vn/webcenter/portal/mof/?_afrLoop=36369253348466610#!%40%40%3F_afrLoop%3D36369253348466610%26_adf.ctrl-state%3DDu8frqtd8h_126.

61 "Xi Jinping delivers important speech at National Assembly of Viet Nam", op cit.

62 *Infrastructure for a Seamless Asia*, http://adb.org/sites/default/files/pub/2009/2009.08.31.book.infrastructure.seamless.asia.pdf.

63 See, eg, "China and Vietnam", http://www.fmprc.gov.cn/mfa_eng/wjb_663304/zzjg_663340/yzs_663350/gjlb_663354/2792_663578/.

64 The problems only got worse after my visit. See, eg, "Chinese-contracted railway project in Hanoi suffers 57% cost overrun", *Tuoi Tre News*, 27 October 2015, http://tuoitrenews.vn/business/31225/chinesecontracted-railway-project-in-hanoi-suffers-57-cost-overrun.

65 City population data is taken from Demographia's "World Urban Areas: 12th Annual Edition (April 2016)", http://www.demographia.com/db-worldua.pdf. In the course of writing my book *China's Urban Billion*, I found Demographia by far the best source of reliable city population statistics.

66 See http://www.fdiintelligence.com/Utility-Nav/Highlights-Bar/The-fDi-Report-2016.

67 "The biggest winner from TPP trade deal may be Vietnam", Bloomberg, 8 October 2015, http://www.bloomberg.com/news/articles/2015-10-08/more-shoes-and-shrimp-less-china-reliance-for-vietnam-in-tpp.

68 "What Vietnam must do now", op cit.

69 "America's global image", 23 June 2015, http://www.pewglobal.org/2015/06/23/1-americas-global-image/.

70 "Global ratings for China", op cit.

71 "Don't start a fire in Asia, China warns Obama after Vietnam arms embargo lifted", 24 May 2016, https://www.washingtonpost.com/world/dont-start-a-fire-in-asia-china-warns-obama-after-vietnam-arms-deal/2016/05/24/3d5a098f-f0d3-4754-aab0-021f98bbe46b_story.html.

72 Obama's speech at the National Convention centre in Hanoi can be viewed at https://www.whitehouse.gov/the-press-office/2016/05/24/remarks-president-obama-address-people-vietnam.

73 Author interview, 25 May 2015.

74 "Testimony before the US-China Economic and Security Review Commission: China–Vietnam relations", http://origin.www.uscc.gov/sites/default/files/transcripts/May%2013%2C%202015%20Hearing%20Transcript.pdf.

75 Beijing secured diplomatic coups with the Philippines and Malaysia in late 2016. In October, Philippines president Rodrigo Duterte returned home from Beijing with an investment and trade package worth US$24 billion after announcing his country's "separation" from the US. In early November, Malaysian prime minister Najib Razak followed suit, declaring himself a "true friend" of China and securing deals worth US$34bn. The significance of these deals, however, should not be overplayed. Duterte and Najib are erratic leaders who may not last, and popular opinion in Southeast Asia still favours the US and is suspicious of China.

76 Author interview, 25 May 2015.

Conclusion

1 Zoellick first publicly urged China to become a "responsible stakeholder" at a meeting of the National Committee on US–China Relations in 2005. His speech can be viewed here: http://www.ncuscr.org/sites/default/files/migration/Zoellick_remarks_notes06_winter_spring.pdf.

2 See, eg, "Security law suggests a broadening of China's 'core interests', *New York Times*, 2 July 2015, http://www.nytimes.com/2015/07/03/world/asia/security-law-suggests-a-broadening-of-chinas-core-interests.html. An unofficial translation is available here: http://chinalawtranslate.com/2015nsl/?lang=en.

3 "Global Ratings for China", http://www.pewglobal.org/2015/06/23/2-views-of-china-and-the-global-balance-of-power/.

4 For analysis of China's growing intervention abroad, see Jonas Parello-Plesner and Mathieu Duchâtel, *China's Strong Arm: Protecting Citizens and Assets Abroad*, International Institute for Strategic Studies, Routledge, Abingdon (2015).

5 "China's growing role in South Asia", talk to Young China Watchers club in Beijing, 19 March 2015.

6   The policy was announced by outgoing president Hu Jintao in his vale-
    dictory Party Congress Work Report. See http://news.xinhuanet.
    com/english/special/18cpcnc/2012-11/17/c_131981259.htm.

7   "In Mekong, Chinese murders and bloody diplomacy", Reuters,
    27 January 2012, http://www.reuters.com/article/us-special-report-
    mekong-idUSTRE80Q00G20120127, and "China parades foreign
    Mekong killers before execution", BBC News, 1 March 2013, http://
    www.bbc.co.uk/news/world-asia-china-21625905.

8   Parello-Plesner and Duchâtel, *China's Strong Arm*, op cit.

9   Traditionally called the Indian Mutiny in Britain but known as the
    First War of Independence, the Great Rebellion or the Uprising of
    1857 in India.

10 The cartoon can be seen here: http://bigthink.com/strange-maps/
    561-kaiser-eats-world.

11 For a response to these arguments, see Jospeh Nye, "China is not
    imperial Germany", RealClear World, 27 February 2013, http://
    www.realclearworld.com/articles/2013/02/27/china_is_not_
    imperial_germany_100580.html.

12 For the full of text of Xi Jinping's speech, see http://www.fmprc.gov.
    cn/mfa_eng/topics_665678/jnkzsl70zn/t1293415.shtml.

13 See David Cohen, "'A peaceful, friendly and civilized lion': Xi
    explains China's rise in Europe", 9 April 2014, *China Brief*, Volume
    14, Issue 7, Jamestown Foundation, http://www.jamestown.org/
    single/?tx_ttnews%5Btt_news%5D=42206&no_cache=1#.
    V5jMBriAOko, and "Xi Jinping is awakening China", 19 August
    2014, http://www.fmprc.gov.cn/ce/cenp/eng/News/t1183900.htm.

14 Xi made his speech at the Fourth Summit of the Conference on
    Interaction and Confidence Building Measures in Asia (CICA). His
    speech, "New Asian security concept for new progress in security
    cooperation", is available here: http://www.fmprc.gov.cn/mfa_eng/
    zxxx_662805/t1159951.shtml.

15 Off-the-record interview, 1 October 2015.

16 For one of the most influential articulations of this view, see Robert
    Blackwill and Ashley Tellis, *Revising US Grand Strategy Toward
    China*, Council on Foreign Relations, Special Report No 72, March
    2015, http://carnegieendowment.org/files/Tellis_Blackwill.pdf.

INDEX